Commando Tactics

Commando
Tactics
The Second World War

Stephen Bull

Pen & Sword
MILITARY

First published in Great Britain in 2010 by
Pen & Sword Military
an imprint of
Pen & Sword Books Ltd
47 Church Street
Barnsley
South Yorkshire
S70 2AS

ISBN 978-1-84884-074-4

Typeset in 11pt Ehrhardt by
Mac Style, Beverley, E. Yorkshire

Printed and bound in the UK by CPI

Pen & Sword Books Ltd incorporates the imprints of Pen & Sword
Aviation, Pen & Sword Maritime, Pen & Sword Military, Wharncliffe
Local History, Pen and Sword Select, Pen and Sword Military Classics
and Leo Cooper.

For a complete list of Pen & Sword titles please contact
PEN & SWORD BOOKS LIMITED
47 Church Street, Barnsley, South Yorkshire, S70 2AS, England
E-mail: enquiries@pen-and-sword.co.uk
Website: www.pen-and-sword.co.uk

Contents

List of Plates vi

Acknowledgements vii

Preface viii

1. Desperate Force 1

2. Norway 29

3. St Nazaire 45

4. Dieppe 57

5. The Making of Commandos 83

6. Close Combat and Lessons Learned............................... 109

7. D-Day: Assault Infantry 133

8. Conclusion 163

Appendices: 179

I: British Commando Clothing and Equipment, European Theatre 179

II: 43 RM Clothing and Equipment, Yugoslav Theatre 180

III: Establishment and Armament of a Royal Marine Commando Troop .. 181

IV: Commando Battle Drill 1945 182

Bibliography 207

Index 211

List of Plates

The original model for the 'Commando'
A Bren gunner aboard a landing craft off Vaagso
Sketch map of Peter Young's street battle at Vaagso
Private Tom McCormack of No. 2 Commando
Commandos pose with the Union Flag on return from Dieppe
Captain Gerald Charles Stokes Montanaro of No. 6 Commando
An NCO of No. 1 Commando rock-climbing during training in Scotland
'The Sentry Hold' from W. E. Fairbairn's *All-in Fighting*
Use of the Commando knife from W. E. Fairbairn's *All-in Fighting*
Commandos jump from assault boats during training
A Commando crawls through undergrowth
Training with the Fairbairn-Sykes knife
Assault course, bridging exercises, and the use of pyrotechnics
Use of the Smatchet
Rifle in close-quarter fighting
Basic section formations in *Section Leading and Fieldcraft for Cadets*
Instruction on disarming a knife-wielding opponent
Use of the Bren during attack and retreat
One way to disarm an enemy rifleman
Advancing rapidly through smoke
Folding 'Assault Boat Mk III'
Cover from the 1942 edition of *Shooting to Live*
Commando raider on the beach at Hastings
Peter Young instructs two camouflaged snipers
Heavily stowed Commando equipped for a landing
Commando memorial at Spean Bridge
Method of forming a 'night-fighting patrol'
Small folding-type assault boat
Rock-climbing exercise
Men of 12 Commando

Acknowledgements

Virtually all works of non-fiction build upon libraries and archives, as well as the help and advice of others: this book is certainly no exception. The following individuals and institutions have been vital, and unstinting, in their efforts to assist – though apologies are offered to any inadvertently omitted from this list.

The Liddell Hart Centre for Military Archives at King's College proved particularly valuable and is here acknowledged specifically for access to, and permission to quote from, the archives of Major General Sir Robert Laycock; Brigadier Derek Mills-Roberts; Brigadier G. C. S. Montanaro; Lieutenant Colonel H. C. J. Hunt; Captain J. G. Burton; also the history of 30 Assault Unit, Royal Navy, compiled by Nutting and Glanville; and the E. J. Embleton collection. The archives collection of the Imperial War Museum proved similarly accommodating and is likewise warmly thanked for access to the papers of Major General J. C. Haydon; Lieutenant S. Weatherall; Lieutenant R. M. Lyons; A. E. Hines; A. F. L. Colson; Lieutenant J. B. Wetjen; Captain F. R. J. Nicholls; Lieutenant D. J. Carnegie; Major General T. B. L. Churchill; G. W. Read; P. H. B. Pritchard; Colonel N. A. C. Croft; J. E. C. Nicholl; I. C. D. Smith; and J. H. Patterson.

Ian Maine, my former colleague at the National Army Museum, and now Curator of the Royal Marines Museum, and his assistant Matthew Little, were extremely helpful to the enterprise. Similarly Dennis Reeves, Curator of the Liverpool Scottish Museum, has proved invaluable with his extensive knowledge of 'No. 4' Independent Company, and early Army Commando organisation and records. Jane Davies, Curator of the Queen's Lancashire's Collection, and Colonel John Downham, have provided information on a number of links between local regiments and the Commando forces. Lancashire Libraries succeeded in unearthing a number of fairly obscure volumes – some of which were ultimately tracked down only through inter-library loans from other institutions. The late Dr Paddy Griffith is remembered, for both inspiration and for organisation of a number of relevant study days.

Preface

Since 1945 there have been dozens of works on the British Commandos of the Second World War. This first 'special' force has been covered in everything from comic books to memoirs, unit histories, and learned dissertations. Indeed a disproportionate amount of ink has already been spilt on this fairly small body of men – who have arguably received better coverage than whole regiments and corps of the 'ordinary' Army – yet their mystique has remained considerable. As a child I recall that our neighbour had served as a Commando in the Second World War, and the very mention of the unit awed many of my elders – who had themselves served creditably – into silence. It was also a term with even greater playground resonance than 'cowboy' or 'spaceman'. The venerable and still much-respected title 'Commando', now more than a century old, remains in use, proudly borne by the modern Royal Marine Commandos, whose deeds continue to add lustre to the name.

Nevertheless, it may reasonably be asked what a new book could possibly have to offer. Yet, whilst the subject matter is not new, there are still significant questions that have not been posed, and material that has not been deeply plumbed – and sometimes not even consulted. It is also remarkable that events so recent in history can give rise to such divergent opinions, and such different accounts, even when eyewitness testimony is involved. What is attempted here is not just 'another narrative' but some attempt at the 'whys and hows' of formation, purpose, minor tactics, and ultimate significance of the Commando force. Not all the answers are comfortable: there were times when the Commandos were clearly more effective as a propaganda weapon than a fighting force – being bluster rather than 'cold steel'. On occasion they were almost victims of their own, sometimes inaccurate, reputation. There were times when even Churchill, at least the pragmatic midwife at the birth of Special Forces, if not their unequivocal champion, lost faith in their efficacy. There were, indeed, some disasters that no amount of positive media, medals, or extreme personal bravery, could possibly conceal.

Yet these falterings are essentially footnotes. For, in asking bigger questions about strategic deployment, tactical methods and doctrine, a different – arguably more interesting – story emerges. In short, there was no single, simple, set of 'Commando tactics'; no single bible of combined operations, assault, movement and close combat, but many. The techniques of the Commando developed with his task and with the equipment available. From the outset, Commando leaders drew a distinction, not always welcome, between their men (with their intelligent application of the novel) and the 'herding together' of the Regular Army – who all too often did not learn to think or look after themselves. Moreover, the true Commando ethos was extreme tactical flexibility combined with self-reliance and team spirit. In this they became the experimental laboratory of both the invasion of Europe and future small-unit tactics. It was no accident that they learned to operate in smaller groups, nor that they sometimes pioneered the introduction of new equipment and techniques, nor that they learned to move in, or on, virtually anything over land or water; and that when all else failed they were usually better at the old skills – forced marches, climbing, swimming and tactical movement than virtually anybody else. Many of their virtues remain those required of Special Forces to this day.

In concentrating on tactics, training, and examples of raids and small-unit combat, it has to be acknowledged that the following account is not a seamless chronicle. Certainly it cannot claim to be a complete history of all Commando units and deployments. Such a work would perforce be much longer, and probably obscure the specific and hopefully salient points presented. The main focus here is Europe, which was where many of the key methods were evolved, and on the 'sharp end' of significant events in which techniques, weapons, equipment, and too often, men, were tried to destruction. Here 'first use' and outcomes are regarded as more important than a repetition of all possible instances. Space is also devoted to training and the notion of 'lessons learned' – that was indeed the main mechanism by force of which knowledge and tactics were advanced. Finally, the effectiveness of the Commando idea is examined: was it primarily a physical phenomenon, or was it more to do with morale? This approach – critical as it sometimes is – implies no slight upon the first Commandos: for emphasis upon difficulty, extreme challenges, close combat and adaptation serves only to distinguish what made these men genuinely a 'special' force.

In Memory of Paddy Griffith 1947–2010

Chapter 1

Desperate Force

The Commandos of the Second World War have attained such legendary standing that it is often overlooked that these forebears of modern 'Special Forces' were born in adversity, and of necessity. In the early days success and failure hung in the balance. Yet, like many of the best military ideas, the Commando concept was conceived to answer specific strategic and tactical needs.

By mid-1940 British fortunes stood at their lowest ebb. Following the Blitzkrieg invasion of Poland in 1939 and the fall of France the following May, British forces had been pushed from Europe, mainly through the beleaguered Channel port of Dunkirk. The survival of the vast majority of the troops may have been a 'miracle' but it was impossible to deny that much of the Army's heavy equipment was lost, and that, for the time being at least, the United Kingdom stood virtually alone against what appeared to be an all-conquering and tactically superior Wehrmacht. Clearly, to come back from such a reverse would take time. To appear weak and supine at such a critical juncture was politically and diplomatically unacceptable. Those who doubted the nation's survival, both abroad and at home, required evidence of the British will to continue the fight. Victories, no matter how small, would be of disproportionate value in demonstrating that Germany could never safely turn its back. Key to the development of what would become the Commandos were two glimmers of hope in the summer of 1940: the survival of the RAF and enemy failure to overcome the Royal Navy. Given these factors, it would remain extremely difficult for Britain to be invaded – but without new innovations it was highly questionable whether the fight could be carried back onto European shores. Equally, there was doubt whether existing formations and tactics would even be enough to confront the enemy, should he succeed in crossing the Channel.

These subjects were close to the heart of the new Prime Minister. Churchill – recently brought to power in the wake of the failure of the Norway campaign – clearly thought such matters worthy, not only of rhetorical flourish, but of concentrated practical effort. Writing to General Ismay on 4 June 1940, he observed that:

> Every creek, every beach, every harbour has become to us a source of anxiety. Besides this the parachutists may sweep over and take Liverpool or Ireland and so forth [...] But if it is so easy for the Germans to invade us in spite of sea power, some may feel inclined to ask the question why should it be thought impossible for us to do anything of the same kind to them? The completely defensive habit of mind which has ruined the French must not be allowed to ruin all our initiative. It is of the highest consequence to keep the largest numbers of German forces all along the coasts of the countries they have conquered, and we should immediately set to work to organise raiding forces on these coasts where the populations are friendly. Such forces might be composed of self contained, thoroughly equipped units of say one thousand up to not more than ten thousand when combined. Surprise would be ensured by the fact that the destination would be concealed until the last moment. What we have seen at Dunkirk shows how quickly troops can be moved off (and I suppose on to) selected points if need be. How wonderful it would be if the Germans could be made to wonder where they were going to be struck next, instead of forcing us to try to wall in the island and roof over it!

In short, an effort had to be made to 'shake off the mental and moral prostration to the will and initiative of the enemy', from which so many now appeared to suffer.

Just forty-eight hours later, a febrile Churchill was suggesting that 'when the Australians arrive' in Britain they should be organised in 'detachments of 250' and equipped with 'grenades, trench mortars, tommy guns, armoured vehicles and the like' – the purpose being to use them as a counter-strike force at home or as a landing force for the Continent. Enterprises were to be planned that would promote a 'reign of terror' on the occupied coasts, using 'specially trained troops of the hunter class'. At first these were to 'butcher and bolt', but later they might seize a major town. Churchill's new 'minute' demanded proposals for 'organising the Striking Companies', as well as the development of tank-landing methods, a parachute force, the deployment of cross-Channel artillery, and revised systems of espionage and intelligence.

On 18 June 1940 the Prime Minister was enquiring about the possibility of forming 'Storm Troops':

We have always set our faces against this idea, but the Germans certainly gained in the last war by adopting it, and this time it has been a leading cause of their victory. There ought to be at least 20,000 Storm Troops or 'Leopards' drawn from existing units, ready to spring at the throat of any small landing or descents. These officers and men should be armed with the latest equipment, tommy guns, grenades, etc., and should be given great facilities in motorcycles and armoured cars.

The following morning, General Paget managed to persuade the Prime Minister that attempting to form British 'Storm Troops' was unwise, proposing instead that the focus should be on 'tank-hunting platoons' and 'Special Irregular Units' that might include American volunteers.

To respond positively to the Prime Minister's ambitious and sometimes contradictory visions at a time when the Army was in a state of such disorganisation was no easy matter. Importantly, it raised serious questions as to where men and materials were to come from to create an aggressive, well-equipped force, when guns and recruits alike were jealously guarded resources. Interestingly, there were answers to hand – embryonic formations on which to build – and it was these that would lend the new force the unique, Janus-like character it maintained for the rest of the war. For, unlike almost any other body, the new Commandos were the scion of both the Army and the Navy. The ancestors, sprung from land and sea respectively, were the recently formed 'Independent Companies', and the already venerable Royal Marines. In the event it would be the Army that created the first 'Commando' force.

Against the long and august history of the Royal Marines, the Army experience of amphibious raiding was but months – and hitherto there was nothing more than brave failure on record. Indeed, Churchill's memoirs state that the War Office offered 'obstinate' resistance to the whole concept. This may well have been so, but professional jealousies were doubtless reinforced by sober realisation of where remarkably similar Churchillian enthusiasm had led in 1915: the blood-soaked strategic cul-de-sac of the Dardanelles. Conversely, it was also true that there were already champions of amphibious hit-and-run and 'irregular' actions within the Army, keen, agitating even, for the opportunity to fight. Significant amongst these were Colonel J. F. C. Holland and Major C. M. Gubbins, both of Military Intelligence, and Lieutenant Colonel Dudley Clarke, an assistant to Chief of Imperial General Staff, General Sir John Dill.

Gubbins, a long-term student of guerrilla warfare, who had seen active service in both Poland and Russia, was thrust somewhat unexpectedly into the guise of amphibious raider early in 1940, after the German invasion of Norway. Nevertheless, he had an up-to-date theoretical grounding, as well as some practical experience in the arts of guerrilla warfare for, in 1939, his work with Military Intelligence had led him to produce more than one treatise on the subject. From the tactical point of view, the most significant of these was the *Partisan Leader's Handbook*. This little booklet was highly revealing of Gubbins' 'no holds barred' view of unconventional warfare, the point of which was to 'embarrass the enemy in any way possible'. Such action was particularly suited to either the 'military acts' of a group under a nominated leader, or 'individual acts of sabotage', which might be anything from destroying equipment to sniping at sentries. His seven 'principles' of the guerrilla fighter were:

a) Surprise is the most important thing in everything you undertake. You must take every precaution that the enemy does not know your plans.
b) Never engage in an operation unless you think success is certain. Break off the action as soon as it becomes too risky to continue.
c) Every operation must be planned with the greatest care. A safe line of retreat is essential.
d) Movement and action should, wherever possible, be confined to the hours of darkness.
e) Mobility is of great importance, act, therefore, where your knowledge of the country and your means of movement – i.e. bicycles, horses etc. – give you an advantage over the enemy.
f) Never get involved in a pitched battle unless you are in overwhelming strength.
g) Never carry incriminating documents on your person nor leave them where they can be found.

The ideal size of his guerrilla band was from eight to twenty-five, varying within this range to suit the task in hand. This would be small enough to travel quickly and find easy concealment, whilst of sufficient strength to carry out a significant mission. Likely targets might include communications of all descriptions; small enemy detachments; dumps and stores of munitions, food, transport, or money; and ambushes of all types. Larger targets might be engaged by bringing several bands together. Key to the success of Gubbins' guerrilla vision was the exploitation of the difference between these fighters and conventional forces, who were 'completely dependent on roads, railways, signal communications etc. to keep themselves supplied with food, munitions and petrol, without which they cannot operate'.

Just as important were the relationships between irregulars and the population of the territory in which they operated. Convincing civilians that enemy occupation was only temporary was a good start, as was encouraging patriotism and 'hatred of the enemy'. Thereafter the populace could become good sources of information, in the best case scenario conducting deliberate spying and acting as lookouts. The very best informants were those who did not arouse suspicion, but in the course of their normal work got close to the enemy – such as innkeepers, barmaids, communication workers, medical personnel, cleaners and 'camp followers'. The ideal lookouts were 'women and children' – less likely to be suspected than adult males. In the early stages of a guerrilla war, fighters might well be able to live at home, under cover, going 'on the run' only if flushed out by raids or arrests. Lack of uniform would enable the partisan to mingle with the general population in all instances. Any who provided information to the enemy were best killed straight away, 'a note pinned to the body' being a good warning to others.

In combat the staples of irregular action were to be the ambush; road blocks; and destruction of enemy posts. In all these events, multiple firing positions, use of cover and darkness were all good tactics. First targets would usually be officers or anybody who appeared to be in charge. Trains were best derailed at speed on bridges or near steep embankments: only then should fire be poured in, the prime targets being any coaches left undamaged on the track. Planning escape routes was critical in all scenarios, whether the attack was successful or aborted.

When it was decided to attempt to stem the northward advance of the Germans in Norway, opportunities for such irregular actions of the type Gubbins had foreseen were thought highly likely to arise. Therefore – and bearing in mind the obvious limitations of terrain – a decision was taken to send not only a regular force to Norway (code-named 'Avonmouth') but small bodies whose main task would be harassment of the enemy using guerrilla tactics. Gubbins, then with the military mission in Paris, was abruptly withdrawn and ordered to select troops for irregular operations against the west coast of Norway. The first and very sensible notion, given constraints of time, was to take one existing parent unit – already skilled in fieldcraft and highland terrain – and to break it down into smaller parts for the task in hand. The Lovat Scouts, whose ranks contained many expert snipers and stalkers, were obvious candidates for the role, but it is believed that this option was shelved in the face of local protest.

So the net had been thrown wider and new 'Independent Companies' were formed from individual volunteers. The main target of this mini internal recruitment drive was the Territorials – part-time soldiers before the outbreak of hostilities – and broadly speaking, each new company was created from an existing Territorial Division. Events moved so rapidly that the main Avonmouth force had sailed even before the surprised Territorials saw an 'urgent telegram' appear on the notice boards of their drill halls appealing for 3,000 men to perform 'special service of a hazardous nature'. The 'No. 1' Independent Company, drawn from 52nd (Lowland) Division, was thrown together under Major Ballantyne of the Cameronians in under a week – and nine more followed before April was out. Interestingly, the flavour of the new units was Scottish, Welsh, Lancastrian and East Anglian, three being made up from Scottish divisions, and two each from Welsh, Lancashire, and east of England divisions. The exception to this pattern was the 5th Independent Company, drawn from the 56th (London) Division, and gathered initially at Lydd in Kent, though Major Pedder, its Commanding Officer, was actually a member of the London Scottish. The disparate origins of the companies were further accentuated by the fact that the cap badges of parent regiments, and at least some divisional insignia, continued to be worn.

The new units were lightly armed but stronger than a normal infantry company. The basic establishment was twenty-one officers and 268 'other ranks', intended to be largely self-supporting and self-contained, being organised in three rifle platoons in such a way as to allow flexible deployment right down to section level. Each platoon had its own headquarters consisting of an officer, sergeant and nine men, and three sections each comprising a second lieutenant, corporal and twelve men. In most instances the men within a platoon were chosen from one regiment: thus it was that 'No. 4' Independent Company, drawn from the components of 55th (West Lancashire) Division, had a King's Regiment platoon, South Lancashire Regiment platoon, and a Liverpool Scottish platoon. The rifle platoons were backed by a support section with additional machine guns, an engineer section, signal section, medical section and ammunition section. Independent companies thus contained virtually every specialism mustered by a regular infantry battalion. The entire company was intended to be carried complete in one ship, greatly simplifying deployment and landings.

The basic uniform and kit, as issued to a soldier of 'No. 4' Independent Company, consisted of the following: personal weapon; battledress; steel helmet; two sets of underwear and two shirts; four pairs of socks; 1937 Pattern web equipment; roll neck sweater and leather jerkin. Specialist items were limited, but even at this early date included sleeping bag; Bergen rucksack; snowshoes; five-day mountain rations, and Arctic boots. Also included in the inventory was a coat lined with kapok. This last was modelled on an overcoat worn by drivers in the Great War and was undoubtedly warm but also long and stiff – no contributor to energetic movement. Platoon commanders also received a bundle of cash and some rather inadequate maps. Almost immediately the first paradox of all Special Forces warfare became apparent. To act independently over difficult terrain and strike hard requires a good deal of equipment but arms, ammunition and rations are heavy – impeding movement. The search for the ever illusive compromise between weight and the ability to survive and fight had begun.

Arguably the greatest deficiency of the Independent Companies was not equipment but training: those departing for Norway had perhaps a week or ten days to prepare, and for the most part the best that could be accomplished was some route marches, navigation, work on the range with various arms, including the Boys anti–tank rifle, and practice digging in. For the majority, Arctic and mountain warfare instruction was as yet completely lacking, though somewhat bizarrely, eight Indian Army officers were belatedly appended to Gubbins' little force as advisors on 'hill fighting'. Also attached were a handful of Norwegian-speaking officers. The first five Independent Companies, code-named, collectively, 'Scissorforce', left Scotland in early May. Companies 6 to 10 did not get to Norway, their deployment being interrupted by German action against France. Though the first of the Independent Companies saw action in Norway in the late spring of 1940, notably around Bodo (and Gubbins intended that the Saltfjord area should become a 'lodgement as a guerrilla sanctuary') they were not really used in the irregular role that had been envisaged. Most of the work consisted of rearguard actions, attempting to cover withdrawal.

The Norway fiasco was one of the factors that brought down Chamberlain's government, whilst Churchill – who, paradoxically, had been intimately involved in the decision to send troops – feared that his political career might be similarly marred. Even Lord Louis Mountbatten, writing in the rather carefully worded wartime official publication on combined operations, was prepared to admit that

> through force of circumstance they [Special Companies] did not perform the duties for which they were brought into being. They did not raid the enemy in the full sense of the word, but fought with him in a more regular manner, and in so doing gave a very good account of themselves.

In retrospect, it is also apparent that there was a gulf between Gubbins' conception of irregular action and the actual composition of the Special Companies – not least of which being that the companies brought with them weighty supplies. Communications between units were also poor. It has famously been remarked that it is much easier to be 'a guerrilla' in one's own country, than to be such in that of someone else. This certainly proved to be so in Norway, even though Norwegian forces were fighting alongside the British, and the local population was generally sympathetic.

Many of the survivors of Scissorforce arrived back at Scapa Flow aboard HMS *Vindictive* on 1 June 1940 – as the BEF was arriving on the south coast of England from Dunkirk. Gubbins had proved himself personally brave and resourceful in a tight corner – and had not long to wait for a DSO, with promotions following later. Yet there was no disguising the shambles and he was quickly shuffled off to become director of training and operations of SOE. There he proved able to use his conception of irregular 'guerrilla' fighting to its fullest extent and in retrospect, Gubbins' departure proved something of a tactical turning point.

Nevertheless, the prognosis for the raiding force itself might have appeared dire, were it not for friends in high places. For just three days later, on the very evening of Churchill's note to Ismay demanding immediate consideration of raiding forces, Lieutenant Colonel Dudley Clarke, military assistant to Chief of Staff, took his work home with him – returning the following morning with a single-page proposal 'on a sheet of Stratton Street writing paper'. South African-born Dudley Wrangel Clarke had been educated at Charterhouse in England. In 1916 he attended the Royal Military Academy at Woolwich and was commissioned into the Royal Field Artillery in November that year. Before the First World War ended he also saw service with the Royal

Flying Corps in Egypt. Between the wars he was deployed to Mesopotamia, undertook special missions in Turkey, and, after several unsuccessful attempts, finally entered Staff College, where one of his instructors was Bernard L. Montgomery. Thereafter he had served in Aden and Palestine, reaching the rank of Lieutenant Colonel in 1939 whilst at the War Office.

The document the versatile Clarke produced in the week after Dunkirk was rapidly improved and swiftly found its way from the Chief of the General Staff to the Prime Minister. It became what is now widely regarded as the founding charter of the Commandos. The speed with which Clarke's famous Commando memorandum was produced, proffered and accepted, was no mere chance. For, in addition to a mission to Africa, Clarke had already been to Norway twice during the early months of the Second World War and had witnessed the debacle that had enveloped the Special Companies at first hand. In his memoir, *Seven Assignments*, he would describe his personal 'Eureka moment' as occurring during his evening journey from the office:

> On the way home I tried to search through scattered memories of military history to find some precedent. What had other nations done in the past when the main Army had been driven from the field and the arsenals captured by a superior enemy? Spain in the Peninsular War [...] answered with guerrilla warfare: in fact she had given this very name to the first and perhaps greatest of all 'Resistance Movements'. Ninety years later the Boers had found the same solution. Their record I knew well enough, for I had been born in the Transvaal just before the war broke out, and my father had been one of the young men who rode out to meet Jameson four years earlier. By the end of 1900 Roberts and Kitchener had defeated the Boer Army and conquered all South Africa, and a dictated peace seemed to be around the corner. But a stubborn enemy still found means of fighting on; and for two years a quarter of a million British troops were to be harried up and down the country by loosely organised bands of horsemen who totalled little more than one-tenth their own strength – the Boer 'Commandos'.

The word 'Commando' itself was said to have been derived from eighteenth-century Portuguese, where originally it meant nothing more than a 'party commanded' – and the expression certainly was encountered during the Peninsular campaign. Nevertheless, the word was also known in Dutch and German at the same period, where it became 'Kommando' or 'group of men under a commander'. Hence, during the Great War, a number of different and sometimes rather *ad hoc* German formations had already carried somewhat similar titles. A *Fernsprech-Ausbildung Kommando*, for example, denoted nothing more novel or offensive than a small 'telephone training detachment'. To English ears, in its Afrikaans guise – and especially after the South African War – the name had taken on rather different and dynamic connotations. Its currency was maintained in literature, not least by Deneys Reitz, who eventually became South African High Commissioner in London and published a memoir in English entitled *Commando* in 1929. Churchill, who had been captured during the Boer war, was undoubtedly only one of many who had been impressed by the performance of these 'Commandos' – groups of irregular troops on horseback, under a leader.

On 9 June the War Office sent out a letter to the generals of regional commands regarding the recruitment of volunteers for 'special service'. This informed them that it was proposed to 'raise and train a new force' for 'independent mobile operations'. To facilitate its formation they were to collect the names of up to forty officers and 1,000 men in their areas. Those who eventually joined this new force were expected to be taken elsewhere in the United Kingdom for training, but were not likely to remain in new units 'for more than a few months'. The men required had to be volunteers, 'young and absolutely fit, able to swim and immune from sea sickness. Those who have already seen active service and are able to drive a motor vehicle are particularly valuable' – as were 'sappers trained in demolition work'. Other desirable characteristics mentioned were intelligence, the ability to work without close supervision, and a lack of propensity to 'looting'. For all officers operational competence was the deciding factor, and the generals were also enjoined to send a letter to branch eight of Military Operations, 'as soon as possible and under secret cover', naming those six to eight officers most suitable to lead a Commando.

A few days later a memorandum from Major General R. H. Dewing, Director of Military Operations at the War Office, outlined the organisation and purpose of the Commandos, who were to be trained to fight independently 'and not as a formed military unit'. Establishments were not to be regarded as 'fixed' but primarily for 'the purpose of allotting appropriate ranks in the right proportions to each other'. Each 'irregular operation' would be initiated by the War Office, with the

Commandos furnishing the relevant manpower. Specific arms and equipment would be issued for an operation, which would probably not last more than a few days, and was not to involve resisting a major attack or 'overcoming a defence of formed bodies of troops'. There would be almost no administrative tail to the structure.

The new organisation was originally intended to be ten Commandos: each with a little over 500 men, and the teeth of which were to be ten 'troops' of fifty. In outline, the Commandos were planned as follows:

'No. 1' Commando: to be made up from the existing 'Independent Companies'.
'No. 2' Commando: designated as a parachute unit.
'No. 3' Commando: to be raised from Southern Command.
'No. 4' Commando: to be raised from Southern Command.
'No. 5' Commando: to be raised from Northern Command.
'No. 6' Commando: to be raised from Western Command.
'No. 7' Commando: to be raised from Eastern Command.
'No. 8' Commando: to be raised from Eastern Command (London District).
'No. 9' Commando: to be raised from Scottish Command.
'No. 10' Commando: to be raised from Northern Command.

The whole outfit would sit as part of 'MO 9' – or section nine of 'Military Operations' – under the view of Brigadier Otto Lund, Deputy Director Military Operations. Lund organised a small headquarters, the personnel of which included not only Dudley Clarke, but a handful of staff officers and a number of female clerical assistants and liaison officers. One of the staff officers was well-known actor Captain David Niven, then serving with the Rifle Brigade. Vessels to transport the raiders were to be found by Captain Garnons-Williams of the Royal Navy.

For a number of reasons the raising of the Commandos did not work out nearly as neatly as the original simple scheme suggested, and the order of battle would remain something of a moveable feast. For example, 2 Commando moved to Ringway for training in July 1940, and soon acquired its new identity as parachute troops. The 'No. 10' or Northern Command Commando was not up to strength, but additional units with higher numbers were created – even when lower numbers in the order of battle appeared vacant. So it was that 'No. 11' and 'No. 12' Commandos were created in August 1940. Moreover, the 'Special' or 'Independent'

Jack Churchill

John Malcolm Thorpe Fleming Churchill (1906–1996), nicknamed 'Mad Jack', was one of the most colourful Commando leaders. Born in Hong Kong, he was educated at King William's College and graduated from Sandhurst in 1926. Thereafter he served with the Manchester Regiment in Burma, but left the Army to work in newspapers in Africa, and also became a champion archer. However, he rejoined with the outbreak of war and fought in the 1940 campaign in France. After Dunkirk, Churchill volunteered for the Commandos and was second-in-command of No. 3 Commando on the Vaagso raid. In 1943 he led No. 2 Commando in Sicily and Italy, where, characteristically at the forefront of the action, he was instrumental in taking forty-two prisoners in one incident. His various actions up to this date earned him the Military Cross and Bar, plus a Distinguished Service Order – and a couple of flesh wounds. His morale-raising trademarks included playing the bagpipes going into action, and the use of unorthodox, and sometimes antiquated, weapons, such as the broadsword and longbow. In 1944 Lieutenant Colonel Churchill was sent with Royal Marine Commandos to Yugoslavia, where he fought in support of Tito's partisans. Here he was captured and held at various times in Germany, Austria and Italy, including a period in a concentration camp. One nearly successful escape attempt ended when he was recaptured near Rostock. He actually got away in April 1945. After the war he served in Palestine, qualified as a paratrooper, was an instructor in Australia, briefly a movie extra, and became interested boating and surfing, being the first man to ride the Severn Bore in 1955. He was twice president of the Commando Association and died in Surrey in 1996.

companies were not dissolved instantly into the new structure, but kept their old names and numbers for some time. Perhaps more significantly, MO 9 would itself be quickly slotted into a new overarching tri-service body headed by Lieutenant General Alan Bourne, Adjutant General of the Royal Marines. Later, Bourne would somewhat wistfully regret the lack of Royal Marines for the early Commando force – but he was left with the impression that the Marines were already under-recruited for the tasks that they had in hand. Even for the use of Army personnel there were tight strictures on both men and resources because it was decreed from the outset that no existing units were to be diverted from defence at this critical juncture, and that the new Commandos would not be given weaponry at the expense of General Ironside's scheme for 'Home Forces'. The basic internal structure of the Commando unit underwent some minor changes during 1940, with more radical alterations early the following year. The directives that accompanied Bourne's appointment as 'Commander of Raiding Operations' and 'Advisor to the Chiefs of Staff on Combined Operations' outlined the new task in a series of numbered points. The object of raiding operations was to 'harass the enemy and cause him to disperse his forces, and create material damage', particularly on the coastline 'from northern Norway to the western limit of German occupied France'. His command was to include the existing Independent Companies as well as the 'irregular Commandos' and was also projected to encompass the embryonic parachute force. Some raids had already been planned and Bourne was to take particular pains to ensure that raiding activities did not interfere with the activities of 'service intelligence departments', with whom he was to co-operate when possible.

Since the Independent Companies had yet to be reshaped into a Commando, and 'No. 2' would take to the air, Lieutenant Colonel Durnford-Slater, appointed to lead 'No. 3' on 28 June, would later claim that he was the 'first Commando soldier of the war'. Though this detail may be debated, Durnford-Slater certainly felt totally alone, since his – and every other Commando Commanding Officer's – terms of reference demanded that he recruit his entire unit from scratch. This was done from the top down, by first sifting through the details of every officer in Southern Command who had volunteered his name. Durnford-Slater's criteria in his search for troop leaders were cheerfulness, good physique, intelligence and keenness:

> If I found a man I thought would do, I telephoned his former civilian employers in my own time during the evening. I looked for some indication of success, of initiative. If he was a regular officer, I checked up on his record of service and tried to find someone I knew to tell me if he was a suitable type. I was in a mad hurry, but I had to find first-class officers. I visited the headquarters towns of the Southern Command, Weymouth, Salisbury, Winchester, Oxford, Exeter, to interview the candidates.

The new troop leaders, or the Commanding Officer, now selected the two junior officers for each troop, and it was the duty of the officers to pick their forty-five-odd men from the many would-be volunteers. In 'No. 3' Durnford-Slater's main requirement of his subordinates was that they should avoid anybody who 'talked too much' or looked like 'a criminal'. In 'H' Troop of 'No. 3' this was cheerfully ignored when Captain de Crespigny and his Lieutenants actually picked out a man awaiting court martial. Character and skill at arms often counted for more than a man's established rank, as Peter Young related:

> We did not take our full complement of NCOs, preferring to promote our own men when they had proved themselves, a stroke of genius for which we were to be deeply thankful later on. The great majority of our men were reservists, who had served seven years with the colours, mostly in India. Their average age was about 26, and they were well trained, keen professional soldiers in the prime of life. They knew their weapons, had seen some fighting and wanted more.

Lance Corporal Weatherall, ultimately a commissioned officer of the Special Boat Service, volunteered for 'special service' with a group of like-minded friends – but got an unexpectedly high-powered recruitment,

> We were interviewed by [...] J. C. Haydon, who later became a major general. We three lance corporals were the first to be marched in [...] When he had finished, we asked him if we would be able to stick together. His reply was that as we were now NCOs we would be split up, and so we promptly refused, and were marched out, only to be marched back in again by the orderly NCO.

A further explanation that 'special service' would entail raiding, just the sort of action they were looking for, persuaded them to enrol. Weatherall then passed into No. 6 Commando. The reasons for those attempting to join were indeed many and various, ranging from extreme patriotism to extreme boredom. W. E. Jones later said he joined because he got 'fed up with doing nothing', and became uneasy seeing men with medals who had 'done something'.

The source material for the Commandos was not only the infantry and Royal Artillery, but the Corps, as for example the Engineers, Royal Armoured Corps and others. No. 8 Commando, drawn from the London

District, covered the traditional stamping grounds of the Brigade of Guards, with the result that this unit inherited some of the social reputation of its donor bodies. Whilst new *esprit de corps* was not instantaneous, a few men knew each other on arrival, and joint training soon created bonds – with the variety of service backgrounds bringing together a range of useful skills. The number of NCOs allowed in each Commando was remarkable – and far beyond that of the ordinary infantry establishment – to the extent that every second soldier had stripes. The full complement was 122 lance corporals, eighty-one corporals, forty-two sergeants and two warrant officers. Each troop had three officers. Such generous command arrangements ensured that even when Commandos were split into very small teams there would be a reliable NCO available as a junior leader, and an officer for any detachment larger than a handful. In the standard Troop structure of the summer of 1940 the command element was the captain (Troop Leader) and one other rank: under the captain's direction were two sections, each led by a subaltern. In turn, each section was divided into two subsections, each of which comprised a sergeant, two corporals, three lance corporals and just five privates. The subsection could itself be further broken down into a 'Bren group' – a junior NCO and two men – and two 'rifle groups' of a junior NCO, usually with a Thompson, and two men each.

When No. 1 Troop of 6 Commando initially mustered, it was probably not untypical in that it boasted four officers, the highest ranking as a captain, fifteen NCOs, and thirty-five men – privates, sappers and guardsmen, many of whom were already trained in different trades; the most promising were soon promoted within the unit to complete the full NCO establishment. Each Commando also had its own headquarters, with attached Royal Army Medical Corps and Royal Army Ordnance Corps personnel, but there were no heavy weapons. The largest arms routinely used were the anti-tank rifle and the Bren gun.

Famously, the first Commandos had no barracks and little transport. Characteristically, Clarke turned these potential tribulations into virtues, rationalising that pampering 'tended to sap the independence of the private soldier'. Instead of demanding facilities, that probably did not exist, he therefore negotiated a sum of 6s 8d per man, and 13s 4d per officer, per day, in lieu of shelter and feeding. Whilst actual Commando pay remained the same as that for 'ordinary' soldiers, living 'outside the wire' with an allowance to pay for board was actually viewed as something of a privilege or distinction by many Commandos. As Young observed, this arrangement worked very well and the men liked it. For training or operations everyone came under starter's orders; nobody had to be left in barracks to do the inevitable chores [...] The administrative tail therefore consisted of some five hundred landladies.

Whilst Young was probably correct in the majority of cases, there were exceptions to the rule. No. 1 Troop of 6 Commando was billeted in Scarborough, where some men were housed above a chip shop – two to a bed. The landlady made a good profit not only from the sleeping arrangements but from the fact that she charged for all meals, whilst the Commandos were out training much of the time and therefore not present to eat them. Conversely, others deliberately sought out the cheapest possible accommodation in order to pocket the difference: some even believed that this was the true motivation for boxing and physical fitness fanatic Lieutenant Colonel Lister spending some of his time camping rather than in a proper billet. There were also occasional accidents, for no barracks meant no armoury, and personal weapons and ammunition also went home at night. More than one Commando memoir features a 'negligent discharge' upsetting a host family.

Mobility was treated in the same pragmatic fashion as billeting: a Commando would simply be dismissed from one point with instructions to appear at another at a certain time the next day. In Dudley Clarke's scheme of things,

> How it gets there is the concern of each individual man. There are after all trains and buses, lifts to be cadged in civilian vehicles, or a man can cycle or even walk if he wants to. Nothing matters except that he should arrive at the right place at the right time.

A byproduct of this completely informal scheme was that the Commando would arrive with less ballyhoo than any other unit, as there were no convoys or troop trains to make its presence obvious. In perhaps the most extreme example of this *ad hoc* initiative approach to transport, one Commando officer recorded being dismissed in the UK with the order to parade in South Africa a week later – and made his own travel arrangements accordingly.

Anonymity was furthered by the fact that until 1942 Commandos continued to wear the headgear and cap badges of their old units – with steel helmets, khaki wool 'Cap Comforter' or Balaclava for operations. It is, however, a little known fact that even as early as June 1940, Charles Montanaro put forward an idea for a unique hat. This extraordinary object was a form of black cloth 'fore and aft' cap, in the Belgian style, adorned with small tassels front and back. The board convened on 11 July to decide whether this and other distinctions should be adopted came close to ridicule in its opinion, declaring the cap 'particularly hideous': it would do nothing either for morale or secrecy. Two days later the whole idea was firmly buried by the Assistant Chief of the General Staff, who should, one surmises, have had better things to do. The letter from the Army Council even described the newly invented headdress as savouring 'somewhat of an accoutrement of the blackshirts'. At this point the suggestion of special insignia fared little better, for whilst Commandos were soon allowed to wear proficiency badges, such as those for trained parachutists, a variety of possible distinctive Commando badges were also rejected. These unsuccessful oddities included winged helmets, stars, arrows, tigers, hawks, foxes, coloured bosses for the battle dress collar, and the letters 'SF' or 'R'. The reason for turning all these embellishments aside was that marking out raiders was deemed undesirable on grounds of security, whilst at the same time the Army as a whole was attempting to move away from metal badges on combat gear as they were not only expensive but a potential giveaway on the battlefield.

Equipment – especially the latest weapons – could not easily be extemporised. However, it could be predicted that it was unlikely that all the Commandos would be deployed on raids simultaneously, so whilst a basic minimum was kept with the troops specialist items were pooled. A stockpile sufficient to equip two Commandos was kept centrally, and the store also contained 'unorthodox' items, such as enemy uniform, materials and specialist explosives. In this way the tiny number of Thompson submachine guns that had as yet arrived in the United Kingdom were made to do maximum service. This shortage of sub-machine guns was particularly embarrassing, indeed inexcusable. The Germans had started to produce this class of weapon as early as 1918, when it was thought, correctly, that rapid fire might be useful for short-range combat in confined areas, such as within a trench system. Thompsons were common currency in the US within a decade. The re-equipped German Army had several types, the most widely used of which was the advanced MP38 model, further improved in 1940. The Finns, Italians, Swiss and Hungarians all produced designs during the 1930s, some of which reached production prior to the outbreak of war. The UK had a military small arms industry with a pedigree stretching back centuries, and a record of mass production in the Great War – but no submachine gun for its Army. Blindness to the usefulness of the 'SMG' was total. In 1938 BSA proposed to manufacture Thompsons but their attempts to find official orders met with no success. In May 1939 the Hungarians offered to license their gun to the British Government, and BSA actually produced samples, but again the idea was rejected. Not until the war was almost lost was UK manufacture of such a weapon for the British Army seriously investigated by government agencies.

Conversely, the option of returning unsuitable or burnt-out men to their units ('RTU') turned out to be a masterstroke. 'Special Service' being regarded as something of a temporary measure, there was nothing to prevent men going back from whence they came: some went with relief, but keen types regarded it as a dishonour to be avoided at all costs, thus spurring them to new efforts. 'No. 4' Independent Company was probably not untypical in returning forty men to 55th Division in early July 1940, with a couple more declared medically unfit following later in the month – a weeding out that represented roughly 20 per cent of total strength, which was then barely 200. In 'No. 3' Commando it was discovered that the indifferent material was concentrated in just one troop, which was thoroughly purged at a similar stage. Replacements were vetted on entry to ensure quality. Apart from being dismissed, men could also put themselves up for return to their regiments, and in this way was maintained what Clarke was pleased to call 'a force of voluntary enthusiasts' where formal discipline was relatively relaxed. Minor matters could usually be dealt with by a warning or some trivial punishment or loss of privilege. In No. 4 Commando, early in the war, for example, repetition of swimming exercises was not just a small and unofficial reprimand but valuable extra training for men who might thereby be saved from the occupational hazard of drowning. Any serious infraction of discipline and the culprit was no longer a Commando – nor his conduct the concern of the Commandos. As Captain March-Phillipps reminded his troop, 'there must be absolute trust and confidence', a man being 'either in or out'.

Following hard on the heels of the evacuation from Dunkirk and the Prime Minister's demand for a 'reign of terror', it was decided that Independent Companies not sent to Norway should be given immediate chance to act. Out of those now in Scotland were drawn men to create a new 'No. 11' Company, under the command of Major R. J. F. Tod, and from this formation were selected about 130 men for what it was hoped would be the first of many swift and deadly cross-Channel missions. For this enterprise, dubbed 'Operation Collar', the troops reorganised into small sections of about eight men, and some were temporarily issued with a few precious Thompson submachine guns.

Sailing in RAF rescue launches under cover of darkness on the night of 23/24 June, from Dover, Folkestone, and Newhaven, they aimed for the Boulogne–Le Touquet area of enemy-occupied French coast. Though landings were achieved safely by most of the parties, the points of disembarkation may politely be described as somewhat random. Some found nothing at all and returned uneventfully. Tod's own craft avoided Boulogne harbour and deposited its team in the dunes, from whence most of them set out to look for a target. Whilst they were on shore a German cycle patrol stumbled upon the launch, with just Tod himself between the enemy and the vessel, so far undetected. Accompanying the mission as an observer was Dudley Clarke:

> Quickly realising the advantage on finding himself no more than a few yards from the cyclists, Tod decided to go into action with his Tommy gun. It was a weapon he had had in his hands only for the first time a few days before the raid, and as he cocked it the magazine came off and fell onto the beach with a clatter. On board we heard it plainly, just a second or two before the Germans opened fire. It is doubtful if they had much to aim at in the darkness, but they must have directed it all at the shadow of the boat, for the bullets started to fly all around us. In the midst of it my own attention was suddenly diverted by something which caught me a violent blow on the side of the head and sent me headlong to the deck …

The founder of the Commandos had very nearly become their first fatality, as a bullet almost severed his ear. The enemy made off rapidly without further casualties to either side.

A little further along the coast at Plage de Merlimot, another party landed near a large building, where two sentries were located, rushed and killed. Lieutenant Ronald Swayne recalled that both had to be bayoneted – not so much because this was part of the plan, but because he had forgotten to load his revolver. According to Clarke's version,

> the noise of the scuffle aroused those inside and soon a machine gun opened up from a first floor window. The Commandos found the

building thoroughly wired in on all sides and failed to force an entry. By then Very lights and alarm signals were going off all round, and it was evident there would not be time to stay much longer. They had therefore to content themselves with throwing hand grenades through the windows before they started back for the boat.

What had been attacked was disputed – some said it was an empty headquarters, others that it was a seaside dance hall or 'boarded-up hotel'. No prisoners, and very little information, was gleaned as a result of this raid. Nevertheless, some limited experience was gained and perhaps more importantly, the newspapers could now be handed a very positive, and mainly accurate, account of a raid on occupied France. This upbeat communiqué claimed 'Collar' as a 'successful reconnaissance', with no casualties, contacts with German troops, and losses inflicted.

Less than a week later, Churchill was again agitating for action. The Channel Islands had been declared 'demilitarised' by Britain on 28 June and occupied by the Germans a few days later. On 2 July the Prime Minister was writing to General Ismay that

If it be true that a few hundred German troops have landed on Jersey or Guernsey by troop-carriers, plans should be studied to land secretly by night on the islands to kill or capture the invaders. This is exactly one of the exploits for which the Commandos would be suited ...

Operation Ambassador, often claimed as the first true Commando raid, followed swiftly. The mission was planned in outline by the new headquarters, where Captain David Niven acted as a briefing officer. It began with a reconnaissance by Lieutenant Nicholle, who was landed on Guernsey from a submarine, his place on the island being later filled by Lieutenants Martel and Mulholland when he was retrieved on 9 July. The plan as first iterated was deceptively simple. The destroyers HMS *Scimitar* and *Saladin* would carry the raiding force across from Dartmouth to the Channel Islands, where the Commandos would transfer to RAF launches. Following landings under cover of dark, forty men of 'H' Troop of the new 'No. 3' Commando would create a diversion. Overflying by friendly aircraft would mask the sound of the launches. The main attack, mounted by eighty-eight men in two parties drawn from 'No. 11' Independent Company, under Major Tod, was to assault the airfield in the Parish of Forest. The enemy, thought to be about 500 strong and dispersed about the island, would have insufficient time to gather and use their superior strength before the Commandos escaped.

Reality bore little relation to the plan. The first problem was that, on the eve of the attack, the original landing points were discovered to be strongly occupied. These had to be changed and the scheme altered. Next, problems were experienced with two of the boats, and a whaler had to be substituted. On the final run in, the 'No. 11' Company launches lost their way and abandoned the attack, whilst H Troop found their landing place at Petit Port too rocky to come close in and had to lower themselves into chest-deep water to wade ashore. This was no easy matter given the weight of equipment and the absorbent property of woollen uniform – the attire worn being normal battledress and steel helmet but with canvas shoes. Subaltern Peter Young went equipped for virtually any eventuality:

> In an old-style officer's haversack I had three Mills grenades, a drum magazine for the Tommy gun and a clasp knife. In my breast pockets were more magazines of the clip type. My armament included a .38 pistol, and I had also some 5 feet of cord with which I intended to secure my numerous prisoners; maps, saws, compasses and other impedimenta were sewn into various secret parts of my costume. For some reason I was carrying an extra fifty rounds of .303 rifle ammunition.

Though sodden, the team succeeded in making their way up the long steps from the rocky beach. From here Durnford-Slater and his men split into two groups and pressed on to their objectives, but found the barracks and machine-gun posts unoccupied. Having achieved nothing except the placing of a few rocks across a road and the severing of phone lines, they made their way back to the beach – uneventfully, bar the fact that Colonel Durnford-Slater tripped down the steps, accidentally discharging his revolver and alerting the enemy.

At the beach there was more consternation. The weather had deteriorated and it was impossible to reach the launches by wading. A dinghy was used to transfer weapons and some of the men, but this was smashed against rocks and one of the men in it was reported lost. Most of the remaining Commandos now resorted to swimming – except for three, who had hidden their inability to swim, and had to be abandoned. In all, the raiders lost six: Martel and Mulholland, who had now been on Guernsey about a week; Private Drain, who had crawled ashore after the dinghy was wrecked; and the non-swimmers, Corporal Dumper, Private

Ross and Gunner McGoldrick. All made attempts at evasion but were eventually captured or gave themselves up. In contrast to the treatment meted out to captured Commandos later, the German reaction was measured and essentially correct. All taken were accepted as normal prisoners of war. Martel and Mulholland, lacking uniforms, handed themselves over to the local island authorities in the first instance, and were kitted out in a semblance of the right attire from old stock once held by the Royal Guernsey Militia. So accoutred, they could surrender to the Germans as soldiers rather than spies. When it was discovered that relatives had sheltered the two officers these people were deported, but only as far as the French mainland, and after six months they were allowed back to their homes.

Peter Young thought that Guernsey had taught much about planning and improvisation, and the dangers of going 'loaded like donkeys'. From henceforth, steel helmets and multiple armament was usually avoided on raiding missions, and swimming tests were made mandatory. Others were less optimistic. Durnford-Slater later referred to the mission as a ridiculous, 'almost comic', failure. Just after the operation, Admiral Sir Roger Keyes, who had commanded on the Zeebrugge raid of 1918 – and was now of pensionable age – was installed as Director of the 'Combined Operations Command', over General Bourne. This was, to say the least, a controversial appointment, and some indeed have suggested that it was essentially political. Keyes was a Member of Parliament, and in May 1940 had been an outspoken critic of the Chamberlain government; he had also backed the Churchill line as early as 1915 over the Dardanelles. It might, therefore, be ventured that the appointment of Keyes as 'DCO' was a payback for his support and loyalty. General Ismay's explanation, as given after the war, was a variation on the theme, for, according to him, there were three reasons for Keyes' new position:

> Firstly, because he wanted to instil the idea of the offensive into everybody's mind; secondly because he wanted to press forward with the training of the Commandos and the design and production of landing–craft and all special equipment required for amphibious warfare, with a view to our ultimate return to the Continent or to landings in another part of the world; and thirdly, in order to give a job to his friend Roger Keyes, who was badgering him day in and day out.

A degree of independence for the raiders was ensured by Churchill's demand that the Admiral would 'form contact with the Service departments through General Ismay as representing the Minister of Defence'. In reality Keyes would be disappointed with what his new title meant in practice, as his role appeared to be mainly confined to technical advice on Combined Operations and the training of troops.

Almost immediately, however, fresh plans were laid for a return to the Channel Islands – using large numbers of Commandos to put out of action airfields on both Jersey and Guernsey. The attackers would stop long enough to do significant damage to various facilities and knock out most of the garrison before withdrawing. Some were inspired, others horrified. Early efforts had demonstrated that amphibious raids – even by small groups – were difficult, and the proper craft for landing large groups swiftly and successfully were, as yet, lacking. Quite what would happen to the civilian population of the islands during the ensuing battle and, perhaps worse, after the raiders had departed, was anybody's guess. 'Operation Tomato' never took place: the Prime Minister, who had been the main instigator of the tiny raids, now dismissed them as 'silly fiascos', fit only to be discontinued. Nevertheless, Churchill had by no means lost his enthusiasm for raiding, and in a letter to Eden, Secretary of State for War, gave his opinion that the main problem was one of scale, since 'pin pricks' and 'fulsome communiqués' achieved little, but at the same time 'worked up' the coasts:

> Sir Roger Keyes is now studying the whole subject of medium raids, i.e. by not less than five nor more than ten thousand men. Two or three of these might be brought off on the French coast during the winter. As soon as the invasion danger recedes or is resolved, and Sir RK's paperwork is done, we will consult together and set the Staffs to work upon detailed preparations. After these medium raids have had their chance there will be no objection to stirring up the French coast by minor forays [...] During the spring and summer of 1941 large armoured irruptions must be contemplated.

Tragically, the meaning and purpose of a 'large armoured irruption', and raids of between 5,000 and 10,000, would still be unclear as late as 1942 and Mountbatten may have felt he was merely carrying political will into effect when he allowed just such a monster to go ahead on his watch at Dieppe. That the idea of raids in general remained popular with politicians other than Churchill would be demonstrated when Major Cazalet spoke in the Commons during a debate on 28 January 1942:

A great many people are puzzled why it is that, with between one million and two million armed men in this country and comparative command of the air and sea, we have not been able to do more in the way of raids. I do not mean invasion, but raids by bodies from fifteen to five hundred men, or any figure you like. There may be adequate reasons, but surely, in the course of the next few months, when the whole coast of Europe from Petsamo to the Piraeus, is less well protected than at any former period of the war, or than it ever will be in future, we should avail ourselves of the immense opportunities of raiding on a considerable scale; thereby, I believe, we shall bring immense relief to the gallant Russian armies.

On 15 August 1940 – somewhat belatedly given that the first flurry of raiding was effectively over – came issuance of the important 'Secret' War Office document, *Commando Training Instruction No. 1*, prepared 'under the direction of the Chief Imperial General Staff'. In its own way, this was just as important as Dudley Clarke's original memorandum – and no doubt much inspired by it. In just three pages it attempted to sum up the aims of the Commando force, the core of its training, and the ideal Commando soldier. The objective was

> To train a guerrilla force, organised in units equivalent in strength to a weak battalion (500) men and to operate independently in 'smash and grab' raiding operations into enemy territory. Raids by Commandos will normally be planned to last not longer than twenty-four hours actually spent in enemy territory, and not more than one Commando is expected to be employed in any one operation. For operational purposes it is intended that the Commando organisation should be as loose as possible, each troop and individual soldier, being trained to work independently – prepared if necessary to rely entirely on their own resources both operationally and administratively in any circumstance which may arise. The Commando will often be operating over a wide area in small groups which must depend on their speed and cunning to avoid action with enemy forces. These groups must seize every advantage and opportunity to achieve their object and inflict damage upon the enemy. In short, their task will be to strike suddenly and get away again before being brought to action.

Commando training was to have the overarching purpose of creating 'a highly developed team spirit and *esprit de corps*', but at the same time produce men who were individually self-reliant and resourceful. These objectives were not seen as incompatible:

> Training will differ from that normally given to the regular soldier in that the greatest stress must be laid on the ability of each man to decide his own course of action without being told what to do. A common and, in some ways justifiable criticism of Regular Army training is that the men are marched everywhere and every detail of their lives is organised and prepared for them, so that the men do not learn to look after themselves. This is to some extent caused by the necessity for economy in time and the fact that administrative centralisation is necessary to keep maintenance costs down. On the other hand, this 'herding together' of the men does allow a close supervision of their daily lives and enables a high standard of discipline (which is absolutely necessary in any form of warfare) to be enforced. If this supervision is relaxed it is clear that an even higher standard of individual discipline must be insisted on.

Perhaps, oddly, the ten commandments of individual training iterated by *Training Instruction No. 1* began by stressing 'high standards of turnout' and saluting along with the more practical virtues of punctuality, fitness and care of arms. The second requirement – development of 'offensive spirit' – is perhaps more what we might expect:

> The men must be taught that their object is the destruction of the enemy and that they must 'get their man' at all costs, regardless of what is going on around them. They must, therefore, attain a very high degree of skill at arms, both by day and night, and be prepared to use any weapon which may be given to them or which may fall into their hands. As offensive raiding will almost certainly include sabotage, instruction should also include simple means of destroying such enemy material as: petrol stocks; MT [motor transport] vehicles including AFVs; aircraft; guns; railway signal boxes; and, if possible, the vital points of power stations and aerodromes. The stalking of isolated enemy posts must also be practised.

Other attributes to be instilled in the effective Commando included silence and secrecy (even towards close family), fieldcraft, camouflage skills and 'hunter's cunning', watermanship, opportunism and inquisitiveness. Activities to encourage development of intelligence and literacy skills were taken as a given. Activities regarded as conducive towards physical and combat fitness included swimming, boxing, and 'if possible' Jiu-Jitsu. Interestingly, 'open-mindedness' was also encouraged, as unfamiliar and unexpected conditions were all to be accepted as part of the day's work.

The temporary cessation of raids was confirmed between Keyes and the Prime Minister in September, and in the autumn of 1940 High Command decided that the Commandos required more formal structure. Bizarrely – and with not a little suggestion of internal conflict between traditionalists and the free-thinking modernists, as represented in *Commando Training Instruction No. 1* – it was decided that the reorganisation should be along the lines of 'battalions' making up a brigade – akin to those used in the rest of the Army. The old 'MO 9' was deleted from the chain of command. This ran contrary to the original conception of independent raiders formed for the task in hand, and was unpopular in many quarters. Unease became more apparent when it was realised that the new battalions and brigade were to be designated 'Special Service' and that this might be abbreviated to 'SS'. Durnford-Slater was adamant that the term should not be used at all in 'No. 3' Commando. Nevertheless, the titles 'Commando' and 'Special Service' would coexist somewhat awkwardly for a long time thereafter, with the latter only completely disappearing in late 1944, even though the Special Service brigade was itself reorganised in 1941. Badges with the 'SS' initials were worn in some formations, notably 'No. 2' Commando.

The new organisation, which took a couple of months to complete, brought together two Commandos, four Independent Companies – or a mixture of both – to make up each battalion of 1,000 men and fifty officers, as follows:

1st Special Service Battalion:
A Company. 1 and 2 Independent Companies (later 1 Commando)
B Company. 3 and 4 Independent Companies (later 2 Commando)
2nd Special Service Battalion:
A Company. 6 Independent Company and 9 Commando.
B Company. 11 Commando
3rd Special Service Battalion:
A (or 1) Company. 4 Commando
B (or 2) Company. 7 Commando
4th Special Service Battalion:
A Company. 3 Commando

B Company. 8 Commando
5th Special Service Battalion:
A Company. 5 Commando
B Company. 6 Commando

A further sifting and refreshing of personnel was achieved at least in part by another round of volunteering for the new formations. In this wide-ranging shake-up, 5, 8, 9 and 10 Independent Companies disappeared altogether. This must have been particularly galling for 'No. 10', commanded by Major May, since it had been away for some time as part of the force committed to the abortive 'Operation Menace' against Dakar on the coast of French West Africa. Here it had been lined up alongside the Royal Marine (Amphibious) Brigade, but its name was deleted from the order of battle at Fort William in October 1940. Also left out of the Special Service brigade were 'No. 2' Commando, which became 11 SAS battalion, 'No. 10', which was understrength, and 'No. 12', which was left separate from the new structure against possible deployment in Ireland.

The commanding officer of the new 'Special Service Brigade' was Colonel J. C. Haydon, a Great War veteran and decorated officer of the Irish Guards, who was quickly promoted Brigadier. Upon Haydon's appointment as brigadier of the new force, the Earl of Cavan wrote to him to offer his commiserations on what he, and presumably many others, regarded as a retrograde or possibly sideways step into a gimcrack command – and an unwarranted interruption to an otherwise conventional and promising career. Cavan's remarks may have been made tongue-in-cheek, congratulations tinged with irony, but on the face of it the match between long-term Guards officer and the unconventionality of the first modern 'special' force was not an obvious one. His subsequent success may therefore have come as something of a surprise. Nevertheless, there can be no doubting Haydon's experience, practical ability as a leader, and personal courage. He had already been involved in battle during the Dunkirk campaign, including the defence of Boulogne, and was later described in an official citation as cool, brave, quick to grasp situations and 'an inspiration to all those around him'.

With the onset of Churchillian displeasure and the bad winter weather of 1940, the first flush of Commando enthusiasm drew to a close. On a positive note, the passage of time and deteriorating meteorological conditions made imminent invasion of Britain impossible – as the Battle of Britain had made it much less likely in the longer term. Nevertheless, objectively, in quantitative terms, raiding had achieved almost nothing. More Special Company and Commando fighters had been lost than German soldiers, and missions to date had cost more in money, equipment and materials than the damage inflicted. In any case, activity had been at a 'pinprick' scale – something admitted by all concerned.

Yet there was more to the story than this, for in two fields it may be claimed that the Commando idea had been a success. The first was in terms of public relations and morale: the Commandos lent substance to the oft-repeated statement that Britain was undaunted, for they were already a source of positive news stories – or propaganda – depending on point of view. The second was in structures and tactics, where there were concrete achievements. An organisation had been developed where the Commando had the best of both worlds: raider units were no longer 'Companies' temporarily detached, but recognised as a unique force in their own right. On the other hand a soldier had no right to be a Commando: if he did not maintain training and effectiveness he could be returned to his former unit. Quality and spirit of competition were inbuilt. Often the Commando travelled under his own steam, and his own self-discipline.

Plenty of experienced officers and NCOs on the establishment facilitated use of multiple, task-oriented, groups on the battlefield, and these could easily be smaller than normal infantry sections if the situation demanded. Finally, it is to be noted that Commandos had pioneered the use of weapons and equipment new to the Army. Perhaps most significantly, these included various sorts of craft in co-operation with the Navy, and mastering the submachine gun, a weapon already familiar to the enemy and ideally suited to close-range, small-unit combat – even before production of such weapons had commenced in the UK. Parachute forces, and ultimately the SAS, were important biproducts of the initial drive to create the force for 'special service', which became the Commandos in the summer of 1940. As if to underline ability to engage with novel technology, the No. 1 Special Service Battalion also spawned 'Force X' in December 1940 – a troop-sized group trained for transportation in submarines and the use of 'Folbots' or folding portable canvas canoes. This little band departed for Malta and Mediterranean operations just before Christmas. In the Middle East, new Commando units had also begun to form: 50 Commando had been founded at Geneifa as early as August 1940, 51 Commando in October and 52 Commando in November. Remarkably, many of the things that are still associated with Special Forces today had come into existence in 1940 within a few short months – the only ingredient lacking now was major success on operations.

Chapter 2

Norway

The year 1941 began with another reorganisation of the Commando force. Haydon had acquiesced in the 'Special Service Brigade' organisation (which had turned him into a brigadier the previous winter) but this did not mean he did not harbour doubts about the effectiveness of the detail of its structure, or that he was deaf to the opinions of his subordinates. The 'Special Service Battalion' – effectively a double-sized Commando – had little meaning in the raiding context, as there were no ships that were both large enough to take such a unit, and able to come close to shore to deposit troops. Transferring Commandos to small craft, which was often the only practical way to get to a beach, only exacerbated the irrelevance of the 'big unit' concept. New recommendations on structure were put forward at the beginning of February and carried into effect over the following few weeks. The revised Commando would be six fighting troops and an HQ. The new Troop, of sixty-five all ranks, together with a few attached specialist personnel, could be slotted neatly into two Assault Landing Craft. Two Commandos could now fit into a 'Glen Type' landing ship. The shake-up required to reform units also offered another unobtrusive opportunity to sift out a few more unsuitable people.

Hard on the heels of these theoretically inspired cogitations and changes came real action. 'Operation Claymore', which eventually came to fruition that March, had, in fact, been in gestation since mid-January, when Hugh Dalton, Minister for Economic Warfare, wrote to the Prime Minister proposing a surprise raid on Norway. Its objectives would be economic and industrial, to the extent that they were to destroy herring and cod liver oil plants and ships in harbour. The disposal of small German garrisons and Quislings could come as a bonus. Churchill was highly responsive, relaying the idea immediately to Sir Roger Keyes for development. Interestingly, this positive attitude was probably less based on the importance of herrings and more on the fact that the raid chimed in with his own predilections. An attack on Norway, overcoming very limited enemy forces, promised at least a local victory against the general

gloom of the time, and would also send the message that no German
soldier was safe anywhere. Churchill did express concern that the upshot
might be a strengthening of German forces in Norway. Yet, in the event,
this was no real impediment, since Norway was not to be the target of
full-scale invasion, and any increase of German defences there could only
serve to dissipate strength elsewhere.

The target area was the Lofoten Islands – inside the Arctic Circle and
sufficiently remote that any support to the garrison would come too late
to have any impact on the result of the raid. The attackers were 500 men
of 3 and 4 Commandos, to whom were attached 55th Field Squadron of
the Royal Engineers and *Kompanie Linge*, a body of fifty Norwegian
volunteers under the command of the intrepid Captain Linge, serving as
guides and interpreters. Altogether, four small ports would be attacked:
the 3 Commando group, under Durnford-Slater, would go for Stamsund
and Henningsvaer; the 4 Commando group, under Lister, for Svolvaer
and Bretesness. Each group had its own personnel-carrying assault ship,
and the Naval cover, 6th Destroyer Flotilla, included five vessels.
Brigadier Haydon travelled on one of these, the destroyer HMS *Somali*.
Submarine HMS *Sunfish* provided assistance *en route*, acting as a radio
beacon in the event of poor visibility. The whole force was code-named
'Rebel'.

For the Commandos the mission began with a week of detailed training
at Scapa Flow, following which they embarked for the three-day voyage to
northern Norway, taking a long and surreptitious route through rough
seas via the Faroe Islands, before heading a further 350 miles north and
turning due east. This approach paid considerable dividends because
when troop carriers *Queen Emma* and *Beatrix* came close to land early on
the morning of 4 March, lights on shore were still lit, and complete
surprise was achieved. *Krebs*, a German armed trawler, blundered
haplessly across the path of *Somali* at a range of 3,000 yards and was
promptly blown to pieces, as the Naval report related, with one shell
landing on her wheel house, one in the vicinity of the boiler, and a third
amongst ammunition. Part of the crew dived overboard and the remains
of the *Krebs*, still with a few men on board, drifted out of control burning
merrily.

Brigadier Haydon had been concerned that it would not be possible to
get supporting vessels close enough to shore to deliver supporting fire.
Therefore, it was arranged that troops be 'prepared to open fire and
mutually support each other from landing craft should the need arise'. As

it turned out, there was no necessity. Most of the Commandos simply walked onto the quaysides, unopposed, and with dry feet – as James Dunning of 4 Commando put it, 'like an exercise'. Indeed, they were warmly welcomed by the local inhabitants, some of whom immediately decided to evacuate to the UK. Food and other gifts were quickly distributed as a token of British-Norwegian fraternity. Whilst many Commandos now formed search parties, others assisted the Engineers in setting up demolitions. Some set off to find the Luftwaffe communications post, as Lord Lovat recalled:

> The Signal station, a converted police barracks on the forward slope of a hill, was flying a Swastika flag. It looked solid and forbidding. From the locals we gathered that only Luftwaffe technicians were within. Led by a subaltern part of the patrol worked its way into a good firing position among some bare rocks, and at a range of about 300 yards opened fire with Bren guns, firing tracers in short bursts at the doors and upper windows of the building. This manoeuvre drove the inmates into the arms of a reception committee from the rest of the patrol, who had slipped round in a detour to cover the rear exit.

With the enemy airmen captured and their equipment smashed by Lieutenant Banks, the Commandos hauled down the flag and set off in triumph.

At Svolvaer it looked as though the German refrigeration and factory ship *Hamburg* might also be captured, but HMS *Tartar* claimed this prize, steaming in, opening fire and destroying her – also sinking the *Pasajes*, as well as completing the destruction of the *Felix Heumann*, which had been started by a Naval demolition party who had already done their work on two other vessels. Many of the crewmen were rounded up by the Commandos. At Brettesnes, one Norwegian trawler was stopped with a shell, whilst another, whose crew was keen to escape, was directed back to the Faroes. Here also Lieutenant Hutton of 4 Commando was in the process of finding the factory manager and assisting Captain Duveen in preparing demolitions when a German coastal defence officer appeared and was promptly captured. Lieutenant Colonel Durnford-Slater and Captain Linge landed at Stamsund, where they set up shop at the police station, assembled reports on collaborators, took the mail from the post office, and identified other possible targets. By 10.30 a.m. dense columns of smoke began to rise from processing facilities and stores marking

John Durnford-Slater

Anecdotally at least the 'first Commando', John Frederick Durnford-Slater (1909–1972) came from a Devon military family. His name was simply 'Slater' at birth, but hyphenated later. He entered the Royal Military Academy, Woolwich, in 1927, and was commissioned into the Royal Artillery. Thereafter, he was posted to India, where he proved himself a skilful horseman. Subsequently, he returned to the UK and, early in the Second World War, was with the anti-aircraft artillery. Lack of action was one of the factors that led him to volunteer immediately for 'special service', and by the end of June 1940 was a brevet Lieutenant Colonel, charged with raising No. 3 Commando. Within days he had his first troops, and within a few weeks was leading some of them in the raid on Guernsey. Towards the end of the year, No. 3 and No. 8 Commandos were banded together as 4th Special Service Battalion under Robert Laycock – a move that appears to have annoyed Slater, who reverted to the rank of major. However, by 1941, he was back to the role of Lieutenant Colonel and, in the Lofoten Islands action, was Mentioned in Despatches. Returning to Norway later in the year he won the Distinguished Service Order for the attack on Vaagso. However, at Dieppe in 1942, he was unable to land (No. 3 suffered many casualties and was eventually moved to Gibraltar after a period of recuperation). During 'Operation Huskey', in July 1943, Slater was prominent in the assault on Sicily, leading his Commando with distinction even when confronted by armour. For his 'courage, determination, and tenacity' he received a bar to his DSO. Thereafter, No. 3 was in the Italian campaign, spearheading the assault on Termoli, with Slater leading both No. 3 and No. 40 Commandos as a brigade. In the divisional-sized Commando organisation finally formed in the preparations leading up to D-Day, Slater was appointed second-in-command under Major General Sturges, and fought with the Commandos in France. He retired from active service in 1946 and published his well-known war memoir *Commando* in 1953. He died in a rail accident in 1972, his obituary in *The Times* being penned by Brigadier Peter Young.

further work of destruction. At midday the work of re-embarkation was well under way.

A BBC bulletin informed the nation of 'a highly successful raid with no casualties'. As the official report submitted to the Lords of the Admiralty recorded, there had been useful results at little cost – indeed, it was rumoured that the only Commando injury was an officer who had accidentally wounded himself with his pistol. Ten vessels – nine German and one Norwegian – had been sunk, sixteen factories and plants destroyed, and nearly a million gallons of various types of oil in seven installations had been burned or otherwise spoiled. German prisoners numbered 213, and twelve Norwegian collaborators were also identified and brought off. About 300 Norwegian volunteers were ferried back to the UK. A few enemy personnel had been killed or wounded, essentially those aboard the *Krebs*. Documents recovered from the wreck of the *Krebs*, which had been suddenly surprised before the crew had any chance to destroy papers, put another piece into the jigsaw of the enemy's *Enigma* code system.

Brigadier Haydon's report noted the value of the training at Scapa; the excellent co-operation between the Commandos and the Navy; the success of all the Commando commanders, and the 'enthusiasm' of Captain Linge. The downsides were few and, in the event, easily overcome. Freezing of weapons might have been a problem if operations had been contested and lasted longer, and there had been concerns that the destroyers might not be able to get in close enough if their guns were needed against shore targets. Fear that the Navy might not be able to get the landing force in and out led the Commandos to carry forty-eight hours' rations: a precaution that proved unnecessary. The Prime Minister was more than satisfied. As he told Admiral Tovey; 'this admirable raid has done serious injury to the enemy and has given an immense amount of innocent pleasure at home'. His 'personal minute' to Admiral Keyes was equally congratulatory:

> The unqualified success of Claymore says much for the care and skill with which it was planned, and the determination with which it was executed. Pray accept for yourself and pass on to all concerned my warm congratulations on a very satisfactory operation.

This approval was put into more concrete form later, when Churchill personally inspected 4 Commando. Peter Young once observed that the only thing wrong with the Lofotens raid was that there was not enough real action: he need not have worried, as there was plenty to follow.

The summer and autumn of 1941 were peppered with small missions. In July a party from 12 Commando landed near Ambleteuse. At the end of August a mainly Canadian force went to Spitzbergen, and about the same time 5 Commando put ashore parties near Boulogne. In September both 5 and 1 Commandos attacked in the unlikely sounding 'Chopper' and 'Deepcut' missions to France at St Vaast and Courseulles on the Cherbourg peninsula. A small German cycle patrol was encountered and shot down, and machine-gun posts fired on. Other minor sallies also featured No. 2 Commando. In November a larger effort saw ninety men of No. 9 Commando make an attempt on the German battery at Houlgate, which miscarried due to lack of time, navigation problems, and heavy ground conditions. On 9 December parts of 6 and 9 Commandos set out for Norway, headed for the town of Floss, but an accidental grenade explosion onboard ship added to navigational miscalculation and led to the mission being aborted.

This somewhat motley selection of actions was followed by a concerted return to Norway between Christmas and New Year 1941. The main objective was to harass coastal defences to such an extent that the enemy would be forced to pull in Naval and Air units from elsewhere, and consider future strengthening of garrisons. Other targets to be picked off along the way included the elimination of military installations, oil facilities and ships, the apprehension of collaborators and the possibility of bringing back Norwegian volunteers to the UK. The plan was double-headed. The main attack, code-named 'Archery', would concentrate on South Vaagso and the small port and Naval anchorage protected by the four-gun coast defence battery on the island of Maaloy. Here the main body of the attacking force would be 3 Commando, supplemented by two troops of 2 Commando with additional medics and engineers drawn from 4 and 6 Commandos, and some Norwegian personnel. The total strength of the raiding force was 573 all ranks, in landing ships, supported by a mixed Naval escort of four destroyers, backed up by the cruiser HMS *Kenya* and a submarine.

According to Brigadier Haydon's post-war notes the detailed planning of the landing points used various sources of intelligence, one of the most useful being tourist photographs. Similar pictures had been used for some of the French raids – one of which had shown an Edwardian lady on a beach, upon which the depth of footprints had correctly shown that it was unsuitable for heavy tracked or wheeled vehicles. What made 'Archery' a truly combined operation was an Air element of Hampdens, Blenheims and Beaufighters, drawn from both Bomber and Coastal Commands, whose job it would be to attack enemy airfields and give 'top cover' to the surface forces. In terms of geography, the target was both well chosen and difficult, in that whilst the enemy might be surprised somewhere sufficiently remote that it would be difficult to aid the garrisons under attack, the place was also too remote to be reached by the most effective single-engined RAF fighters.

The second prong to the late December assault was 'Anklet' – a 300-man diversionary mission back to the Lofotens by 12 Commando, supported by Norwegians. Interestingly, since it should not have come as a complete surprise to the enemy – who had been caught this way before – 'Anklet' was a remarkable success. Some minor installations were destroyed, and the tiny German garrison in the landing areas at Reine and Moskenes made itself scarce or surrendered. A total of twenty-nine enemy personnel were captured and more than 200 Norwegians were evacuated to the UK. The 'Anklet' force remained in the vicinity for some time until enemy aircraft finally appeared on the scene and the attackers then withdrew before they could be set upon.

Vaagso proper was a much more sanguinary affair, in which new combined techniques were tried, and largely succeeded, despite what became a small but brisk battle. For, unlike Dieppe the following year, planning and preparation was coherent and objectives realistic, given the forces to hand. The opening moves saw the flotilla approach the Norwegian coast in formation, with the destroyers creating an anti-submarine screen ahead of the cruiser. On entering the fjord, *Kenya* took the lead and gave the coastal defences a good dawn battering with her 6-inch guns. Meanwhile, Hampden bombers deflected attention by overflying the Ulversund, and also bombing the battery at Rugsundo to the east. Nevertheless, enemy guns managed to reply gamely, engaging *Kenya* to the best of their ability. Though the coast defences were not immediately silenced, bombardment from sea and air effectively distracted from the assault landing craft, which were now headed towards the shore, and when more Hampdens appeared and dropped smoke bombs onto Maaloy Island and South Vaagso from low level, the defenders were completely unsighted.

Unfortunately, this well-calculated stroke was not without mishap – since simultaneous engagement of bombers and landing craft was not entirely risk free. As the official report explained:

The smoke bombs dropped at the landing place at South Vaagso were only 50 yards out of the desired position, but one of them unfortunately struck a landing craft, setting it afire and causing some 20 casualties from burns [...] Despite this serious accident it is considered that these bombs were of great value, for they enabled the troops to be put ashore with few casualties from automatic weapons which were bringing fire on the landing place and which might have inflicted even heavier losses had they been given a clear and unimpeded view of their targets.

Colonel Durnford-Slater not only described how the errant smoke bomb caused mayhem, but that it also set alight munitions on the craft, which 'detonated in a mad mixture of battle noises'. Nor were the other bombs distant enough for comfort:

About 100 yards from our landing place, I fired ten red Very light signals. This told the ships to stop firing and the aircraft to come in with their smoke bombs. As I leaped from the leading landing craft three Hampden bombers passed over me at zero feet with a roar. As they did so they loosed their bombs, which seemed to flash then mushroom [...] Some of the phosphorus came back in a great flaming sheet. The next thing I knew both my sleeves were on fire. Fortunately I wore leather gloves and beat the flames out before they could eat through my four layers of clothing to the skin.

The low-level air attack also cost a bomber which caught fire and crashed into the sea with just one survivor.

It was shortly after 8.45 a.m. when the first landing craft hit the rocky beaches. The raiders were divided into five separate parties, each with different tasks. 'Group One' – a small detachment under Lieutenant Clement – landed at Hollevik to investigate a reported enemy gun site near to the southern tip of Vaagso island, cleared the village of Halnoesvik, and were then ordered along the coast road to join up with headquarters. 'Group Two' – consisting of four troops led by Colonel Durnford-Slater – made landfall by the canning factory, whilst Major Jack Churchill's 'Group Three' landed on Maaloy Island to complete the destruction of the coast battery. 'Group Four' – two troops of 2 Commando under Captain Hooper – was a reserve, ready to support Durnford-Slater's main assault, and 'Group Five' was a detachment under Captain Birney, destined for

North Vaagso, intended to block the road and thereby cut off the target areas from the outside world. Some thought had gone into how the raiding parties should be equipped, the general premise being that the raid was to be relatively brief and swift, so personal impedimenta could be pared to a minimum. Conversely, some fighting was anticipated, so ammunition had to be adequate. Riflemen therefore carried 100 rounds for their own use and fifty magazines per Bren gun were spread amongst the sections and held in an immediate reserve. This allowance of over 1,500 rounds for each gun turned out to be a wise precaution, and really the minimum that was needed. Only a small ration was carried, and since so much happened in a short space of time, many came back to the ships unopened. Officers mainly carried pistols with a supply of twenty-five rounds, and many of them also helped to carry the Bren magazines. Some also carried a rifle. Perhaps predictably, the pistols were the least satisfactory part of the arrangement. As Durnford-Slater recalled:

> On this operation I carried a Colt .45 pistol with three spare magazines. All these magazines were discharged by the end of the day but I never again went into action carrying a pistol only, as these weapons do not give confidence when opposed to a man with a rifle.

Captain Peter Young claimed to be the first out of Major Churchill's landing craft, the Major being busy 'stowing his bagpipes away' and drawing out a fearsome, if theatrical, broadsword, with which he intended to lead the onslaught. Not to be outdone, Young got ashore dry-shod, clambered up the small cliff, and ordered his men to fix bayonets: but as he did so, Churchill regained the lead, charging past, 'with impatient and warlike cries and vanished into the smoke'. Young spread his troop out and was able to advance quite steadily and unmolested as the smokescreen was still thick. They found the barbed wire protecting the battery still in place, but sagging and damaged by the bombardment, and were able to push their way through. The first of the gun pits was entered without mishap and a white signal was fired to show that the Commandos were on the position. However, by the time the No. 3 gun pit had been reached, the enemy had begun to emerge:

> A little way to the right a grenade exploded, and almost simultaneously a German soldier appeared 20 yards away charging towards us – perhaps the leader of a counter-attack. I was glad that I had got the men

under cover ready to receive it. Kneeling inside the gun position, my rifle resting on the wall I was able to shoot him. He screamed, spun round, and fell.

It was later discovered that this man had seen the raiders and was running towards an alarm bell. A handful more made a fight of it and two were killed by Young and Lance Corporal Harper with his Thompson, but as the official report put it Major Churchill's men had found most of the surviving coast battery gunners on Maaloy 'demoralised and dazed' by the pummelling they had received from sea and air. Many were found inside their shelters, believing that an air raid was still in progress, and surrendered more or less quietly. Sergeant R. G. Herbert found sixteen, including the senior officer, hiding in one bunker, and took them all alive. The battery commander's office was now located, ablaze: nevertheless some of its paperwork was quickly lifted and dumped into sandbags ready to go back to the UK for further study.

By 9.20 Major Churchill was able to report that all resistance had ceased. With the guns out of action two of the supporting destroyers, *Onslow* and *Oribi*, were able to enter the Ulversund safely. It now proved possible to spare a troop from the Commandos on Maaloy and ferry them across to Mortenes, where they destroyed a fish oil factory. Captain Birney, with 'Group Five', was landed after Maaloy had been forced but was similarly successful. His little party blocked the road, and managed to apprehend a number of Germans escaping off the beaches from vessels that the destroyers had now begun to engage. A patrol from 'Group Five' also entered North Vaagso, where they occupied the telephone exchange, destroyed it before leaving, and also arrested a collaborator.

For the main party at South Vaagso it was a very different story. Here the primary tasks were demolitions, the knocking out of an anti-aircraft gun, and the elimination of a couple of machine-gun nests. Yet nothing was simple, as the official report related:

Group Two, from the start, encountered very stiff opposition, both from German infantry who fought to the last man in the buildings in which they were established, and from snipers, armed often with automatic rifles, who took up positions on the hillside west of town where they were very difficult to locate owing to the excellent natural cover. It must be emphasised that the opposition in South Vaagso was severe in degree and skilful in quality. It appears from the interrogation of prisoners that the garrison had been augmented by a detachment who had been moved into the town for Christmas, but, however that may be, there is no doubt that the fighting spirit, marksmanship, and efficiency of the enemy in this area was of a high order.

The key problem was that everything degenerated very quickly into street fighting and in leading from the front many of the officers, and several NCOs, had become casualties. Of six officers in the first two Troops into action two were killed and three wounded. One officer was killed trying to break into the back of a house, others were put out of action soon afterwards, as Durnford–Slater later recalled:

> Algy Forrester went off like a rocket with his No. 4 Troop down the street of the town, leaving a trail of dead Germans behind him. The Troop had just lost Arthur Komrower, who had suffered severe leg and back injuries when he was pinned between a landing craft and a rock. The third officer of 4 Troop was Bill Lloyd, who, with Algy, had developed the technique of landing on rough and rocky shores. Bill had hardly got going before he was shot, clean through the neck. That was the end of him for this operation. Algy waded in, shouting and cheering his men, throwing grenades into each house as they came to it and firing from the hip with his Tommy gun [...] He led an assault against the German headquarters, in the Ulversund Hotel, and was about to toss a grenade in when one of the enemy, firing through the front door, shot him. As he fell he landed on his own grenade, which exploded a second later.

The popular Norwegian officer, Captain Martin Linge, soon stepped into the breach but he too was shot down and killed, attempting to force open a door. According to the citation for his Distinguished Conduct Medal, command of the attack on the hotel finally devolved to Corporal E. G. 'Knocker' White – who took part in a 'series of assaults' and finally destroyed it. 'He personally accounted for some fourteen of the enemy,' with gallantry and leadership 'of a high order.' Nor was White the only one upon whom heavy responsibility was foisted, for, as the official report observed, much of the weight now fell on 'small parties' often 'under the leadership of junior NCOs', who now made understandably slow progress when moves against the houses were also countered by crossfire from the hill. Sergeant Cork located an enemy armoured vehicle, which had been previously identified in an intelligence report, in a garage, and promptly blew it up – but using too large a charge was himself killed in the explosion.

It was clear that the main assault of 'Group Two' needed every available man if the struggle for South Vaagso was going to be won, and the fighting soon sucked in the 'Group Four' reserve, reinforcements from 'Group One', and even remaining spare hands from Maaloy Island. Amongst the first of the reinforcements into the fray was Lieutenant Denis W. V. P. O'Flaherty and a section from 'Group One'. This party had moved extremely swiftly along the coast road, chasing a few surprised German Marines from their billets, wounding two of them, and at one point accidentally throwing a grenade at a Norwegian civilian, who quickly made himself known. On arrival at the original 'Group Two' landing point they were directed on up the main street, passing the bodies of men who had already fallen – and sprinting across open areas. O'Flaherty now gained Captain Bradley's position, finding him in a firefight with a sniper, and buildings beginning to burn. Making his way via a baker's house he now attempted a solo reconnaissance of factory buildings occupied by the enemy – but immediately bumped into Germans defending the end of an alleyway. He shot one but was knocked over by the explosion of a stick grenade, falling flat on his face and breaking his nose. His section was lucky to extricate itself, under fire, with one more casualty.

Captain Young arrived with half his troop under Sergeants Herbert and Connolly, and two of the official photographers, landing just about the point where the fighting appeared to have stalled, and quickly met up with the main party. Durnford-Slater decided that the best way forward was along the waterfront, rushing from building to building, taking the route least exposed to the snipers on the hill. When Hooper's Troop arrived it was to move in support of Captain Bardley: Young's party would be supported by O'Flaherty – who had just received his second minor wound· when nicked by a bullet – the two joining up at the warehouse from which one of the enemy positions had now been pinpointed. As Young later recalled:

> In street fighting it is extremely difficult to locate the enemy, and so as soon as we got into a warehouse with a reasonable view I posted Lance Corporal Hills with a Bren in an upper window from which he could cover our advance. There was a small building about 20 yards away to our left front and this I made our next bound. We had to dash out through the door one at a time.

On arrival at the next building Germans were seen disappearing inside, but were persuaded to emerge when one of the Commandos fired a long burst from his Thompson. Three men were captured, including, remarkably enough, one who had been a professional opera singer in civilian life; but a shot now rang out from an unexpected angle and one of the raiders was mortally wounded. Lack of windows in the new building prevented observation of the sniper, so the party dashed on again only to be checked by grenades thrown from cover. Three fell not far from Young, though luckily that which landed closest failed to detonate. The Commandos replied in kind, throwing about a dozen Mills bombs into the building that harboured most of the enemy. Confident that this would have put the Germans out of action, Young walked in:

> There was a little hallway with a wooden staircase leading up to the right and a doorway straight ahead. The door, if there was one, was open and the room was black as night. I was silhouetted in the doorway. Two shots rang out from a point across the room to my right. I fired and sprang back into the open. The Germans had retreated to an inner room.

For the moment the attack had stalled again, but now Durnford-Slater managed to extricate himself from where some of the Commandos had been pinned by sniper fire, and again caught up with the lead troops behind a large woodpile. During the course of making his way from group to group that day, both his orderlies were wounded and he narrowly escaped death from a grenade landing at his feet. The bomb-thrower had then attempted to surrender but was shot down by a Commando. It gave the Colonel pause for thought: 'Can a man throw a death-dealing grenade one second and surrender the next? I hardly think he can expect much mercy.' Given the situation, the only quick way to get the Germans out appeared to be to burn them out. A bucket of petrol was fetched, but in the lapse of time it took to appear a brave but impetuous O'Flaherty, 'fighting mad' as he was described in one account, had led another impromptu attack on the enemy-held building. As he entered, a bullet went clean through his face, breaking his jaw and taking out one eye. Amazingly, he and the wounded Sergeant Sherrington were able to struggle back out again soon afterwards, right under the noses of the defenders. With the injured clear Sergeant Herbert heaved the petrol through the entrance and a grenade ignited it. A Bren gunner cut down two of the enemy who fled the flames.

Gradually, resistance slackened. Enough space had been claimed for demolitions and evacuations to be achieved unmolested, so roadblocks were established against the possibility of counter-attack. Captain Bradley's team set light to the Firda factory, and other installations exploded or burned. As Durnford-Slater remarked:

> We carried out demolitions so effectively that we used most of the stores we had brought ashore for this purpose, 300lb of plastic explosive, 150lb of ammonal explosive, 150 incendiary bombs, sixty guncotton primers and 1,400 feet of fuse. Before any German-occupied building was blown up a member of our intelligence section searched through it for documents. This precaution paid off beautifully when we found the master code for the whole of the German Navy ...

The Commandos then withdrew in sequence, one troop at a time. The Colonel, first in, was also last off.

The official report on Vaagso listed nine enemy, and enemy-controlled, vessels of various sizes destroyed. The largest of these was the 3,000-ton SS *Remar Edzard Fritzen*, the smallest were armed tugs and trawlers. A total of ninety-eight enemy personnel were captured, along with four 'Quislings'; seventy-seven Norwegians who wished to escape to the UK were also brought out. Five various factories and canning plants were destroyed, along with the Maaloy battery, an anti-aircraft gun, a number of barrack buildings and offices, a telephone exchange, a radio mast, various stores and a headquarters. German casualties were estimated at well over 100, and a number of enemy aircraft claimed. Much of the action had been witnessed by a Reuter's correspondent, an Army Film Unit under Captain Harry Rignold, correspondent Jack Ramsden, and Lieutenant H. E. G. Malindine of the Army Photographic Unit. The official British communiqué declared the raid 'entirely successful in all respects'. *The Times* carried a piece on 'a brilliant little raid' in which 'clockwork precision' had played a vital part. Actions at Vaagso resulted in the award of twenty-two gallantry medals and thirty 'Mentions in Despatches'.

This, however, was just one side of the story. Reports from Berlin claimed, inaccurately, that the raiders had been 'ejected': however, references to British losses had better basis in fact. Eight aircraft had been destroyed in the air battle overhead, there was some damage to British ships and two Naval personnel died with four wounded. One of the Naval officers, interviewed some years after the event, was clear that though ship-to-shore communications with the Commandos had been maintained, Air-to-Naval communications had suffered 'complete breakdown due to lack of training and rehearsal' and there was 'utter lack of control over participating air forces'. Interestingly, and despite the reputation of Vaagso as a traumatic bout of street-fighting, the Commando dead numbered eighteen, with fifty-seven wounded. Arguably this was minor for a street battle of the period – Durnford-Slater calling the loss 'reasonably light'. Perhaps the most significant results of 'Anklet' and 'Archery' were that they convinced Hitler of the need to improve the defences of Norway unnecessarily. They also gave Allied powers at least one good news story with which to compare Malaya, Pearl Harbor, and the titanic events of the Eastern Front.

Perhaps oddly, October 1941 saw the end of Admiral Keyes as Director Combined Operations. Yet Keyes had never been satisfied with the way his role had worked out. The title appeared to signify great things, but in practice Churchill had never got round to carving the Admiral a clear niche. Keyes had complained to the Prime Minister that he could not continue to hold the office, unless he was 'given the power' to be a 'real Director'. Indeed, the Chiefs of Staff had managed to limit his scope quite effectively, and had made sure that larger-scale operations in particular would fall to the responsibility of the Commander-in-Chief Home Forces, working with the relevant Air and Naval Chiefs. By September 1941 the main responsibility that Keyes had left was training centres, such as the one at Inveraray. It was here that the C-in-C Home Forces, General Alan Brooke, spent three days with Keyes that month. The result was not happy, as Brooke later recalled:

> The whole of my visit to Roger Keyes was an attempt on his part to try and convince me that our Commando policy was right. He failed to do so and I remained convinced to the end of the war that the Commandos should never have been divorced from the Army in the way that they were.

The outspoken Keyes soon left in disgust, defeated by power politics and inter-service rivalry – later blaming officers who had briefed against him and the impossibility of his position. Churchill and others blamed the Admiral's sometimes abrasive attitude and failure to work with others. Many had thought his schemes beyond reckless, his acknowledged acuity past its best, and were pleased to see the back of him. Sadly for Keyes, tragedy quickly overtook professional disappointment, for it was just a month later, in November 1941, that his son, Major (Temporary

Lieutenant Colonel) Geoffrey Keyes, was killed in North Africa. His end came on one of those very Commando missions that was so bold in conception, but risky almost to the point of folly.

Field Marshal Erwin Rommel had become so regarded as a bogeyman, and General Auchinleck had become so sick of him, that an order was issued that he was not even to be mentioned, as his very name might sap morale. At the beginning of 'Operation Crusader' the depleted No. 11 (Scottish) Commando was tasked with dealing with Rommel once and for all: they were to capture or assassinate him at his billet at Beda Littoria. This would not only be a serious blow to German morale, but would dislocate command of the Afrika Korps at the very moment that their charismatic leader was most required. Almost at once, however, plans went awry. The small landing force was transported to the coast by submarine under the overall command of Colonel Laycock, but had not got ashore in the numbers expected. The remainder beached at Hamma – well over 200 miles behind the lines – and had advanced over difficult country, only to discover that Rommel was not at the Beda Littoria headquarters, but was thought to be nearby at a house at Sidi Rafa. Accordingly, Major Keyes and eighteen all ranks slipped into the village to hunt him out, bluffing their way past an Italian and some Arabs.

With the majority of the Commandos positioned nearby and in the grounds of the house, Keyes, with Captain Campbell and Sergeant Terry, had crept around the back, attempting to gain a stealthy entry. None was found but they bumped into a German who was not to be taken prisoner easily and shouted warnings until shot. The occupants of the house were roused and a shooting match ensued with a man rushing down stairs. Keyes and Campbell began to clear the downstairs rooms with grenades, but on opening one door and putting in a bomb, were greeted by a burst of submachine-gun fire that mortally wounded Keyes. The grenade exploded and Campbell and Terry tried to shoot their way out, but Campbell was badly wounded in the leg – according to one account by friendly fire – and could not escape. The surviving Commandos were quickly pursued by both German and Italian troops, and only Terry and Laycock managed to get away – by walking for forty-one days and avoiding the enemy. It later transpired that Rommel was not even in Africa: he had been in Rome consulting with his Italian allies. Sergeant Terry was awarded a Distinguished Conduct Medal. Keyes, 'by his fearless disregard of the great dangers' and 'magnificent leadership and outstanding gallantry', became the first Commando to win a Victoria Cross.

Chapter 3

St Nazaire

The problem that the raid on St Nazaire set out to solve was a knotty one. The port had the largest dry dock in Europe and was located in Brittany, yet was 6 miles upstream from the mouth of the River Loire. This made it ideal for the servicing of German warships, and indeed the *Bismarck* had been headed for this haven when sunk – and the *Tirpitz* might yet repeat such a venture. To make matters worse, St Nazaire was also a U-boat base and one of the facilities that helped the enemy in the struggle for the Atlantic, making it difficult for supplies, and American troops, to reach the UK.

Massive air raids might eventually have knocked out the St Nazaire facilities – but such a course of action, even if ultimately successful, would have had several very undesirable consequences. The first was the diplomatic and humanitarian disaster following the almost inevitable heavy loss of French civilian life. Similarly, bombing was not yet sufficiently accurate to take out individual lock gates with any certainty, and U-boat pens were of such massive construction that the aircraft and bomb types available in 1942 were not really suitable for their destruction. Moreover, the target was approximately 250 miles from the British mainland: assuming a total distance travelled of about 600 miles, proper fighter cover would have been difficult. Repeated raids would have made it virtually certain that German aircraft would have been able to intercept incoming planes, and flak guns were already in position. Significant RAF losses could be expected, whilst targets in Germany went unmolested. An attack by major warships with heavy guns was similarly problematic. The target lay up a long channel with tricky shallows, and possibly mines, to negotiate. The river entrance itself was commanded by copious emplaced artillery and was frequented by the U-boats on their way to and from their Atlantic stations. Standing off and bombarding St Nazaire from a range of miles would have created a similarly inaccurate spread of devastation to an air attack – with no guarantees of destroying the vital facilities.

There was, however, another way to hit the St Nazaire docks – a surprise Commando raid, delivering explosives right to the spot where they would do the most damage, and without significant risk to either bomber forces or major Naval ships. This idea had been floated as early as August 1941, but serious planning did not commence until Captain J. Hughes-Hallet RN suggested combining raiders with a massive bomb. The method of delivery would be a relatively modest sacrificial vessel to blow and block the main gates, to which would be added small craft to take the Commando demolition squads into the heart of the enemy position. Initially, it was also planned that 350 aircraft would support the main mission, though this was later scaled back to just sixty-five. The small craft were sixteen Fairmile Motor Launches, of wood, lightly armed, and stowed with tanks of petrol for the long round trip. These 'MLs' were of several slightly differing models but the usual armament was a 20mm Oerlikon gun forward and aft, plus several Lewis guns mounted for both surface and AA work. One extraordinary addition, of rather dubious utility, was the Holman projector – designed to lob Mills bombs into the path of low-flying aircraft.

The Commandos themselves were now much better equipped than they had been in the dark days of 1940, but still maintained considerable flexibility in the way that weaponry was allotted by keeping central stores – now within each Commando – so that armament could be fitted to the task. As one American report observed:

> Every man who joins the Commando brings his own rifle or pistol, and he is also provided with a fighting knife, which is used by the Commandos with particular effectiveness. Each Commando headquarters has a separate store of extra weapons so that extreme flexibility in armament is assured. A typical store contains: Bren guns; Thompson submachineguns; caliber .50 [*sic*, Boys .55] antitank rifles; 2-inch and 3-inch mortars with a supply of both smoke and high-explosive shells; defensive (fragmentation) Mills hand grenades; offensive (plastic body, concussion-type) hand grenades; smoke pots; Very pistols; 'knuckle dusters' (brass knuckles); 'Limpets' (magnetic, acid, high-explosive mines), one type suitable for use against ships and another against tanks; and demolitions of all types. Each troop is equipped with Bren guns, Thompson submachineguns, an antitank rifle, and a 2-inch mortar; normally each subsection is allocated one Bren gun and a submachinegun, the allocation of the antitank rifle and the mortar being left to discretion of the troop commander.

For St Nazaire, the Commandos were organised strictly by task, men of the right skills being grouped into parties of sizes that could be accommodated in the transport available – these being essentially units of fifteen. The 265 all ranks were divided into three main groups. Two groups would travel in MLs, the third aboard the destroyer HMS *Campbeltown* – sheltered as far as possible behind armoured screens. The broad plan of attack was that 'assault' parties would take on the enemy and clear out his strongpoints, whilst 'demolition' parties, following in their wake, would seek out specific dock facilities and destroy them with explosive charges. The biggest single contingent for the raid would be drawn from Lieutenant Colonel Newman's No. 2 Commando, but with specialists added from 1, 3, 4, 5, 9 and 12 Commandos.

The main objective of Captain Bertie Hodgson's 'Group One', eighty-nine all ranks, transported in six MLs, was the seizure of the Old Mole and Old Town on the south-eastern corner of the dock complex. Here the demolition teams would destroy the power station and boiler house and the gates and bridges of the 'New Entrance' lock. Hodgson was then to secure the Mole for as long as was required for the withdrawal of the Commandos, who would re-embark here after their missions. From ML 447 Captain Birney and a fourteen-man assault team was to land and attack the two pillboxes on the Old Mole, then form a bridgehead for the protection of its landward end. With a similar fifteen-strong team, Captain Hodgson in ML 341 was to make landfall on the long East Jetty, destroy its flak positions, and secure its landward end before sending out patrols to the north. Taking advantage of the work of the assault teams in knocking out the main German positions, Lieutenant P. Walton and ten men from ML 457 would land and demolish the northernmost lock gate and lifting bridge. The remaining troops on this vessel, under Captain Pritchard and Lieutenant Watson, formed the 'demolition control party'. A second demolition team of seven, commanded by Captain Bradley, travelled in ML 307 together with a couple of medical orderlies. Their target was the southern lock gate. Lieutenant Bronwin and fifteen men in ML 443 were to target the power station and boiler house. The final fourteen-strong team, under Lieutenant R. Swayne, on ML 306 would blow up the lock gates and swing bridge at the South Entrance.

'Group Two', comprising eighty-five all ranks commanded by Captain 'Micky' Burn, was intended to bypass the Old Town and land a little further to the north around the 'Old Entrance' capturing the area between the Normandie dock and submarine basin. Here they were to blow the Pont de Douane, knock out flak towers, bridges and lock gates. Burn's own fourteen-man assault team, in ML 192, was assigned the flak towers at the north end of the Ile de Penhouet, and the position commanding the swing bridge, followed by the creation of a defensive block at the northern end of the Normandie dock. A similar size group, under Lieutenant Woodcock in ML 262, was to blow the lock gates and their operating mechanisms, as well as the swing bridge across the old entrance. RSM Moss and another fourteen men formed a reserve, which would engage enemy vessels in the St Nazaire basin as required. Meanwhile, Lieutenants Jenkins and Pennington would take their team from ML 268 to destroy the swing bridge at the north end of the basin. In ML 156 the mission of Captain Hooper and his team was conditional on whether guns had been mounted on the waterfront between the Old Mole and the Old Entrance. If they were, he was to attack them; if not, his men were available to fire on vessels in the dock or be used as a reserve. In the event of heavy resistance, they could call upon Troop Sergeant Major Haines and the team in ML 177.

Major Copland's 75-strong 'Group Three' was to travel aboard HMS *Campbeltown*. Two demolition teams and their supports, commanded by Lieutenants Chant and Etches, would attack each end of the Normandie dock, targeting the main pumping house, lock gate machinery and winding huts. Lieutenant Roderick and fourteen men would assault east of the dock, where they would single out the flak positions and fuel storage. Captain Roy and his team would take out flak positions on the south-west corner of the dock, then take up positions to cover the withdrawal and protect against any attack from enemy vessels from that quarter. With *Campbeltown* now effectively a massive time bomb wedged in the Normandie dock, soon all the main dock gates would be ripped from their mountings, mechanisms spoiled, gun positions wrecked and the various damaged facilities isolated on a series of separate islands: St Nazaire would be all but useless for months. The main docks and dry dock would be inaccessible to Axis shipping, a major submarine base would be out of commission, and whatever vessels were in port might be trapped or destroyed. With bridges blown and parties in strategic covering positions the Commandos could then withdraw, the planned retirement being carried out in two steps. First a fall back from Penhouet Island, then a final bridgehead evacuation from the Old Mole. Such was the scheme, but the execution would be tragically different.

The two lines astern formation used by the attackers might have been vaguely reminiscent of Nelson at Trafalgar, were it not for the fact that most of the vessels were smaller, flimsier, and constrained by the channel leading to the dock. Moreover, unlike the Nelsonian scenario, the plan was to approach undetected rather than overawe the enemy. Up to a point, this was what happened. The defenders were initially mystified by the behaviour of the aircraft of the diversionary raid (which dropped few bombs but spent a lot of time over the target area) and were at first taken in by what appeared a routine signal from the vessels that they had orders to enter the harbour. Just before 1.30 a.m., however, the game was up: a further exchange of messages had left the Germans unconvinced and a recognition flare used by the attackers was not of the correct type. With the formation well into the narrow estuary, bathed in the glow of multiple searchlights, and German guns giving rapid fire, there was nothing left but to shoot – with *Campbeltown* opening the return. Thereafter, all the main armaments blasted away, whilst Commandos manning Bren guns on

---

Joseph C. Haydon

J. C. Haydon (1899–1971) attended Downside and Sandhurst and was first commissioned into the Irish Guards in December 1917. Though promoted to full lieutenant just after the end of the Great War, it took him a another decade to reach the rank of captain. In the early 1930s he was a Staff Officer, having charge of weapons training for London District, obtaining his majority in 1934. Just before the outbreak of the Second World War he was Military Assistant to the Secretary of State for War at the War Office in London. With the coming of the war, Haydon soon came to notice, commanding a composite battalion during operations at the Hook of Holland; and later, 2nd Battalion of the Irish Guards in the defence of Boulogne in May 1940. His performance in both duties gained him the Distinguished Service Order for his 'bravery, coolness, quick grasp of the situation, and ability to give well thought out orders at a moment's notice'. With the formation of the Commandos he was appointed first commander of the Special Service Brigade. In 1944 he commanded 1st Guards Brigade in Italy, but later moved to Washington as as a member of the Joint Services Mission. In 1946 Haydon was appointed British Army representative on the Joint Chiefs of Staff Committee in Australia, and finally, in Germany, was made Chief of the Intelligence Division of the Control Commission. Created a Commander of the Bath in 1948, he retired from active service in 1951, but worked at the Foreign Office until 1958.

the decks attempted to knock out the searchlights. Some were hit, but others switched off immediately the tracer bullets arced towards them.

In the vanguard, gunboat MGB 314 took the brunt of this punishment, and lost the hydraulic power to her machine-gun turrets due to punctured lines. *Campbeltown* was hit repeatedly from several points of the compass, an effect that Major Copland described as like being in the centre of a bowl, into which was poured a 'hailstorm of illuminated fire'. One shell, bursting on the deck, injured most of a section, and also mortally wounded Lance Corporal Donaldson. Lieutenant Etches was hit and now the shooting became more concentrated and accurate as *Campbeltown* neared its target. Riding ahead of *Campbeltown*, ML 270 and ML 160 were armed with torpedoes as well as guns – but not carrying any troops. They therefore did their best to cover the vessels behind, but ML 270 suffered steering damage from fire from the Old Mole and was forced to break off. ML 160 carried on alone past the Normandie dock, drawing fire as she went, and managed to shoot off torpedoes and engage flak posts.

ML 192 was very uncomfortably placed just behind *Campbeltown*, and seemed to be absorbing not only aimed fire, but rounds that missed the fast-moving destroyer. Then she was struck by a shell on the waterline, one amidships, another on the port quarter, and yet another in the engine room, which stopped the engines and set her ablaze. With control lost she smashed into the shore, many of her crew already dead or wounded. Not far away, ML 447 was having an even less happy time: concentrated close-range fire killed many of those aboard, then she was also hit in the engines and started to burn. ML 457 was slightly more fortunate – she was riddled with holes, and had begun to list, but with luck, as well as judgement, got under cover of the Mole itself. There she landed her Commandos, unaware for the time being that so many of their comrades had already perished or were unable to get ashore. ML 446 was raked by fire. As medic Lance Corporal Webb reported:

> Lieutenant Oughtred was badly wounded in the neck [...] I was called to Captain Hodgson on the other side of the main deck. He was evidently badly wounded: I found it difficult to see what I was doing even though the searchlight was full on us. We were in the deep shadow of the bridge. I could detect neither pulse nor heartbeat, and when, feeling for his wounds, I had found more than a dozen entrance holes in his body.

ML 307 did manage to get close in – but as she carried a demolition party and a medical team was not best placed to execute the landing. Indeed, the launch was soon under fire from a gun on the blockhouse, where it was supposed to land. As Medical officer David Paton recalled:

> The first shot fell into the water only 10 yards away, the next was 5 yards away. I don't know what happened to the third, but the fourth produced a draught as it shot by me [...] All hell broke loose. Searchlights by the dozen illuminated us from both sides and we became shooting targets for a variety of guns. At first I took cover behind a depth charge on the deck, but a bit of that went whizzing past my ear, so I stood up [...] The air was thick with tracer shells coming from all directions, rather like cricket balls. You could see them coming and jump out of the way [...] We pushed our ladders up against the mole, but anyone who tried to climb up fell off because the ladders were pushed out from above. Now bombs began to be rolled over onto our decks and we were all dancing about kicking them into the water.

Several Commandos were wounded.

On the *Campbeltown*, Lieutenant S. W. Chant of No. 5 Commando, with a squad of four NCOs, was under orders to destroy the main pumping house and caisson operating machinery of the Normandie dock. The impact of a warship doing 20 knots into solid dock gates was 'shattering': most on board were already prostrate, sheltering behind armour on the deck when the vessel hit. Chant recalled forcing himself to stand up and pick up his rucksack:

> Others like me were likewise struggling to their feet, but there were some who lay still or struggled to rise only to fall back. Firing was still going on all around us and one of my first reactions was to note the almost toy-like chatter of our Commandos' Tommy guns and stripped Lewis guns as they landed and joined in the firing. Meanwhile the heavy German counter-barrage continued.

Covered by the attacks of the fourteen-man assault parties of Lieutenant Roderick and Captain Roy, plus fire from the decks of *Campbeltown*, the demolition groups virtually fell down the ladder over the bows. Chant's party blew open the lock of the pump house with a small charge and raced inside. Some of the team were already wounded, and Sergeant Chamberlain was left guarding the entrance. The remaining demolition men went down the steps and laid about 40lb of explosives on each of the giant pumps, set 90-second fuses and ran back up into the open air, only just getting far enough away before gigantic explosions sent blocks of masonry around the dock.

The work of Lieutenant Smalley was accomplished with similar success in the wrecking of the winding wheels and motors of the southern caisson of the Normandie Dock. At the northern end, matters were far more fraught. The run-up to the target crossed several areas of open ground that were under enemy fire, not least from vessels moored in the dock. Particularly troublesome were two tankers mounted with 20mm guns, and to cover the work of the demolition men meant silencing them. This was accomplished by storming the ships, but in the process Lieutenant Burtinshaw and half a dozen men lost their lives. This action, nevertheless, enabled Lieutenant Purdon to destroy the northern winding gear, and reduce its hut to a small pile of tangled rubble. Charges were also blown against the northern gate of the Normandie Dock – the results here were less spectacular but telltale streams of bubbles showed that this, too, had been damaged below the waterline, and was now leaking badly.

Given the battering that the launches had received on the way in, and the failure of a couple more to land their charges, less than half of the Commandos had managed to get ashore – and not all of these in fighting condition. Even so, serious damage had been inflicted on shore installations: but now emerged another horrendous problem. The plan had envisaged that the Old Mole would be securely in British hands early in the raid, with plenty of launches held there ready to execute an orderly withdrawal. In fact, most of the port side column had been wrecked, and whilst many Commandos had succeed in fighting their way on to their objectives, their retreat was effectively blocked. Captain Birney and his team were charged with covering the Old Mole, but his vessel, ML 447, had long since been set afire, and those Commandos aboard not already dead had had to swim for their lives. The wounded Birney was himself almost rescued by another launch, but in the end crawled ashore only to expire from his injuries and exhaustion. There was no covering team, and no waiting transport. In fact, not even the rockets for signalling the retirement had survived.

Colonel Newman had now been joined by Major Copland from *Campbeltown*, but even so, still had less than 100 live troops on French soil, with no obvious exit. These few had long since been outnumbered by the flak crews, German sailors and various guards of the port, though for a while they had kept the initiative due to surprise and darkness. Yet, with the larger German ground forces of the 679th Infantry closing in, dawn only hours away, and little ammunition remaining, it was a choice of surrender or attempt to fight a way out overland. As Newman recalled:

> There were no MLs alongside the Old Mole and the general view of the river so far as I could see presented only a picture of sinking craft. I therefore decided that transport home would not be forthcoming, so calling Major Copland and Stan Day [adjutant of 'No. 2' Commando] into a confab by a railway truck, I decided to break inland with the idea of making for Spain.

With so many casualties the attacking order of battle had become meaningless, and to execute the desperate plan of escape and evasion the Commandos were now roughly reordered into groups of about twenty. Creeping along behind stranded railway trucks, different routes out were attempted – but 'Bridge G' had already become a death trap, so it was quickly determined that 'Bridge D' across the mouth of the Bassin de St Nazaire offered the only credible chance of success. This the Commandos crossed in short rushes, using 'fire and movement' – but not without casualties – as was remembered by Lieutenant Purdon:

> A hail of enemy fire erupted as we crossed the bridge, projectiles slamming into girders, bullets whining and ricocheting off them and from the cobbles. There was a roar of gunfire of varying calibres and the percussion of 'potato masher' grenades as we reached the far end. One of the latter burst at my feet and the explosion, combined with my own forward velocity, lifted me clean off the ground, wounding me in the left leg and shoulder.

Six of the raiding vessels were lost in St Nazaire harbour, and a couple more on the way out. Just nine of the seventeen committed to the attack survived long enough to clear the French coast on the return leg – and of these half were already badly damaged. Several managed to rendezvous with the destroyers at 'Position Y' and here the crews from MLs 156, 270, and 446 were taken aboard, together with the wounded from Motor Gun Boat 314. These four leaking hulks were then scuttled. ML 341, which suffered engine trouble and had failed to enter the Loire as a result, managed to transfer her troops to another vessel. She then made her way home alone. Motor Launches 160, 307 and 443 missed the rendezvous but nevertheless limped home – harassed more than once by German aircraft, on whom they returned a spirited fire. This left only ML 306, which escaped from the Loire – making smoke and with much of its armament inoperative – only to encounter a larger vessel in the early hours of the morning. Unfortunately, this warship was the German destroyer *Jaguar*, with which the little ML now engaged in a highly unequal duel. Commandos manned Lewis guns and Brens until they were cut down and the destroyer actually rammed its opponent, striking it a glancing blow that knocked men into the water. With Lieutenant Henderson the Commander of the British vessel dead, and most of the crew now wounded or helpless, ML 306 was finally surrendered.

With daylight the land battle had degenerated into a hunt for fugitives. *Campbeltown* was still stuck against the dock, and it was questionable whether 'Operation Chariot' had been anything but brave failure. Partial damage of the St Nazaire dock facilities, and relatively modest German losses in guns and men, had been traded against the cream of the raiding force, plus a flotilla of small vessels. By 10 a.m. the Germans were confident that a large raid had been successfully defeated, and that there was nothing more to do but sort out the casualties and assess damage. Prisoners were gathered, and anybody who looked like an officer was interrogated about the purpose of the raid. German soldiers and sailors now strolled around the docks taking photographs of each other, the dead, and *Campbeltown*, which looked for all the world like a huge buckled hatchet embedded at a crazy angle into the dock gates. Some even stood triumphantly on her deck. At 10.35 this picture changed abruptly in a huge explosion, as the 9,000 lbs of ammonal that had sat peacefully for most of the night erupted the water of the dock violently into the air. Where *Campeltown* had been there was now nothing, and surrounding parts of the quay were liberally littered with both debris and human entrails, odd chunks of which rained down for several seconds. In fact, the explosion had finished what the ramming had begun: the dock gates had given way catastrophically and the destroyer, now without any bows, had ridden up into the Normandie Dock atop a wall of water. This mini tidal wave took with it at least two vessels, which were swamped by the rushing water. Though not all targets had been destroyed, the Normandie Dock would still be inoperative when visited by Commander Ryder in 1946.

A total of 135 awards were made to men who went to St Nazaire. Five Victoria Crosses headed this list. Three went to Navy men and two to the Commandos. Sergeant T. F. Durrant won the Victoria Cross attempting to engage the German warship with a Lewis gun from ML 306, despite multiple, and ultimately mortal, wounds. Colonel Newman's VC citation noted that he need not have landed, but

> was one of the first ashore and, during five hours of bitter fighting, he personally entered several houses and shot up the occupants and supervised the operations in the town, utterly regardless of his own safety [...] An enemy gun position on the roof of a U-boat pen had been causing heavy casualties to the landing craft [*sic*] and Lieutenant Colonel Newman directed the fire of a mortar against this position to such an effect that the gun was silenced. Still fully exposed, he then brought machinegun fire to bear on an armed trawler in the harbour.

Though slightly wounded by an enemy grenade he tried to fight his way out but was captured by dint of overwhelming numbers. Major W. C. Copland of No. 2 Commando, 'conspicuous throughout the entire fighting', and instrumental in getting the wounded off *Campbeltown*, was given a DSO. ML 192 was hit repeatedly and set ablaze near the Old Mole: Captain M. C. Burn of No. 2 Commando ended up in the water with most of his men killed and wounded. Nevertheless, armed with grenades, he pressed on alone to the flak towers that were his objective, ascertaining they were empty before eventually being captured. Like Chant, who suffered multiple wounds, Lieutenant Etches of No. 3 Commando, and Captain Day, also of No. 2 Commando, he was awarded a Military Cross. A number of Distinguished Conduct and Military Medals were won by other ranks. Remarkable amongst these was Sergeant Randall, who scaled the pumping station with Captain Roy, under fire, and 'forced the enemy gun crew to withdraw', and later manned a machine gun, giving covering fire, allowing his comrades an opportunity to escape.

Of 611 Army and Naval personnel in the raid, 168 were killed and 214 taken prisoner. Of thirty-nine Commando officers taking part, twenty-two were killed. Only three of the sixteen Motor Launches made it back to England. With 28 per cent dead and 33 per cent wounded, losses were proportionately higher than those suffered in the 'Charge of the Light Brigade' during the Crimean War. Colonel Newman recovered from his wound, but was still in captivity in Oflag 9A in March 1944, when, remarkably enough, he managed to send out an official prisoner-of-war postcard to Brigadier Haydon. It read: 'We are all very fit and cheerful and will be drinking a toast to you on the 28th.' Thus was celebrated the second anniversary of the remarkable raid on St Nazaire. 'Operation Chariot' had been an extremely expensive mission for the Commandos, but it was also one where genuine objectives of military importance were achieved. Many of the dock facilities targeted, including the most significant, had been destroyed. These included the vital lock gates, pumping and power stations, and the port had been rendered useless. *Tirpitz* would remain in Norway until sunk by the RAF. Moreover, casualties in the land battle had actually been balanced by destruction of the gun emplacements and the large numbers of the enemy killed when *Campbeltown* had detonated.

Chapter 4

Dieppe

Planning for what ultimately became the major raid on Dieppe was commenced by Combined Operations Headquarters as early as April 1942, with an outline plan being approved by the Chiefs of Staff on 13 May. The original objectives for code-name 'Rutter' were relatively modest, being a classic raiding operation – entailing the destruction of defences, aerodrome, dock facilities and such like. The shore batteries were to be tackled by parachutists. Yet other concerns were afoot in the background, not all of which were fully articulated. One of these was undoubtedly geopolitical in scope. With the war on the Eastern Front growing continually in scale and ferocity, and Soviet survival apparently hanging by a thread, Stalin's demands for a 'Second Front' were becoming ever more difficult to ignore. A larger raid would not be a new front, though if successful it might very well convince the enemy that they needed to retain forces in France, which could not then be used in Russia. It has also been said, more clearly in retrospect than at the time, that Dieppe was actually a 'dress rehearsal' for the second front, and an attempt to ascertain how realistic the seizure of a significant French port might be. Nevertheless, the Dieppe raid came perilously close to cancellation that summer when an unsuccessful exercise, followed by poor weather, led first to postponement, then dispersal of the troops.

In its final form, 'Rutter' became 'Operation Jubilee' – a beast that was neither fish nor fowl. It was not small enough to be a swift 'hit and run' with limited objectives, nor was it large enough to bite and hold a significant port in the face of serious opposition. Perhaps unfortunately for the Commandos, the parachute element of the venture was deleted, and the shore batteries either side of Dieppe were allotted to them to silence by means of amphibious attack. To make matters worse, the role of 'Combined Ops' in planning was scaled back as the size of the venture grew. Another failing was something of a hiatus in command – as a major raid employing Canadian troops and tanks as well as all three arms of service this was an exceptionally big 'Combined Operation', over which Mountbatten strove to assert his authority. Who explicitly approved the execution of the resurrected Dieppe plan has been a subject of controversy. Churchill would finally admit that he gave assent, but perhaps more importantly, no one was prepared to order cancellation of this dubious venture – though some of the generals did, in fact, speak up against it.

Planners certainly believed the idea that success was not only possible, but likely, given recent outcomes in Norway and at St Nazaire. Arguably the greatest failing of Dieppe was that its reasons never crystallised into one specific objective, with tangible results. St Nazaire had been difficult to organise, under-resourced, bloody, and hovered on the brink of failure – but its key objective, that of putting a major port out of action without deploying masses of bombers or killing large numbers of French civilians, had been achieved in spectacular fashion. The weapon, relatively weak as it was, had been fashioned explicitly for the task. The Dieppe force, conversely, remained a very uneasy compromise: neither small, swift, and light enough to get in and out quickly; nor large enough to crush all opposition. Perhaps most naively it was assumed that tanks could not only make an opposed landing, but perform tasks in support of the infantry, re-embark, and return in short order. This would have been a very tight mission for an unopposed exercise, but proved suicidal in battle.

Contrary to some later reports, the enemy had no explicit warning of the assault, but Dieppe was garrisoned by a full regiment of the German 302nd Division. The 302nd, formed in November 1940, was a so-called 'static division', created specifically for defence and was up to strength – though largely reliant on captured French equipment. Against these defenders and their fixed defences, Combined Operations was to despatch 5,000 Canadians, 1,000 Commandos and fifty US Rangers, plus a battalion of Churchill tanks. Air and sea support was significant. Naval forces deployed totalled 237 vessels, including eight destroyers and over 170 tank and infantry landing craft, whilst in the air, some dozens of squadrons were available, including seven from the US.

The Commando contribution was highly significant and ultimately the most successful of the whole sorry performance. The satisfactory achievements of the Commandos were all the more remarkable because they had not formed part of the original plan, for only in mid-July 1942 were they substituted for the paratroops. Three Commando units would be deployed at Dieppe: No. 3 and No. 4 protecting the flanks by disabling the heavy coast batteries at Berneval and Varengeville, and the new Royal Marine Commando acting as floating reserve in the centre. This unit was a novel departure, as it was the first Commando to be drawn from the Navy rather than the Army. First mustered on Valentine's Day 1942, and initially known as 'A' Commando, it would later be titled as No. 40 RM Commando. It was thought, rather optimistically, that on successful outcome of the mission this unit could be used to secure and remove captured enemy vessels. The Commandos would also be supplemented by some novel additions. These included fifteen Frenchmen of 'No. 10' Commando – sporting blue Marine uniforms and a national identity flash, and six men of the 'X' troop. These latter, though given 'English' identities and papers, were, in fact, Sudenten German-speaking Czechs. Amongst their special duties would be translation, and where possible 'shouting instructions calculated to mislead and confuse the enemy'.

Also very small in number, but arguably of even greater significance, were US soldiers fighting alongside the Commandos. Colonel Lucien Truscott was the first American to receive an official invitation 'to join the Commandos', as the preliminary phase in the establishment of a similar US force. The suggestion was proffered by General Mark W. Clark in Washington in April 1942, and by 17 May Truscott was in London. The brief of the original Rangers was to combine training and amphibious combat operations with their British hosts, and then – assuming they survived – return to spread their experience. The required manpower was drawn from units already in the UK, notably V Corps, 34th Infantry, and the newly-arrived 1st Armoured Division. Interestingly, it was proposed in some circles that the new US 'Special Force' would also be known as Commandos, but Eisenhower reportedly decided that this title was best left as distinctively British. Instead, the 'Ranger' name was selected as genuinely American, evoking the traditions of many different units of the old frontier, and specifically the deeds of the eighteenth-century 'Roger's Rangers'. The title was also consciously different to that of any other unit then in the US Army. The commanding officer selected for the new battalion was Major William Darby. Like the Commandos, the first Rangers went through selection, in this instance with a particular eye to 'pioneer' skills, climbing, scouting, perfect vision and healthy blood pressure. As many were in their mid-twenties, the average Ranger tended to be a little older than the normal infantry recruit, and most were unmarried. In this age before integration, there were no African Americans picked, and no Japanese Americans either – any particularly strong links with Italy and Germany were also examined before candidates were admitted. Nevertheless, there were men of native American ancestry in the ranks.

The US 1st Ranger Battalion was founded just a couple of months before Dieppe. Its establishment of 520 men, divided into six small companies, would be similar to that of the Commandos. The new Rangers were now rapidly packed off to Achnacarry to absorb as much training in limited time as possible – long and fast heavily laden marches, explosives training, live firing exercises and small boats all featured strongly in this induction. Commandos and Rangers alike also learned to work in pairs on many of their tasks, but quite a few did not get through the gruelling highland training and were promptly dropped. Those who did well did very well but, unsurprisingly, most grumbled about the quality of the British food. The successful now passed on to coastal landing exercises with their Commando comrades. Though there was much to learn in a short time, it is arguable that the Ranger weaponry and equipment was actually better than that used by the Commandos from the outset. The semi-automatic Garand rifle was already on issue – and in addition to knives in the Fairbairn-Sykes mould, many also possessed a set of 'brass knuckles'.

There have been many conflicting reports regarding the deployment of the US Rangers at Dieppe. According to recent research, the contingent was divided up amongst the participating units as follows: the bulk (of forty all ranks) was with No. 3 Commando, an officer and half a dozen or a dozen men being attached to the HQ, 3rd, 4th and 6th Troops. The senior officer present, Captain Roy A. Murray, went with the No. 3 HQ. The remaining Americans were allotted in penny packets. Sergeant Kenyon was the sole representative of the Rangers on Blue Beach with the Royal Regiment of Canada, and two others were the token presence with other Canadian units on 'Red' and 'White'. Lieutenant Flanagan and two NCOs were earmarked for Green Beach. Four Rangers – all of them NCOs – are known to have accompanied No. 4 Commando, the most senior of these being Staff Sergeant K. D. Stempson. Also attached were the Frenchmen, deployed at least in part for their language skills and scouting abilities. One of them, Sergeant François Balloche, would be awarded a Military Medal for his part in the action.

As on earlier missions, play would be made of the Commando reputation and media representatives were carried with the troops for maximum public effect. As War Correspondent A. B. Austin put it:

We had all heard about the Commandos, the raiding shock troops of the British Army, the hand-picked, disciplined guerrillas of our war, volunteers from every famous regiment, trained together for jobs which needed fast movement on foot, physical endurance, and quick thinking by every man. We had heard of the Vaagso, Lofoten, St Nazaire and Boulogne raids, all of them carried out by comparatively small Commando forces and we supposed there would be more raids of the same sort, perhaps bigger ones. But beyond that most of us had not, at that time, thought much about the practical problems of raiding on a scale large enough to amount to a second front diversion, or even of establishing a more permanent Second Front.

The final instruction for the Commando part of the operation was aided by a large model. Looking back Derek Mills-Roberts was suitably impressed:

Every road, house, track and every tree of any size was shown in detail and to perfection. I had memorised the terrain shown on the model so thoroughly that, like the Lord's Prayer or the National Anthem, it came to mind instinctively.

All in all, the model would have looked like a 'summer fairyland' suitable for 'any travel agent's window' – were it not for the brooding presence of a large six-gun battery located 1,200 scale yards behind the chalk cliffs.

It was also immediately before the raid that Austin formed an impression of Lord Lovat and his men. Lovat being a

tallish Commando officer with slightly wavy brown hair, a small Guards moustache, a full, youngish face, and a pleasant, speculative, slightly quizzical smile. He was wearing a woollen cap, an old battle-dress blouse and a pair of corduroy slacks. He wore no rank badges.

The Commandos were certainly equipped for raid rather than invasion and moved exceptionally light:

They didn't take anything at all. They just travelled in their woollen caps, battle-dress and rubber boots or shoes, with no personal equipment – not even a water bottle. The rest of the Dieppe force quite rightly wore tin hats. The Commandos didn't. They argued that their job is to go in fast and first, before the enemy has time to start any bombing or shelling, and if they are too late they probably won't need tin hats anyway.

It has wrongly been claimed that the Germans had explicit forewarning of attack at Dieppe. This is untrue, although they were on a generally raised level of vigilance. A order of the day from General Haase, issued on 10 August, gave notice that the Western Allies would be forced to 'do something' due to the situation on the Eastern Front, and for 'Home Front reasons'. Nevertheless, luck certainly was involved in the initial interception of the transports. So it was that things began to go awry even before the beaches were reached. Portsmouth radar detected a small German convoy of five motor vessels and signalled warnings to the raiders – which were not acted upon due to defective communications. To the east of Dieppe the target of No. 3 Commando, led by Lieutenant Colonel Durnford-Slater, was the four-gun 150mm 'Goebbels' battery at Berneval. The landing grounds were beaches 'Yellow' 1 and 2, from which the troops were expected to march about 500 yards inland to attack the battery. The raiders travelled in twenty-three 'Eureka' boats, each of which carried twenty men, with three immediate escorts, a gunboat, flak craft, and a motor launch. Two destroyers shadowed the operation a little further off. All went well on the journey from Newhaven until 3.47 a.m. when there was a sudden encounter. As Major Young recalled:

> Immediately a heavy fire was opened upon us; 3- and 4-inch guns, ack-ack guns and machineguns poured a stream of shells and tracer into the flotilla, while further star shells lit the sky. It was by far the most unpleasant moment of my life. Five enemy craft were converging on us. It seemed impossible that our wooden landing craft could survive more than a few minutes.

In the ensuing sea battle, and despite the valiant efforts of the gunboat and flak vessel, several of the little landing craft were sunk, others badly damaged or scattered. The American-designed Eurekas (also known as 'Landing Craft Personnel Light' or 'R' Boats) were fast, but wooden and vulnerable, and holed pipes magnified the effect of shrapnel on the boats. In between 'ducking and weaving' to avoid being hit, Colonel Durnford-Slater took the detached view of the professional that, 'The German ships teamed together most efficiently. They chose the gunboat as their principal target.' Signaller Charles Hurstwick was dismayed to see the 'grim spectacle' of their protector 'full of holes, like a colander. The bridge had been destroyed, the steering gone, and only one gun was still firing.' Having tended the wounded, Durnford-Slater was eventually left bobbing about on the ocean with one intact landing craft still under command, 'feeling useless'. Far too late to be of practical value in the assault, he now made towards Dieppe to report to General Roberts. Just seven landing craft had managed to run the gauntlet, and arrived nearly half an hour late on the beaches. Six of these made land at 'Yellow 1' near Berneval, and one at 'Yellow 2' near Belleville.

On 'Yellow 1', with the larger surviving party, the senior officer present was Captain R. L. Wills. With only parts of 2, 5 and 6 Troops present, a total of 120 men, the carefully-prepared timetable ruined, and much equipment missing, Wills had only one fleeting chance of success – and so advanced rapidly on the gullies, which were supposed to lead him up the cliff. One was completely blocked, but after battling through the wire of the other, the Commandos negotiated a minefield and sent out scouts. They were unaware that not only were the Germans thoroughly alerted, but by now a reinforced company of 570th Infantry was well on its way to confront them – significantly strengthening the existing battery garrison.

On emerging from cover, the Commandos immediately came under well-directed fire from several carefully placed machine guns. One of these was charged and put out of action by Corporal Halls, but others began to inflict serious losses. Captain Osmond was badly wounded, and Captain Wills took a grenade fragment to the neck. Lieutenant Loustalot of the 1st US Ranger Battalion was killed – the first US serviceman to fall in land combat on mainland Europe. The last officer from 'Yellow 1' yet remaining, Lieutenant Wright, carried on fighting, but no way could be found through the defence. Since further progress was impossible, and enemy mortars – against which the Commandos had no defence – had joined the battle, the decision was made to fall back to the beach. Still under ground fire and air attack, the remains of this group carried their wounded back down to the shore, but there were no boats near enough to pick them up – even though Sergeant Connolly made a valiant attempt to swim to landing craft spotted about a mile off shore. Just eighty-one Commandos – many of them wounded – were captured: thirty-seven were dead. Only one, Lance Corporal Sinclair, managed to escape back to the UK in the company of the Naval beach party.

Whilst 'Yellow 1' had quickly turned into the sort of disaster that the Canadians were beginning to suffer in front of Dieppe itself, actions at 'Yellow 2' were rising from the surreal to the heroic. Major Peter Young's craft, commanded by Lieutenant Buckee RNVR, had been at one end of the landing craft flotilla, and after some 'tepid soup', Young had attempted to sleep. After being so rudely startled by the start of the sea fight, his craft had attempted to follow behind the gunboat, but as the riddled escort faltered and began to wallow to one side, Buckee had pressed on through the destruction as fast as possible. Though the canopy was shredded, the headquarters troops in the vessel were very lucky to escape unharmed. Remarkably, Buckee was able to locate 'Yellow 2' fairly quickly, and five minutes early – just 50 yards from a gully in the cliff– made landfall. Young had just eighteen men, not counting the Naval personnel (whom he thought best to leave guarding their vessel) and, as he quickly discovered, some alarming absences in the equipment inventory.

The first of these was any implement to blow the tangles of wire that choked the gully. Nor were there wire cutters. As a headquarters unit, it had been expected that none would be needed. Now Driver Cunningham linked the men's toggle ropes and the Commandos climbed painstakingly around the wire, and up to the minefield at the top of the gully. Young quickly got his men – who 'did not look particularly pleased' at the turn of events – under cover of a nearby wood. Here they reorganised into three small sections, two under Captains Ruxton and Selwyn, with Young taking the third, and checked their equipment. It was an odd assortment, but for a very small detachment, contained remarkably heavy firepower. There were ten rifles, including an American Garand (which Young himself had souvenired from US Rangers), a Bren gun, six Thompsons and a 2-inch mortar. The 3-inch mortar had proved impossible to get up the cliff with the enemy wire still intact.

Emerging cautiously from the wood behind Privates Clark and Craft (now acting as scouts but actually the HQ batman and runner), the Commandos were soon blessed with two remarkable pieces of luck. First, Hurricanes appeared and strafed the battery, which replied, so pinpointing its position; and second, a boy on a bicycle happened by, who, though terrified, quickly told them that the enemy garrison numbered about 200. Realising that they were completely unexpected, and hearing the battery open fire, the Commandos threw caution to the wind and simply doubled up the street of Berneval, enquiring of villagers as they went as to the positions of both friendly and enemy forces. The 'excellent rifle shot', Private Hopkins, took point ahead of the group. However, abreast of the church they were brought up suddenly by a burst of machine-gun fire from a post not 60 yards away. The Commandos returned fire with their Thompsons, and rapidly brought the Bren and mortar into action, using the church as cover for the latter. Young also tried to get a sniper up into the church tower to engage the machine-gun crew, but discovered that the ladder had been removed. Given this minor setback, the Commandos first tried to creep through an orchard, were fired upon again, stumbled upon a dummy gun position, and finally crawled closer to the main battery through standing crops. At some point, Private Hopkins came across the battery telephone wires and managed to sever them.

Young positioned his tiny army in 'two lines in extended order, with a good distance between each man and with the second line firing between the intervals in the first line. We now opened a hot fire at the smoke and flashes around the gun positions.' There was some ineffective return fire but the Commandos had managed to flank the guns and popped up and down amongst the corn, snap shooting at the enemy. This harassing fire continued for some time until the gunners were goaded into swinging the nearest heavy gun to use on their tormentors, but luckily the Commandos were so close that the barrel could not be depressed to land shells safely so near to the gun. The rounds therefore sailed over the top of the raiders with an almighty roar. It was what Young later called 'an unusual experience'. This unequal David-and-Goliath performance continued for more than an hour, with the Commandos far too few to assault the battery and the Germans intermittently disrupted in their continuing attempts to get on with the job of battering the main attack in front of Dieppe.

As ammunition began to run low, and with the increasing possibility that German reinforcements might force them out of the corn, the Commandos began their withdrawal. First went Selwyn's group to secure the way and fire a signal to let everyone know all was well. Young and Ruxton, accompanied by three other ranks, including J. Abbott the Bren-gunner, brought up the rear, first shooting up a pillbox, then providing covering fire for the retreat. None of this was too soon, for as the rearguard reached the beach it became apparent that the landing craft was being engaged by German riflemen atop the cliff. Private Hopkins gave suppressive fire with the stripped-down Lewis gun kept on the boat, as did Driver Cunningham, already on board with his rifle. Despite a wound from a mine, Lance Corporal White, assisted by Private Adderton, used the 3-inch mortar from the beach before bundling their awkward burden back into the landing craft. It was now almost too late to escape so they began to cast off from the beach. The last of the Commandos struggled to reach the vessel. It was, as Young's account recalled, like one of those dreams you have of desperately trying to walk and making no progress. Eventually we laid hold of the lifelines and were towed out to sea. About 300 yards out the craft hove to and we were dragged aboard. Quite a number of shots hit the craft at this point, and a sailor a yard from me was severely wounded in the thigh. The battery fired a few shells at us but pretty wide of the mark. A bullet hit the smoke canister in the stern and we began to give out quite a respectable smokescreen.

As Young later admitted, it was unlikely that his pocket raiding force had killed many Germans, but this was not the point. Under the most adverse of conditions, the tiny 'Yellow 2' party had carried on and, at least partially, fulfilled the important task that had been set for an entire Commando – reducing, if not eliminating, fire from Goebbels battery. Of all Peter Young's exploits in a much celebrated career, this was certainly his finest hour: what he was most proud of was the fact that, in doing the job, his group had suffered no casualties from the moment of landing until the very moment of leaving, and even then nobody was killed. On return to the UK the little party was profusely decorated – half of its members earned gallantry awards. Major Young received a Distinguished Service Order, Selwyn and Ruxton were both decorated with the Military Cross. Of the other ranks, Cunningham got a Distinguished Conduct Medal; Abbott, Adderton, Clarke, Craft, White and Hopkins all won Military Medals. One is tempted to think that the main thing that prevented almost any one of them from receiving a Victoria Cross was the fact that none was killed.

The new Royal Marine Commando (otherwise known as 'A' Commando) had embarked at Portsmouth with part of the unit carried in 'Chasseur' boats, brought to Britain at the fall of France. These were armed with a 75mm gun and two heavy machine guns. The remainder, including the commanding officer, went aboard the shallow-draft gunboat *Locust*. In the central landing grounds of Dieppe they had a baptism of fire that came close to proving terminal. The main force of Canadian infantry, attacking frontally, and without benefit of sufficient covering fire, had suffered heavy losses immediately. Survivors succeeded in crossing the beaches and the first wire obstacles but most were pinned by pillboxes and a second belt of wire at the sea wall, and hammered by well concealed guns. Some managed to fight their way into town, but were met by concerted counter-attacks. Perhaps worse, the tank landing craft were rapidly engaged by heavy guns, and though they managed to land twenty-eight Churchill tanks, several vessels were sunk. On shore the tanks found it difficult to gain traction on pebbles and shingle, and most were prevented from getting off the beach by concrete roadblocks. Engineers attempting to assist them suffered badly. Casualties to the 2nd Canadian Division, killed, wounded and captured, totalled approximately 3,400.

As the Canadian troops were cut to pieces on the beaches, the Royal Marine Commandos were ordered in towards 'White' beach to lend them support – but, as is so often the case, reinforcing failure proved a serious tactical mistake. As the Chasseur boats cleared the smokescreen, it became horribly apparent that the German defenders were thoroughly alert, firing for all they were worth, and there was little or nothing left to support. Lieutenant Colonel J. P. Phillips made valiant attempts to signal his men to turn around but was killed standing on the wheelhouse of his craft. Some boats carried on to the beach, others were able to heed the warning to turn round.

The situation was hopeless but there were remarkable deeds of bravery. Some of those who had the worst experiences were the Marines who attempted to engage targets on the beaches and cliffs from their landing craft during the final approach. The vessel carrying Marine Reginald Bevin came in close to shore, attempting to pick up survivors, but itself came under fire. Using a light machine gun, he silenced one enemy machine gun, which was shooting from the East Cliff – but an unlucky shell hit the boat and Bevin's weapon was blown off its mounting. Marine Commando Terence Breen performed a similar service against a German gun position on the Casino, and stayed in action until his ammunition was expended. Marines Bradshaw and Singleton were two of many who glued themselves down to the decks in the hope of somehow avoiding machine-gun and rifle fire from the land, but had to stand up, fully exposing themselves to enemy fire in order to hit back. All four were awarded Military Medals. Flak ships attempted to bring heavier fire-power to bear, to redress the position, with LCF 2 going close to use its Oerlikons and pom-poms, but it was outgunned by the shore defences, and its commander, Lieutenant E. L. Graham, was killed. Eventually, LCF 2 was sunk.

The assault craft carrying Major R. D. Houghton, second-in-command of the Royal Marine Commando, came under attack as it approached the beach, but grounded sickeningly about 100 yards offshore. This was the worst of all worlds, to be caught too far out to disembark easily, too close to escape the lashing of enemy rounds:

Major Houghton, with complete disregard for his personal safety, was the first to attempt to land. He found the water too deep to achieve a landing, so under heavy fire he re-embarked and gave orders for the LCA to be beached on another position [...] This second attempt was successful and on landing Major Houghton immediately organised his party and engaged the enemy with all weapons at his disposal. In spite of overwhelming enemy fire, he only gave up when all other troops in the vicinity had surrendered.

Major Houghton was later awarded a Military Cross.

According to Brigadier Haydon, writing after the event, 'what happened was inevitable'. In one early version of the plan, the main attacks had been on the flanks. In another, the approach was in darkness and under Naval and air bombardment. The result of such ideas had been 'the usual argument' as to whether the Navy would find the right spot in the dark, plus concern that if tanks were landed on flanks they could not join up behind Dieppe quickly enough to avoid massive enemy retaliation.

Unaware of the catastrophic mayhem breaking about other parts of the fleet and landing grounds, 4 Commando's 252-man 'Operation Cauldron' was making excellent progress – at least in part due to the fact that lights were still showing on the shore. Its exploits would become quite literally a 'text book' illustration of Commando tactics, described in the manual *Notes From Theatres of War: Destruction of a German Battery*, as, with no exaggeration, 'a classic example of the use of well trained infantry; fire and movement; the killing power of weapons in the attack' and 'thoroughness in training, planning and execution'. Its scheme was in two parts. 'Group 1' (comprising a reinforced 'C' Troop with a total of eighty-eight all ranks commanded by Major Mills-Roberts) was to land, make its way through the cliffs, and as soon as it was discovered by the enemy, or the Varengeville battery fired, engage the guns frontally. The Commandos would be supported by a 3-inch mortar team, as well as men with smoke generators, signallers, and ammunition carriers, and was assisted ashore by a Navy 'Beach Master'. The larger 'Group 2' was almost three fighting Troops in strength, totalling 164 men, including the handful of attached US Rangers and Canadians. This would be led by 4 Commando's commanding officer, Lord Lovat. 'A' Troop would land first, quickly securing the left-hand end of the beach and making sure that two pillboxes were unable to fire on the main party. The remainder, 'B' and 'F' Troops, would land three minutes later and move 'at all

Robert Laycock

Sir Robert Edward Laycock (1907–1968) was the Eton-educated son of a brigadier, and thus it was probably natural that he should have attended Sandhurst, followed by a commission into the Royal Horse Guards in 1927. However, despite being on the Continent prior to May 1940, he missed the French campaign due to recall to a staff appointment in the UK. David Niven later claimed that he was instrumental in introducing Laycock to Dudley Clarke, but in any event Laycock volunteered for special service that summer, and was soon charged with raising No. 8 Commando. Early the next year Laycock – now ranking as colonel – led a Commando group the size of a small brigade to the Eastern Mediterranean. Drawn mainly from 7, 8 and 11 Commandos and the Middle East Commandos, this was known as 'Layforce'. Though a raid was mounted on Bardia, its biggest action was in covering the retreat from Crete in April 1941 – a mission in which it suffered very heavy casualties. Later, Laycock led the unsuccessful raid attempting to assassinate Erwin Rommel, and in its aftermath escaped only by spending a prolonged period evading the enemy behind their own lines. In 1942 Laycock was redeployed to lead a brigade in the attack on Sicily, and was awarded the Distinguished Service Order. If not always successful, his courageous and wide-ranging service was certainly acknowledged in October 1943 when, as major general, he was promoted to Chief of Combined Operations as replacement for Lord Louis Mountbatten. He was therefore instrumental in the remoulding of the Commando force prior to D-Day. He remained in his post until 1947. From 1954 to 1957 Laycock was Governor of Malta. Back in the UK, he was appointed Lord Lieutenant of Nottinghamshire in 1962. He died suddenly of a heart attack in 1968.

possible speed' up the Sanne valley, moving between the settlements of Ste Marguerite and Quiberville. With a timed pre-planned assault they would then take the battery in the rear. Their success could be made much more likely by the fact that the battery was already being engaged from the front by 'Group 1'.

The landing of 'Group 1' on beach 'Orange One', just after 4.30 a.m., was achieved unopposed and largely dry. The only mishap was that a Bren got wet, but following a dab of lubrication was soon functioning again. According to Mills-Roberts:

> we landed on a narrow little beach. Here we were out of the racket allright, and it seemed rather like stealing round to the back door of a house where a rather noisy party is in progress and finding nothing but silence.

To traverse the beach rabbit-wire netting was thrown across its barbed wire obstacles and the men clambered over. Reconnaissance of the two gullies through the cliff now determined that the right hand passage was less obstructed than the left, so a bangalore was swiftly planted there:

> With a loud report magnified by the narrow gully it blew. We raced in to spot the damage – a poor gap but we widened it, and placed the second torpedo in the next bank of wire. This one blew a wide enough gap for us to scramble through singly, and soon a small party was told off to widen the gap.

The Commando parties now climbed up through the gully – possibly the most dangerous part of the whole operation, since, had the enemy been able to fire into or along the passageway, much of the group could have been trapped in the defile. Aware that such an eventuality could spell catastrophic casualties, or complete failure, men were pushed out to the sides of the gully as soon as practicable. Still, the Commandos were not discovered, and on reaching the top, a section was deployed as a defensive perimeter to secure the retreat. Others spread out to search nearby houses for enemy snipers or observers: none were located. The Commandos had instructions to neutralise the battery with fire by 6.30 a.m., and were advancing to take up positions of advantage ready to deliver their blow, still with about forty minutes in hand, when there was an unexpected interruption to the timetable that required immediate adjustment. At about 5.45 a.m. the battery shattered the surrounding air, and began to lob shells in the direction of the fleet. This was precisely what the raiders had come to prevent.

In the hope of distracting the German gunners, three snipers, led by Sergeant Lindley, were now quickly pushed into vantage points at a converted barn at the edge of the wood overlooking the battery. As Mills-Roberts recalled:

> We ordered one of the snipers to get ready and pointed out his target. He settled himself on a table, taking careful aim. These Bisley chaps are not to be hurried; we waited whilst he took the first pressure – it reminded me of the immense and awesome time it took General Sir Bindon Blood to take the first pressure at Bisley [...] At last the rifle cracked, it was a bull's eye and one of the master race took a toss into the gun pit. His comrades looked shocked and surprised – I could see it all through my glasses. It seemed rather like shooting one of the members of the church congregation from the organ loft. The barn was only 140 yards away from the perimeter wire and about 170 yards from the guns. This range is nothing, even to a moderate shot with Bren or rifle.

With this exhibition shoot, preambles were at a conclusion and Lieutenant Style's section now brought the battery under general fire with three Bren teams and a few rifles – forcing the crews to duck down below their sandbagged parapets. The Commando shooting was not, however, an indiscriminate plastering, but a calculated balance between systematic neutralisation of the battery and expenditure of the limited amount of ammunition it was possible to bring up from the landing place:

> The three Bren guns fired in short bursts to a prearranged plan, only one gun firing at a time; it was necessary to weigh the conflicting claims of making the maximum delay possible from this direction at the same time as conserving ammunition. Each gun had sixteen magazines of which about 12 were fired. One was continually in action in a position in long grass only 150 yards from the battery and was not observed. Three men with sniper's rifles did excellent work. One of them, his face and hands painted green, and wearing suitable camouflage, crawled forward to a fire position 120 yards from the gun emplacement.

The Commando who crawled forward was Lance Corporal Mann, whose Military Medal citation remarked that he 'succeeded in killing a great number of the enemy gun crews. His sniping was so accurate that it became impossible to service the gun.' Lance Sergeant P. F. McCarthy, directing the Bren teams, received a similar award.

These efforts had the desired effect for a while, but before long the Commandos were themselves receiving fire as the enemy managed to direct machine guns and light flak into likely hiding places around their perimeter. As the rounds crept closer, Style moved half his section into nearby scrub, so the raiders would not make such a concentrated target:

> Two of our other detachments were now ready and joined the fray – the antitank rifle, a ponderous but powerful weapon with great penetrating power, and the handy little 2-inch mortar. The antitank rifle was to pierce the steel plated armour with which we knew the enemy perimeters were protected [...] Gunner McDonough was firing this gun, with Private Davis as his 'No. 2', and he operated against the flak tower with great effect. It ceased to revolve and gave the appearance of a roundabout checked in full flight. Then he directed his attentions to the German machineguns, ably assisted by the Brens.

The little mortar was set up a few yards from the barn:

> Their first round fell midway between the barn and the target, but their next round was a good one and landed in a stack of cordite, behind number one gun, which ignited with a stupendous crash, followed by shouts and yells of pain. We could see the Germans as they rushed forward with blankets and extinguishers, and everything we had was directed onto this area. The fire grew, and meanwhile the big guns remained silent.

The detonation of the No. 1 gun position – described by War Correspondent Austin, still some distance away, as the 'mother of all explosions' – was the turning point in the battle with Hess battery, for she never fired again. The 2-inch mortar team, with all due humility, described their shot as 'pure luck', since they had no prearranged plan and simply aimed at the centre of the battery. Though battery 813 'Hess' was no longer a threat to the landings, the German garrison in the vicinity was now thoroughly alerted and fought back with renewed determination, mortar rounds beginning to drop around the Commando positions. But help was at hand, for at 6.28 the air support arrived, which had, according to the original timetable, been planned to start the action. Fighters strafed the battery, adding a new dimension to the fight, and the Commandos' 3-inch mortar – initially brought too far forward – finally came into action. Eventually, the Bren teams and snipers silenced the German machine guns, whilst a rifle grenadier managed to put a bomb neatly through the window of a house from which fire had been opened. The antitank rifle got off sixty rounds at the flak towers, and resolutely chipped away at any target too hardened for ordinary bullets to penetrate. Gunner McDonough was lucky to survive. As his Military Medal citation observed:

> Each time he fired the antitank rifle, heavy fire was immediately brought to bear on the flash from the rifle. McDonough repeatedly changed his position and continued to engage the enemy, each time incurring heavy enemy fire. He scored a great number of hits and his endurance (after ten rounds of an antitank rifle the average man becomes giddy) was quite phenomenal.

Whilst this largely successful fire-fight was in progress, 'Group 2' of 'Cauldron', led by Lord Lovat, had battled its way towards the Hess battery. The group's landing had been much more difficult than that of their colleagues but still carried off with dash. At about 4.30 a.m., as the assault landing craft were approaching their beach, white star shells went up from the lighthouse. Nevertheless, 'A' Troop landed as planned and began to tackle the formidable wire obstacle when the alerted enemy opened up with machine-gun and mortar fire, and four of the Commandos were wounded before they could clear the beach:

> The remainder of the group at once began to go ashore 150 yards further up the beach, using rabbit netting to get across the wire. They also came under fire and received eight casualties. The enemy used a concentration of tracer ammunition which, in the half light, had a most unpleasant effect on men not accustomed to it [...] Most of the casualties were from the mortar – which, fortunately, soon lifted and continued firing at the retreating landing craft. Two medical orderlies, who were brothers, remained with the wounded. One was taken prisoner with them; the other escorted three walking wounded along the cliff top to Beach One, two of whom were unfortunately killed on the way. One officer, leaving his boat, was hit by mortar fragments, his right hand becoming useless. Nevertheless he went on, and led a charge in the final assault on the battery, using his revolver and grenades with his left hand accounting for a number of the enemy.

Undaunted, 'A' Troop was led on by Lieutenant A. S. S. Veasey to complete its task. Using tubular metal ladders, they mounted the cliff and rushed the two pillboxes. One of these was empty but the second was occupied and the defenders killed with grenades.

Despite these dramas and mishaps, 'Group 2' pressed on, pausing only to sever telephone communication along this sector of the coast by sending a man up a telegraph pole to cut the wires. The trooper who climbed was William Finney, and as his Military Medal citation for the deed remarked, he 'bore a charmed life' – since the pole was struck by several bullets as he worked. Proceeding at the double, 'B' and 'F' Troops crossed a road and followed the east bank of the River Sanne, through long grass and mud. As it was now light, gaps between cover had to be crossed in rapid bounds, but morale was improved – and the pace hastened – by the fact that small-arms fire could be heard from up ahead, suggesting that their comrades of 'Group 1' were already in combat. The massive cordite explosion that lit up the trees a few minutes later increased confidence that the enemy would already be battered and distracted by the time they arrived. On reaching the wood behind the battery, 'B' and 'F' Troops split off according to plan:

> 'B' Troop moved forward inside the southern edge of the wood and then filtered through the orchard by sub sections. Using cover they approached the perimeter wire, where they came under inaccurate fire from an MG position, the flak tower and from various buildings. From thereon they advanced by fire and movement with covering smoke. One MG was stalked and silenced with a grenade.

'B' troop was thus in its final jumping-off positions ninety-five minutes after landing.

Meanwhile, 'F' Troop took the slightly longer, but arguably somewhat safer, route around the northern fringe of the wood using smoke wherever the way appeared exposed. Yet, quite unexpectedly, 'F' Troop was also engaged as they came upon a party of Germans in a farmyard, who appeared to be preparing their own local counter-attack on the 'Group 1' Commandos. As one laconic official report put it, 'They were killed with Tommy guns.' Now the Commandos reached the battery:

> Vigorous opposition was encountered from the buildings and enclosures just inside the perimeter wire, and several casualties were

sustained. The Troop commander was killed with a stick grenade, and one of the section officers mortally wounded. The Sergeant took over but was also killed. The third officer was shot through the hand, the bullet lodging in his wrist, but he closed with his opponent and killed him.

This 'third officer' was Captain P. A. Porteous, who was, in theory, supposed to be acting as a liaison between the Commando parties. Finally, even part of 'A' Troop with its attached Rangers managed to make a fresh contribution to the action by working around the west side of the battery, thus engaging the Germans from yet another direction – and doubtless increasing the enemy apprehension that they were steadily being outflanked, if not surrounded. One American Corporal, Franklin M. Koons, scored the remarkable distinction of being the first US serviceman to kill a German soldier in a land battle in the Second World War.

Exactly 100 minutes after the appointed landing time, Lord Lovat fired white Very lights to signal the final attack, and troops 'B' and 'F' – by now lacking several of their officers – charged Hess battery from close range. Instrumental in this antique, bloody, and ultimately successful final assault was Porteous – the officer with one bullet already lodged in him. Given the treatment the battery defenders had already been dealt, the remainder might have been forgiven for attempting immediate flight – but in their predicament of fire from several directions they fought back, initially at least, with great determination. Troop Sergeant Major Stockdale, now in temporary command of a troop following officer casualties, was badly wounded by a stick grenade that blew away part of his foot. Porteous fell at his moment of triumph, wounded by a shot through the thigh, but survived to be awarded the Victoria Cross, for gallantry, 'brilliant leadership and tenacious devotion to duty'.

Others quickly stepped up to the mark and by now, after a battle which had lasted the better part of two hours, the Commandos were clearly in something of a blood fury. Conspicuous in the often confused hand-to-hand fighting in the battery itself were Corporal Charles Blunden and Lance Sergeant Portman. Blunden displayed considerable courage and leadership in the fight amongst the battery buildings, and though himself wounded, refused medical attention 'and continued to destroy the enemy until there were no Germans left alive'. Portman took up the baton until so recently held by Troop Sergeant Major Stockdale and Captain

Porteous, and was the first man into the German gun pits, where he 'disposed of the gun crews'. This achieved, he took part in the demolition of the guns. Both Blunden and Portman received Military Medals. Amongst the last Germans to fall was an officer who fought back with his pistol during what one Commando would later describe as an 'exhilarating chase around the battery office', which ended when the German was bayoneted.

As Mills-Roberts later recalled, it had been 'a rough party with no quarter asked or given. The many dead – mostly German but some of our men – lay in and around the gun pit.' The guns were demolished with charges:

> One man, Sergeant Watkins, was lying on a stretcher. He had been shot in the stomach. His face looked grotesquely ill beneath its covering of camouflage paint, but he was quite cheerful. He asked me how the battle had gone and told me that he was all right – the stretcher bearer silently shook his head.

According to later assessments the Commandos had actually lost twelve dead including two officers and just over thirty were wounded or missing. Though a few more died of wounds, a dozen of those injured were well enough to return to duty over the next couple of months. The majority of 4 Commando made their getaway from the beach. The enemy had clearly lost many more men – 150 dead were initially claimed in one official publication, along with three prisoners, though the death toll was later revised down to about seventy. Nor had the opposition been feeble: many of the German troops were from 110th Division, a formation that had already learned from bitter experience in Russia.

So successful had 'Cauldron' been – though overshadowed by the general disaster of Dieppe – that it was promoted as an exercise to be studied and replicated by others. Naturally the upbeat, not to say jingoistic, *Notes From Theatres of War* stressed training and planning, but it was in use of weapons and minor tactics that the real lessons were thought to be found:

> Rifle. The large number of Germans who fell to our rifles had their death sentences signed many months before when the Commando struggled to perfection in judging distances and shooting straight.

Sniper. A special mention must be made of snipers. It was made very clear to the Germans that a stalker with a quick and sure eye, cunning and fieldcraft, and the sniper's rifle with its telescopic sight, can do much to swing the battle against them.

Bayonet. There is something about a bayonet that defeats not only the armchair critic but, what is more important, the enemy. The Hun has always hated it. He may be old fashioned but it can't be helped.

EY [grenade projecting] Rifle and Grenades. The EY rifle and 68 grenade were useful against enemy behind defences but the incendiary bullet was not a success. 36 grenades were useful, though it appears the Germans can throw their stick grenades further.

Bren gun. The Bren gun did what was expected of it. Thanks to concentration on judging of distance, accuracy of fire, and the use of cover, many Germans were killed by Bren fire. Considerable training in firing it from the hip during the assault produced striking results.

Tracer. It was agreed that the psychological effect of tracer at night is very great. It is necessary that this form of battle inoculation should be undertaken without delay. The demoralising effect of tracer, which always appears to be going to hit you, is very great.

Mortars, 2-inch and 3-inch. Extensive training and practice was undertaken to ensure a high degree of accuracy and speed in obtaining fire effect. During the operation, as the narrative shows, this training probably went far to ensure the successful end of the operation.

TMC (Thompson Machine Carbine). Extensive training in the use of the TMC in assault and in-fighting was undertaken. Results obtained were good, but the Bren proved a more effective weapon when used from the hip in similar circumstances.

Minor Tactics. Training in fire and movement was carried out over country similar to that fought over with special regard to close country fighting. All ranks were thoroughly prepared for their various parts in all phases of the action. This careful study and preparation was the main reason why such a small infantry force was able to defeat approximately equal numbers of an enemy who was organised behind wire and occupying strong prepared defences. Training in the use of smoke at the right time and place, and in suitable quantity, resulted in the saving of many casualties at critical moments. The success obtained in this operation bears out the principle of thorough and detailed training in the basic infantry requirements – FIRE and MOVEMENT.

Despite the glories of No. 4 Commando, it has been claimed, probably correctly, that there were proportionately more casualties at Dieppe than in any other significant Allied operation of the war. The Canadian killed, wounded and captured amounted to 68 per cent of those committed – or rather more than double the rate suffered by the Commandos. Three US Rangers, including Lieutenants Loustalot and Randall, died at Dieppe. Three others became the first US ground troops to be captured in Europe. Corporal Franklin M. Koons was awarded a British Military Medal. At the time, the catastrophe that was Dieppe stayed largely concealed from home audiences. Within the House of Commons awkward truths were glossed over and positive aspects fully highlighted. In Churchill's official report of 8 September, the mission received only second billing:

> It is a mistake to speak or write of this as 'a Commando raid', although some Commando troops distinguished themselves remarkably in it. The military credit for this most gallant affair goes to the Canadian troops [...] The raid must be considered a reconnaissance in force. It was a hard, savage clash such as are likely to become increasingly numerous as the War deepens. We had to get all the information necessary before launching operations on a much larger scale. This raid, apart from its reconnaissance value, brought about an extremely satisfactory air battle in the West, which Fighter Command wish they could repeat every week. It inflicted perhaps as much loss on the enemy in killed and wounded as we suffered ourselves. I, personally, regarded the Dieppe assault, to which I gave my sanction, as an indispensable preliminary to full-scale operations. I do not intend to give any information about these operations, and I have only said as much as I have because the enemy can see by his daily reconnaissance of our ports many signs of movement we are unable to conceal from his photography ...

Other reports went further, claiming full success. The idea of the 'dress rehearsal' for D-Day was always somewhat far-fetched and, specifically, the suggestion that Dieppe taught the Allies to avoid attempting to take a significant port straight away was plain wrong. Dieppe had been chosen, at least in part, because it was already known by 1942 that it was not to be a target of the main invasion when it came – and the planning for prefabricated 'Mulberry' harbours had already commenced.

Though Dieppe has come to overshadow other events in Western Europe in late 1942, it was far from the only operation involving Commandos at this period. Indeed, the 'Small Scale Raiding Force' (SSRF) – which had come into existence in March 1942, was commonly known as No. 62 Commando, and operated largely under the auspices of SOE – was particularly busy that year. Parts of No. 2, 4 and No. 6 Commandos were also active on other work. Missions included forays to Cherbourg, Hardelot, Norway and an abortive foray to Bayonne. The SSRF also went to the Casquets in 'Operation Dryad', where they seized a German lighthouse crew, and to reconnoitre Burhou, in 'Operation Branford'. Major March-Phillips, commander of the SSRF, was killed during a mission to Normandy in September; but for equally sorry reasons, it is 'Operation Basalt', mounted by the SSRF and men from No. 12 Commando, that is better remembered.

'Basalt', which took place on the night of 3 October, saw a small group land from a Motor Torpedo Boat on the island of Sark – having signalled the German garrison on the way in that they were a friendly vessel seeking shelter for the night in Dixcart Bay. The ruse worked and the Commandos soon found an old lady who was able to tell them much about the dispositions of the enemy. One of the detachments located was the billet of a small group of engineers in the Dixcart Hotel. Here, outside an annexe, the Dane Anders Lassen dealt with a sentry before five enemy soldiers were surprised inside, searched, and then taken out with their hands bound. As Major Appleyard's report explained:

> In the darkness outside the house one of the prisoners, seeing an opportunity, suddenly attacked his guard and then shouting loudly for help and trying to raise an alarm, he ran off in the direction in which it was known there were buildings containing a number of Germans. He was caught almost immediately by his guard, but after a scuffle again escaped, still shouting, and was shot. Meanwhile, three of the other prisoners seizing the opportunity of the noise and confusion, also started shouting and attacking their guards. Two broke away and were shot immediately. The third, although still held, was accidentally shot in an attempt to silence him with the butt of a revolver. The fifth prisoner remained quiet and did not struggle.

Now thoroughly roused, enemy troops started to pour out of the hotel and the Commandos made off rapidly with one captive. By running all the way back to their boat, a clean escape was made, though one Commando was slightly injured. By morning, the enemy was making a thorough investigation of what had happened. Three Germans were dead, a fourth wounded. In addition to the testimony of the captive who had been left behind, two Commando knives, toggle ropes, and other items were found to complete the story of what had happened. The British countered by a statement from Combined Operations HQ, pointing out that illegal deportations from the Channel Islands to Germany could now be categorically proved. On top of reports that the Canadians had manacled captives at Dieppe, 'Basalt' roused the Nazis into reprisals, and a tit-for-tat binding of prisoners commenced, this only being ended by the intervention of the Swiss.

On 18 October 1942 Hitler issued the infamous *Kommando Fuehrerbefehl*. The main clauses were as follows:

1. For a long time now our opponents have been employing in their conduct of the war, methods which contravene the International Convention of Geneva. The members of the so-called Commandos behave in a particularly brutal and underhand manner; and it has been established that those units recruit criminals not only from their own country but even former convicts set free in enemy territories. From captured orders it emerges that they are instructed not only to tie up prisoners, but also to kill out of hand unarmed captives who they think might prove an encumbrance to them, or hinder them in successfully carrying out their aims. Orders have indeed been found in which the killing of prisoners has positively been demanded of them.

2. In this connection it has already been notified in an appendix to Army orders of 7.10.1942 that in future, Germany will adopt the same methods against these sabotage units of the British and their Allies; i.e. that, whenever they appear, they shall be ruthlessly destroyed by the German troops.

3. I order therefore – From now on all men operating against German troops in so-called Commando raids in Europe or Africa, are to be annihilated to the last man. This is to be carried out whether they be soldiers in uniform, or saboteurs, with or without arms; and whether fighting or seeking to escape; and it is equally immaterial whether they come into action from ships and aircraft, or whether they land by parachute. Even if these individuals on discovery make

obvious their intention of giving themselves up as prisoners, no pardon on any account is to be given. On this matter a report is to be made on each case to headquarters for the information of higher command.

4. Should individual members of these Commandos, such as agents, saboteurs etc., fall into the hands of the armed forces by any means – as for example, through the Police in one of the occupied territories – they are to be instantly handed over to the SD. To hold them in military custody – for example in POW camps etc. – even if only as a temporary measure, is strictly forbidden.

5. This order does not apply to the treatment of those enemy soldiers who are taken prisoner or give themselves up in open battle, in the course of normal operations, large-scale attacks; or in major assault landings or airborne operations. Neither does it apply to those who fall into our hands after a sea fight, nor to those enemy soldiers who, after air battle, seek to save their lives by parachute.

6. I will hold all commanders and officers responsible under military law for any omission to carry out this order, whether by failure in their duty to instruct their units accordingly, or if they themselves act contrary to it.

The *Fuehrerbefehl* was circulated on a strictly limited basis to 'commanders only' and was under no circumstances to be allowed to fall into enemy hands. Headquarters mentioned on the distribution list were to be responsible for seeing that the order, or even extracts taken from it, were destroyed. These covering instructions were given under the hand of Jodl, Chief of Staff of the Army.

In many similar historical instances the Germans, as occupiers, had an interest in portraying all guerrillas and raiders as criminal and outside conventions; whereas the Allies, who were attempting to liberate, defined the same troops as freedom fighters. It should, of course, be pointed out that Commandos fought in uniform as the paid troops of a sovereign country; they had formal ranks and serial numbers and were, in every sense, soldiers of the Crown. The majority were indeed already members of another unit before they became Commandos. Their existence as a recognised military formation was not only admitted by the British government, but trumpeted in the international press. In this respect, the Commandos were entirely distinct from real partisans or members of secret organisations such as SOE. Though Commando tactics were often 'irregular', the units themselves were not. Whilst it cannot, of course, be claimed that no Commando ever committed any infringement of international law, the correct course of action would have been to accuse and bring before a court, military or otherwise, specific men charged with stated crimes. Others were clearly entitled to be treated as prisoners of war in the normal manner.

Nevertheless, Hitler's 'Commando order' has remained a point of controversy, and to some extent the Commandos became victims of the propaganda that was created on their behalf. More than one Allied document had referred to Commandos as 'guerrilla' fighters, and their training was definitely unorthodox. Written instructions, secret at the time, do also carry hints that Commandos were sometimes ordered to play fast and loose with the strict conventions of war. The mid-war document *Lessons Learned from Combined Operations* contains the direction: 'For stay-ashore raiding parties, one suit of civilian clothes should be taken ashore by the leader of the party.' The orders for the exercise code-named 'Rommel', planned for Brodick on the Isle of Arran in July 1942, outlined a dummy mission to attack the castle, which stood in as an enemy radar station. The secret training document included the words, 'No prisoners will be taken.' Originals of both these papers are retained in the Mills-Roberts collection at the Liddell Hart archive at King's College. The widely distributed book, *Commando Attack* by Telegraph Exchange Correspondent Gordon Holman, of May 1942, contains throwaway lines put in the mouth of 'a general' regarding the necessity to kill or capture any Germans attempting to invade the UK, and ends with the remark that 'we are not much concerned with taking prisoners'. There can be little doubting that, with such potentially incriminating material waiting to fall into enemy hands, it would be used to justify the ideas that Commandos could dress in civilian clothes and execute captives.

As it turned out, the boot was sometimes on the other foot. Commando prisoners who fell into enemy hands during raiding activity, rather than in action on the battlefront, were placed in a separate category, and not a few tortured and executed. Instances were documented by Allied powers and recorded as war crimes. At Nuremberg, Jodl attempted to shift some of the responsibility for the Commando order, and other criminal instructions, onto General Walter Warlimont, Deputy Chief of Operations at OKW. Nevertheless, Jodl was hanged for war crimes and crimes against humanity in 1946, whilst Warlimont received a life sentence, from which he was actually released in 1954.

Chapter 5

The Making of Commandos

At first most Commando training was done within individual units in various parts of the country, and much of it had a distinctly improvised character, which has been described under the apt euphemism of 'emerging doctrine' – since, initially, there was very little in the existing manuals or established training schemes about amphibious work or the use of small non-standard units in a raiding role. Worse, much of the equipment that would be needed on operations either did not exist, or had to be held in a central pool. Most instruction was initiated by the commanding officers of the individual Commandos. As Durnford-Slater, leading No. 3 Commando, recalled:

> Jack Churchill had been appointed my second-in-command. Commonly known as 'Mad Jack', he continually evolved new and very unusual ideas for training. I gave all the troop commanders a pretty free run at this time as the great thing was to avoid boredom. Peter Young continued to study his troop attack and I often went and worked with his troop. Their technique had come on a lot since the Plymouth days and I found work in one of his movement groups the hardest exercise I have ever taken. Another of Peter Young's activities was the training of potential NCOs. I frequently took him off all other duties for this purpose, giving him a squad of about twenty-five promising men. They would do an intensive three-week course, after which Peter could tell me with almost unfailing accuracy which men would make good NCOs and which would be just ordinary, good, private soldiers.

Nevertheless, some of the Commando preparation of 1940 now appears positively quaint, if physically strenuous, in retrospect. J. G. Appleyard described a 'typical' day on the south coast as starting at 6.30, with a brisk mile-run at 7, followed by some PT and breakfast. The parade at 9 included an inspection, after which the Commandos did a route march of 8 to 10 miles, including map-reading and compass work and tactical movement through cover. After lunch came 'swimming parade' and attendant exercise at 2.30. 'Tea' was followed by a lecture, and freedom for the evening after 6. Appleyard looked forward to the weapons training, range practice, 'hare and hounds', 'treasure hunts', and 'mock operations' by night and day, which were promised for the future.

No. 6 Commando undertook training at Plymouth, where one of the most memorable and useful drills was swimming fully clothed, before moving to Scotland in the winter of 1940 for a course that included demolitions and landings. At Inveraray a night exercise in snow was devised, where the Local Defence Volunteers defended a telephone exchange that the Commandos attacked via a river crossing. As Corporal Wetherall related:

> Captain Montanaro was the first to cross the icy river, and we all followed. Titch Harley who was in front of me turned round [...] and promptly disappeared under the water [...] on reaching the other bank, we had to crawl a long way in snow. I think everyone was shivering with cold except me, because I had donned a pair of woollen 'Long Johns', which kept the sodden trousers from flapping round my legs.

Later, some of the men accompanied the officers deer-stalking, before the trainees moved on again to Loch Fyne and Arran. In these places the work included climbing and walking on Goat Fell and the Devil's Punch Bowl, and canoeing. One experiment involved firing a Bren gun from the bows of a canoe – not entirely successfully, as the recoil was apt to push the vessel backwards.

Physical training or 'PT' was part of the schooling of virtually every soldier of every nationality in 1940, yet the Commando version was different, and arguably better, for a number of reasons. As a number of accounts have noted, Commando PT was usually more practical than that indulged in by the rest of the services. Often it was performed rifle in hand and involved some sort of task, almost always out of doors. For example, 'Log PT' – not particularly fondly remembered by many – was remarked upon in *The Times*. Logs were lifted, carried, tossed like cabers, laid across streams and otherwise used, not just to develop fitness and strength, but as a team-building activity in which small groups learned to work together and develop mutual reliance. Rope work was possible wherever there were trees or other handy uprights, and exercises involving rope bridges, scaling nets, abseiling, and the infamous 'death slide' were soon included. One simple piece of equipment forever to be associated with the Commandos was the 'toggle rope'. As described by the US journal, *Tactical and Technical Trends*, this was 'a four-foot length of rope with a loop at one end and a toggle at the other [...] By linking several of these together, ropes of various lengths are made, which are very useful in overcoming obstacles, crossing streams etc.' Laudable as all this undoubtedly was, it was partly a case of necessity being the mother of invention. In 1940 Commandos had no barracks, and no base meant no drill hall beyond a church hall, and certainly no well-equipped gymnasium or ready supply of PT equipment. Commandos had already done basic training with their parent units or depots, and a sure way to create boredom or resentment would have been to patronise them by repeating the same activities – imagination, improvisation and basic equipment made Commando PT different and relevant.

A particularly useful adjunct to local efforts was the 'Irregular Warfare School', later known as the 'Special Training Centre', at Lochailort, which had opened its doors in May 1940, and first admitted small groups of Commandos on short courses a couple of months later. One of the moving forces here was Lord Lovat, whose clerk recalled that he devised many of the training programmes personally, and that these had to be typed and then printed up for distribution to the various instructors. These courses were very much a precursor of what would later be offered at Achnacarry: close combat, demolitions, signals, swimming, long-distance marches, climbing and seamanship all being high on the agenda. A small glen nearby is still known as 'sniper's valley', due to its use in sniping exercises. The use of live ammunition increased realism, and achieved what was described at the time as a degree of 'battle inoculation'. This was not without its dangers. In mid-1941, for example, Brigadier Haydon was forced to issue a temporary order banning use of live ammunition following an incident in which three soldiers, playing the 'enemy' in a Commando exercise, were injured.

Though early Commando training was disparate in character, there were soon efforts to ensure that key subjects were covered, methods of doing so becoming more unified over time. Early in 1941, for example, a brief document was issued from Haydon's headquarters under the heading *Special Service Brigade Spring Training Instructions*, supplemented by *Additional Notes*. These specified subjects to be taught and points requiring attention. One of the most important was 'Field Firing' – Commandos were to integrate weapons practice into other activities such as climbing or landing, shooting from boats, and master the arts of rapid and snap firing, engagement of surprise targets, use of cover, tactical features, and street-fighting. 'Sea Training' was to focus especially on boats and landing in 'difficult places'. Under the general heading of 'Reconnaissance' were to be included the skills of climbing, swimming, signalling and first aid. 'Marching' was a subject in its own right, being increased gradually so as to increase stamina and condition the feet. The 'normal Commando pace', over all distances up to 20 miles, was set at 3.5 miles per hour. The shortest marches worthy of the name were set at 5 miles, with the longest 'endurance' march being 35 miles in fourteen hours. In practice, the shorter 'marches' were often relatively rapid, with plenty of doubling and jogging and a minimum of equipment, not merely on grounds of variety and improving overall fitness, but because this mimicked the likely circumstances of a raid, in which the approach was not particularly long and the troops might be required to get into and out of action very quickly. Experiment determined that practical exercises were best when the 'enemy' was given some latitude of action, as things became unrealistic when the defender was told what to do in advance.

Primary focus on tactical weapons and explosive training appears to have remained a constant wherever Commandos trained. R. M. Lyons was witness to 11 Commando's courses in Syria prior to the Litani River operations, which covered 'explosives, fuses, switches, grenades, rifle, pistol and knife'. Naturally, plastics and guncotton were included, as were such subtleties as booby traps comprising grenades attached to trip wires. The pistol trainer also showed some imagination, teaching 'close work', for which pupils were instructed 'to lower the body, turn sideways to the target, and cock the weapon [...] on entering a room, shoot the nearest person first, next the person who moves, leaving those who were bemused to last'. Such attention to detail was coupled with tactical schemes, raids, map-reading, field work and demolitions. Lyons believed, almost certainly correctly, that the whole training scheme was based on that also used by Commandos in the UK.

Though less well known than Colonel Newman's famous and oft-quoted *Service in a Commando* memoranda – used as a basis for training by the newly raised 2 Commando after its predecessor had been converted to parachute troops – some parts of the *Spring Training Instructions* are identical, and it would, therefore, appear that one was based upon, or evolved from, the other. Newman's document also included reference to the importance of 'night sense', unarmed combat, the setting of 'booby traps', basic medical training, and an ability to forage, so that the Commando could 'live under a bivouac for a considerable period'. As

The original model for the 'Commando' – a group of Boers under a leader, lightly equipped, and usually mounted, during the South African War. Transvaal-born Lieutenant Colonel Dudley Clarke claimed to have come up with the title for the new 'Special Force', though Churchill's experiences in the Boer War doubtless made official acceptance of the name more likely.

A Bren gunner aboard a landing craft off Vaagso, 1941. Several buildings are alight and the church is clearly visible in the middle distance. *(P&S)*

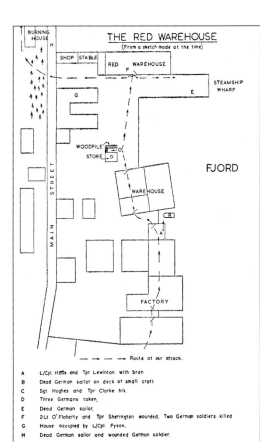

THE RED WAREHOUSE
(From a sketch made at the time)

BURNING HOUSE

SHOP | STABLE

RED | WAREHOUSE

STEAMSHIP WHARF

G

WOODPILE STORE

FJORD

WAREHOUSE

MAIN STREET

FACTORY

— ▪ — ▪ — ▶ Route of our attack.

A   L/Cpl. Halls and Tpr. Lewinton with bren
B   Dead German sailor on deck of small craft
C   Sgt Hughes and Tpr Clarke hit.
D   Three Germans taken.
E   Dead German sailor.
F   2Lt O'Flaherty and Tpr Sherington wounded. Two German soldiers killed
G   House occupied by L/Cpl Fyson.
H   Dead German sailor and wounded German soldier.

Sketch map of Peter Young's street battle at Vaagso, showing the route through the warehouses of the quayside. From *Storm from the Sea*, courtesy of Greenhill Books.

Stoic, but bleeding heavily, Private Tom McCormack of No. 2 Commando, seen just after capture at St Nazaire. McCormack had previously served in the Queen's Own Cameron Highlanders, and the Territorial Liverpool Scottish. During the battle he was wounded more than once. Lieutenant Chant described seeing him with 'half of his face blown off' by a grenade. This photograph later appeared in the German propaganda magazine *Signal*. In fact, McCormack was mortally injured and died soon afterwards. *(P&S)*

A brave face – Commandos pose with the Union Flag on return from Dieppe, 19 August 1942. Despite the triumph of No. 4 Commando at Varengeville, none of the units involved had escaped unscathed, and No. 3 Commando and the new Royal Marine Commando suffered very serious losses. (P&S)

Captain Gerald Charles Stokes Montanaro of No. 6 Commando, and later 101 Troop, during Combined Operations training at Inverary, October 1941. Montanaro wears a rather fluffy-looking private purchase version of the 'Cap Comforter' and is armed with a German long-barrelled Luger pistol of First World War vintage, complete with drum magazine. In the background is a Commando with a Thompson.

An NCO of No. 1 Commando rock-climbing during training in Scotland at Glencoe, 19 November, 1941. He carries a slung Thompson submachine gun but little other equipment. *(P&S)*

Fig. 47   Fig. 48

Fig. 49

'The Sentry Hold' from W. E. Fairbairn's *All-in Fighting*, 1942. The sentry is approached stealthily – preferably in soft footwear and from cover or darkness – and at '3 or 4 feet' a 'lightning attack' is launched. Simultaneously striking with the left forearm across the throat, and punching in the back (fig. 48), gives the attacker the advantage. He may now grasp his opponent around the neck, smothering him with the free hand and dragging him backwards.

The use of the Commando knife from W. E. Fairbairn's *All-in Fighting*, 1942. Figure 113, the 'artery number one' attack to the arm with a 'slashing cut outwards'. Fig. 114, 'artery number two' – a 'downwards and inwards' cut to the left wrist. Fig. 115, with the knife in the right hand, edges parallel to the ground, 'seize opponent around the neck from behind with your left arm, pulling his head to the left. Thrust point well in; then cut sideways.' Fig. 116, downward stroke, followed by a cut – a fatal stroke for which the application of a tourniquet is impossible.

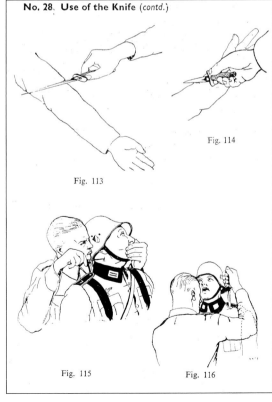

Fig. 114

Fig. 113

Fig. 115   Fig. 116

Commandos jump from assault boats during training; getting clear of craft quickly was vital, especially if opposed. In theory, small assault boats could be carried overland by their crews using the rope which ran along the outside of the hull – not an easy operation at the best of times. (P&S)

A Commando crawls through undergrowth with Tommy gun and machete during training in Scotland, February 1942. The fearsome machete was primarily a tool for clearing vegetation – but doubled as a weapon. Note also the 'Commando' cloth shoulder-title: later in the war a universal design of red on dark blue, either printed or embroidered, prefixed by the number, replaced the various types already in use. *(P&S)*

Training with the Fairbairn-Sykes knife: severing of the carotid artery was estimated to bring an extremely messy death in about twelve seconds. The man playing the 'victim' in this exercise also has a Commando knife in his thigh pocket.

The assault course, bridging exercises, and the use of pyrotechnics were all regular elements of Commando training. Many things remarkable in 1940 have since become established staples of basic infantry training. *(P&S)*

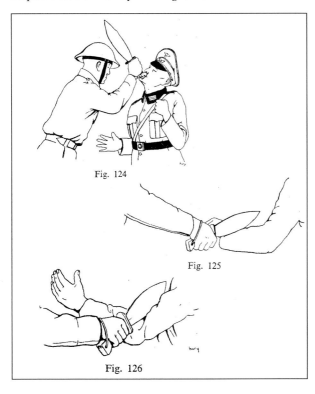

Fig. 124

Fig. 125

Fig. 126

The use of the Smatchet from W. E. Fairbairn's *All-in Fighting*, 1942. At this period the Smatchet was often issued to Tommy-gunners, who lacked a bayonet to their main weapon. Though the Smatchet could be used for more conventional attacks, such as thrusts to the stomach or 'sabre cuts' to the neck, it was also equipped with a heavy pommel, which could be brought up sharply under the chin of an opponent. Similarly, it could be smashed into the face, as in figure 124. Figs 125 and 126 show 'sabre cuts' to arm and wrist.

The rifle in close-quarter fighting, from an addendum to all *All-in Fighting*, by Captain P. N. Walbridge. Most mainstream rifle training concentrated on aiming and firing – Walbridge offered practical hints for combat to supplement Fairbairn's remarks on knife-fighting and unarmed combat. Whilst firing from the shoulder was undoubtedly more accurate, and often quicker for repeat rounds, it was sometimes necessary to move and fire simultaneously. Firing speedily from the hip (fig. 155) was useful in some circumstances, as where the target appeared suddenly at close range. The 'stalking' advance (fig. 156) could be used on a stealthy approach, with the rifle slightly raised to fire (fig. 157). Very rapid, if not particularly accurate, fire against close targets could be achieved by manipulating the bolt with thumb and forefinger and the trigger with the second finger.

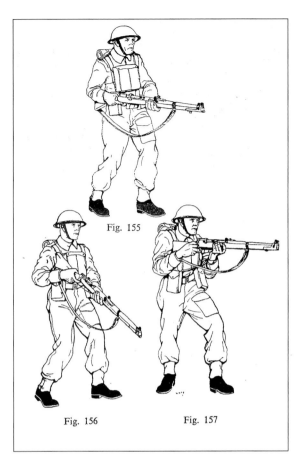

Fig. 155

Fig. 156   Fig. 157

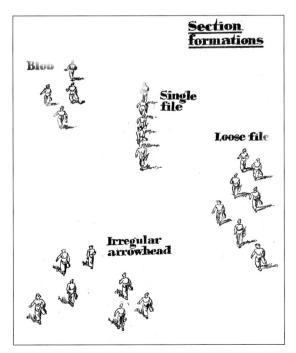

Section formations

Blob

Single file

Loose file

Irregular arrowhead

Some basic section formations shown in *Section Leading and Fieldcraft for Cadets*, 1945. These, plus the irregular prone 'skirmish line' and methods of 'fire and movement' were drills used throughout the Army. Most Commandos learned them in basic training before volunteering for 'Special Service' – thereafter it was possible to graft on new variations suited to conditions, mission, and equipment available.

W. E. Fairbairn was by no means the only producer of special close-combat manuals. This instruction on disarming a knife-wielding opponent comes from the *Manual of Commando and Guerrilla Warfare – Unarmed Combat,* published in London *c.* 1942.

Sketch A.—Opponent goes for you with a knife in his right hand, in an upward direction. Step to the right. Ward off his thrust with your left hand, gripping his right shoulder with your right hand.

Sketch B.—Press his shoulder down, so that his chest is against your right thigh. Simultaneously, slip your left arm underneath his right arm, putting your left hand just below his right shoulder.

Sketch C.—Get hold of his right wrist with your right hand, pressing his arm rearwards, and as high as you can. This will make him release the knife. Grip your opponent's little finger and wrench backwards. He is then in your power.

N.B.—Reverse hands, if opponent attacks you with knife in left hand.

Methods for use of the Bren during attack and retreat: prone, with every possible cover used to advantage, including folds in the ground (fig. 12), isolated cover such as thick tree-trunks (fig 13), and slopes (fig. 14). From *Light Machine Gun*, Small Arms Training Pamphlet 4 volume I, August 1942.

25

No unnecessary exposure.

LINE OF FIRE.

Muzzle clear of cover.

Gun mounted using a fold in the ground.

Fig. 12.

Body straight — Carrying handle upright to suit cover

Gun close to cover.

Feet together.

No undue exposure.

Gun mounted round isolated cover

Fig 13.

Position to suit cover

Bipod leg lengthened to suit slope.

Fig 14. Gun mounted on the side of a slope.

One way to disarm an enemy rifleman, as shown in a Commando training demonstration. The unarmed man has unbalanced his opponent by forcing him backwards over his left leg, simultaneously pushing the butt of the weapon upward. In other versions of the manoeuvre the bayonet is parried and the muzzle pushed away and upwards, combined with kicks. *(P&S)*

Advancing rapidly through smoke during landing training. Given how lightly equipped most Commando units were, initially, there was considerable emphasis on concealment and surprise during both training and operations. Darkness was the best cover but smoke could be useful, particularly on landing, when men were likely to be moving, bunched, and vulnerable to fire. *(P&S)*

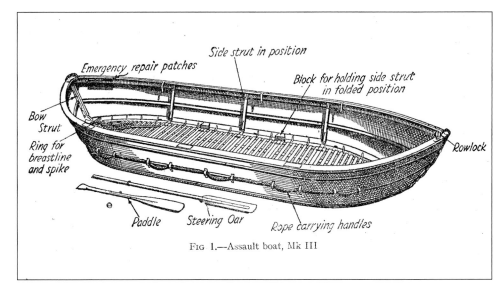

Side strut in position

Emergency repair patches

Block for holding side strut
in folded position

Bow
Strut

Ring for
breastline
and spike

Rowlock

Paddle   Steering Oar   Rope carrying handles

FIG 1.—Assault boat, Mk III

The folding 'Assault Boat Mk III' from *Rafting and Bridging, Part III, Assault Crossing Equipment,* January 1944. This was just one of many craft used by Commandos: at various times canoes, rubber dinghies, motor launches (MLs), rescue boats, whalers, *Eurekas,* Landing Craft Assault (LCAs), and Landing Craft Personnel (LCPs) all formed part of the repertoire.

FIG. 17.—Side View.

Using the semi-automatic pistol from cover from the 1942 edition of *Shooting to Live* by W. E. Fairbairn and E. A. Sykes. This manual was based on experience with the Shanghai Police, hence the uniform in the illustration, but was later used in training Commandos. Subsequently it was used as inspiration by Colonel Rex Applegate for the US instruction book, *Kill or Get Killed,* another bible of the combat handgun.

A returning Commando raider on the beach at Hastings, summer 1942. He carries a Thompson submachine gun and a lifebelt.

Lieutenant Colonel Peter Young giving instructions to two camouflaged snipers near Breville, Normandy, 17 June 1944. As Young recalled, 'From this time on the nature of the fighting changed completely. The Germans delivered no more attacks, but dug in more than 1,000 yards east of us beyond the Breville–Gonneville road. It became a war of sniping and patrolling. In No. 3 Commando we made it our object to see that the enemy was confined to his own lines.'

A heavily stowed Commando equipped for a landing – note the Tommy gun, eagle, and anchor 'Combined Operations' badge on the left upper arm. The original was designed by Lieutenant D. A. Grant of the Royal Naval Volunteer Reserve as the result of a competition, and approved by Mountbatten in 1942, being introduced before the end of the year. The type shown here, on a circular ground, was associated specifically with the Army Commandos. The kit shown includes a lifebelt, and a 'Yukon' type pack frame from which are suspended various items and tools including a small pack, bayonet, and gas mask bag. Interestingly, the rifle carried is not the standard SMLE with a ten-round box magazine, but one of the US Enfield variants with a five-round magazine which saw use in training and as sniper weapons. *(P&S)*

The Commando memorial at Spean Bridge near Fort William. The monument was unveiled in September 1952 by Queen Elizabeth, the Queen Mother. Its central figure, with binoculars, is based on Sergeant Lewington of No. 4 Commando. The inscription on the plinth reads 'United We Conquer', under which is a panel with the legend, 'In memory of the officers and men of the Commandos who died in the Second World War 1939–1945. This country was their training ground.'

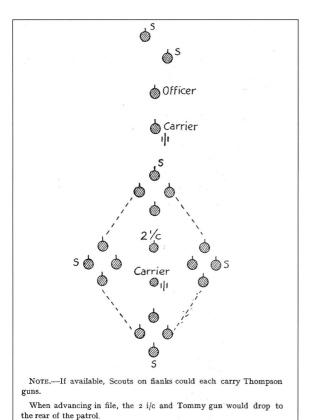

One method of forming a 'night fighting patrol', from Major Nevill A. D. Armstrong's *Fieldcraft Sniping and Intelligence*, November 1940. Note the positioning of the Thompson gunners marked 'S', vital at night when close-range encounters were likely and long-range targets were not visible.

One of the small folding-type assault boats is dragged ashore during training. These craft were relatively light, could be stowed in small spaces, and sometimes unobtrusively concealed whilst a small party of raiders was ashore. On the downside they were of modest capacity, slow when rowed, and easily damaged. *(P&S)*

Rock-climbing exercise using knotted rope laid by one of the more expert team members that the remainder then use as a scaling aid. Sometimes, when dedicated climbing ropes were lacking, individual 'toggle ropes' were joined to create longer sections. Commando mountain and rock-climbing training became increasingly sophisticated with the participation of some of the leading military and civilian exponents of the day, at a variety of venues in Scotland, North Wales, and Cornwall, allowing simulation of many different mountain combat and coastal landing scenarios. *(P&S)*

Men of 12 Commando re-embark from a small LCA onto one of the larger ships on return from the Bruneval raid, February 1942. Note the gear often worn by Commandos in cold weather – leather jerkin and scarf or balaclava over battle dress. Bruneval was small scale, but a great success, and a truly combined operation. Parachutists attacked the radar station capturing the enemy apparatus, then fought their way out to meet Commandos and Naval gunboats securing the beach. Casualties were gratifyingly light. *(P&S)*

James Dunning of 4 Commando has observed, the major problem with early Commando training was not unwillingness to learn new things, nor lack of application in drawing up demanding training regimes, but the sheer number and diversity of skills that the first Commando leaders aspired to instil in their men. Nevertheless, most of the officers were highly enthusiastic, and usually drove themselves just as hard. Geoffrey Keyes wrote of sleeping 'like a dog' after days of violent exertion. Colonel Newman demanded that the whole of 2 Commando foot-slog from Paignton in Devon to a new base at Weymouth in Dorset, camping on the way.

Many American observers were upbeat about Commando training techniques from an early stage, doubtless regarding them as a model that could be profitably emulated in the near future:

Training of Commando personnel is designed to develop individual fighting initiative, and is based entirely on offensive principles. The training program seeks the development, to the very highest possible degree, of stamina and endurance under any operating conditions and in all types of climate. It aims to perfect all individuals in every basic military requirement, as well as in the very special work likely to be encountered in operations, namely: wall climbing, skiing, obstacle running, demolition, street fighting, both night and day shooting, solution of tactical problems, surmounting barbed wire, handling grenades and torpedoes, etc. Every man is expected to achieve some particular qualification, as motorcyclist, driver, boat operator, engineer, etc. The training succeeds in developing at one and the same time confidence, initiative and ingenuity in the individual and perfect teamwork in the group. Commando leaders are given a free hand and a reasonable cash allowance to organise their own training program. Particular stress is placed on swimming and boating, although other exercises are also practiced in order to develop rugged physical condition. Stalking and use of cover and concealment are stressed, but greater emphasis is placed on night problems, for success in raiding operations depends on an ability to work silently, with precision, in darkness.

Quite what a Commando should consume to sustain himself during the extreme exertions of both combat and training was given serious consideration. Though 'living off the land' was taught, and hunting game also featured in training, it was realised that this could only really be an emergency measure – as, for example, when rations ran low or small groups were evading the enemy. As a general method of feeding, individual foraging was next to useless, since it required so much time and effort as to preclude the undertaking of any but the most inconsequential mission. Moreover, items such as fresh rabbit, seafood, berries and green vegetables, though highly nutritious, were bulky, prone to go off after a fairly short time, required some preparation, and were far from ideal for carrying during long marches or action. What was needed, therefore, was a basic combat ration that contained the necessary calories, was quick, compact and easy to transport, not particularly vulnerable to spoiling, and at least palatable enough that hungry men would eat it in short order. Preparing the food should also need little extraneous equipment – and be perfectly possible by individual soldiers under inhospitable conditions.

Solutions to the problem were tested experimentally at Lochailort early in 1941. Obviously, long marches or other fatiguing actions required plenty of calories, but the problem was not that simple. Since the Commandos took no land transport with them on raiding missions, everything had to be carried on the man, and balance had to be struck between weight and mobility. Moreover, water was heavy; there was concern that salt was lost through sweat; and really tired men were more likely to want sleep than food – even if this left them hungry later. On 3 May 1941 Royal Navy Surgeon Commander G. M. Levick gave his opinion, this being circulated as the memorandum *Rations – Emergency* to Commandos in the UK, plus '101' Troop and the Brigade Signal Section. The ideal one-day ration on operations 'when simple cooking in mess tins is possible' was determined to be:

Bully Beef	4 oz	310.4 calories
Chocolate	2 oz	313 calories
Oatmeal	4 oz	452.8 calories
Army Biscuit	8 oz	848 calories
Dried fruit	4 oz	314.8 calories
Sugar	4 oz	453.6 calories
Margarine	2 oz	435.8 calories
Tea	.125 oz	000 calories
Salt	.25 oz	000 calories
[Total]	28.38 oz	3,128.4 calories

As sustenance for some of the most strenuous soldiering known to man, this was not regarded as overgenerous, but Levick discovered that adding extra biscuits, for example, made no improvement because the men were too exhausted to eat them. Large amounts of sugar in wartime Britain is similarly strange at first glance, but as Levick explained, it was important for marching: 'the effect of eating sugar, when very fatigued physically, is surprisingly valuable for the reason that it is rapidly converted into blood sugar and can be utilised to provide muscular energy a few minutes after it is taken'. The men were to be advised to 'take half their sugar in empty matchboxes to eat on the march when they are very tired, the rest being taken with the dried fruit for preference and in tea'. A pint of tea was

---

Bernard Leicester

Bernard William Leicester (1901–1977), nicknamed 'Jumbo', was born in Worcester and joined the Royal Marine Light Infantry in 1918. He served first in HMS *Barham*, qualified at the Naval Physical Training School, and later took up an appointment there. In 1929 he volunteered for the Sudan Defence Force, serving for five years, before going to HMS *Rodney*. Following the staff course at Sandhurst, he was given the post of brigade major in 9th Infantry Brigade, and so found himself in France in 1939, but was invalided out before the German invasion. During 1940 and 1941 he occupied various staff appointments, but was eventually appointed commanding officer of 1st Battalion Royal Marines. In 1943, after the formation of the Royal Marine Commandos, 'Jumbo' moved to lead 4th Special Service Brigade. His finest hours were arguably the D-Day campaign and the assault on Walcheren, in November 1944 where, as his obituary remarked, his leadership inspired both the confidence and affection of his men. The Distinguished Service Order and bar were awarded for these operations. Leicester commanded the Commando Group until 1947, then went to Washington as representative of the Chief of Combined Operations. This was followed by further tours in the Sudan, and at the Royal Marine base at Lympstone. Amongst his ceremonial duties he served as ADC to both King George VI and Queen Elizabeth II. His personal charm and ability to work on both sides of the Army/Navy service divide were widely remarked.

recommended morning and night, with a drink of hot water at lunch, as this was perceived as 'banishing fatigue'. Salt was intended to be used up with porridge, the bully beef, and an odd pinch with water, though how much was really necessary must have varied tremendously with energy and perspiration expended. According to Ernest Dale, who served as a clerk at Lochailort, the experiments on efficacy of salt were brutally simple. Levick selected two men of equal physique, and deprived one of all salt for a week, feeding the other normally. The pair were then run around, and up steep mountain slopes wearing full packs – with the 'desalinated soldier' collapsing far more quickly than his comrade.

There were a few different options with the rather basic list of ingredients, but Levick suggested a 'standard apportionment'. This was a breakfast that consisted of oatmeal porridge, sweet tea, biscuit with margarine, and an ounce of dried fruit; lunch of biscuit, bully beef, chocolate, fruit and water; and an evening meal of a 'stew' of bully beef, oatmeal and salt, followed by more biscuit, fruit and sweet tea. The remainder of the 'marching' sugar was to be eaten between meals. It was perhaps fortunate that missions tended to be short, as apart from the danger of constipation, the menu lacks any fresh food, and as Levick was forced to admit, 'Vitamin C is unavoidably absent.' The whole thing appears marginally less appetising than food eaten by Tommy in the trenches over two decades earlier. On the positive side, the day's ration weighed less than 2 lb, had nothing to go off, was simple to prepare, and reasonably compact.

By the following year there appear to have been both minor nutritional improvements, and nods in the direction of taste and roughage. The US study *British Commandos* of mid-1942 gives the following as the standard daily operational ration, this version being stated as developed by 'an officer who had considerable experience in mountain operations in all climates'. Possibly this was another sideways reference to the somewhat eccentric and perennially shorts-wearing Levick, who had been on Captain Scott's Antarctic expedition:

Pemmican (dried meat 60% lean, 40% fat) 3 oz
Chocolate 3 oz
Oatmeal 5 oz
Biscuit 6 oz
Dried Fruit 5 oz
Margarine or butter 1.5 oz

Tea or Coffee (compressed) 0.25 oz
Salt 0.25 oz
Sugar (lump) 1.5 oz
Total weight 25.5 oz

As before, the various ingredients were broken into three major portions to be prepared in the individual mess tin and served as meals spread over the day. Further,

> the soldiers were encouraged to use dandelion shoots, grass nettles, and other herbs in conjunction with pemmican and oatmeal for making a stew. These herbs in the stew contributed Vitamin C. While the standard Army ration was used during training, the concentrated ration was substituted during tactical operations because of its small bulk and light weight.

At Achnacarry, trainees also recall rations being handed out prior to overnight exercises that included raw meat and vegetables as well as some bread and tinned milk, though often this food had to be prepared without the aid of solid fuel cookers or similar devices. Later still, some Commandos were able to train on American 'K' rations, and most found these distinctly preferable, at least for limited periods. As A. E. Hines of 41 RM Commando remarked, they were 'quite a change from ours', with 'dehydrated foods, fruit juice, spam, biscuits and cheese'.

Not insignificantly, much Commando training doctrine found its way into American literature, notably the pages of the US War Department publication, *Tactical and Technical Trends*. The first edition carried a detailed feature entitled, 'Organisation and Training of British Commandos'. As it explained:

> Commando Training is conducted along the following lines: it seeks the development of a high degree of stamina and endurance under any operating conditions and in all types of climate. It seeks to perfect all individuals in every basic military requirement as well as in special work likely to be encountered in operations *viz*: wall climbing, skiing and so forth. It aims to develop a high percentage of men with particular qualifications, *viz*: motorcyclists, truck drivers, small boat operators, locomotive engineers, etc. It aims to develop self confidence, initiative and ingenuity, in the individual and the group. It seeks to

develop perfect team work in operating and combat. An officer or enlisted man volunteering for Commando duty is personally interviewed by an officer.

In its training the SS Brigade is prepared to accept casualties rather than suffer a 50 per cent or higher battle casualties because of inexperienced personnel. All training is conducted with the utmost reality and to the end that the offensive spirit is highly developed. Wide latitude is accorded commanders in the training methods employed, and thus the development of initiative, enterprise and ingenuity in the solution of battle problems, and the development of new techniques is encouraged. A corresponding latitude is accorded troop commanders. Only the highest standards are acceptable and if officers and men are unable to attain them, they are returned to their units immediately. Leaves are accorded Commando personnel during prolonged training periods and after actual operations in order to prevent men 'going stale'.

The specific courses noted by *Tactical and Technical Trends* were the assault course, cliff-climbing, demolitions, street-fighting, field combat firings, marches, obstacles and wall-scaling. Demolition training was given to all Commandos, though an advanced course was also run for a 'demolition group' within each troop. This special team was also taught how to blow up bridges, rail installations, machinery and oil tanks. A particularly useful skill was blowing craters or demolishing buildings in such a way as to create temporary roadblocks. At Troun, on 3 December 1941, a night exercise village attack involving three troops was reported by the American 'Special Naval Observer', during the course of which the following techniques were employed:

> Bangalore torpedoes for gapping wire, booby traps installed in the likely avenues of approach, and well camouflaged piano trip wires set to explode land mines. The Bangalore torpedoes were real enough but booby traps and land mines were represented by detonators. Very few booby traps exploded as the men kept their wits about them and their eyes open. Sufficient training allowance of all types of high explosive, fuzes, and detonators is made available so that this important training is continuous. A plastic type of HE is used extensively.

Later, an American witness attended a Commando lecture on scouts and observers. Here he learned that scouting was treated as a special skill with the object of obtaining 'accurate and reliable information in all types of warfare', and in any type of country with or without aids such as binoculars and maps. Observation near to the enemy was particularly vital, whether he was 100 yards or 100 miles away. The best scouts were not only keen, resourceful and trustworthy with good powers of reasoning, but knowledgeable about their job and the various functions of other arms. Such background would enable him to know what to look for and immediately interpret what he was seeing. Moreover a scout should be able to conceal himself successfully and ability in sketching, photography, first aid, sailing, swimming, horse and motorcycle-riding were all valuable. Scouts were to excel in five tactical areas:

1) Patrols, observation in small detachments, sniping and verbal reporting.
2) Fieldcraft, if necessary to the extent of being able to pass through enemy lines.
3) All scout personnel must attain a high degree of skill in movement by night over difficult country by use of stars and compass, and must be trained to carry out certain tasks under cover of darkness and in silence.
4) Construction of field defences, and erection of obstacles.
5) Demolition and sabotage.

Similarly, one of the Americans attended a standard lecture on street-fighting 'given by a British Major' during Commando training, and his notes again appeared as a feature in *Tactical and Technical Trends*. The vital essentials of all attacks in a built-up area were surprise and speed. Advanced warning allowed the enemy to 'turn every house into a fort' and Independent Companies, lacking heavy support, would then find it 'very costly', if not impossible, to shift him:

Once the attack is launched, the enemy must be kept continually on the run, and not given the least respite in which to rally and organise his resistance. Troops must be trained to display the greatest boldness and initiative, since the slightest hesitation may prove fatal to the whole operation; junior officers, especially, must combine a daredevil recklessness with a cool head. In this type of warfare the motto is 'Hit first, hit hard, and keep on hitting.' Nothing is more demoralising to the attackers than a long drawn out and indecisive battle in the streets.

In advancing along streets, Commandos were taught to move in single file along both sides, leaving an interval of about 3 yards between individuals, who were to be vigilant in checking for snipers in doors and windows opposite. A light machine gun might expediently be placed near street crossings to provide covering fire:

> When movement is possible along the roofs of houses, picked snipers of special agility and marksmanship should be sent up to the rooftops to cover the advance below. Never approach a doorway into a house or room, directly from the front. If there is an enemy behind it he is sure to see you several seconds before you can see him, and he will shoot first. Approach from one side, hugging the wall; then take one or two hand grenades and throw them inside, and follow yourself immediately after the explosion, with pistol or knife at the ready – the pistol is preferred. It is fairly certain that if the grenades do not actually kill or seriously wound the defenders, they will knock them out for a few seconds at least. A house that is strongly defended will have to be taken floor by floor, or even room by room; hence the danger of allowing the enemy to organise any resistance; but once a house has been entered, and fighting is proceeding on the upper floors, the attackers should post one or two men on the ground floor to watch the street and guard against surprise.

When strong resistance was encountered, the best method was to reduce the enemy by working around the flanks, squeezing the defenders into small pockets to be tackled one at a time. Mortars were thought particularly useful in street combat, due to their accuracy and the demoralisation induced by the rapidity of fire, and efficacy against street barricades:

> Finally, it must be emphasised that a small attacking force in street fighting cannot afford to take prisoners; it is too easy for them to escape and, having escaped, to do great damage to their captors. Furthermore, men cannot be spared for escort.

Leaving aside the obvious brutality of street-fighting, this quotation could have been taken direct from Henry V at Agincourt.

It has been claimed, quite erroneously, that many of the classic elements of street-fighting were actually devised by the Commandos and only perfected after the Vaagso raid of December 1941. Whilst Commandos were innovators in many fields, and certainly became expert early practitioners, the evidence does not in any way support the contention that the key techniques of street-fighting were invented by Commando officers. In point of fact, some basic ideas were in existence by the First World War, and brief instructions had appeared in the manual *Infantry Section Leading* of 1938. More was gleaned in the Spanish Civil War, and specifically from incidents in the Madrid area in 1936 and 1937. These recent examples were subsequently taught to the Local Defence Volunteers, Home Guard and regular Army, by veterans of the campaign, such as Tom Winteringham, John Langdon-Davies, Hugh Slater and others. By 1941 a modern street-fighting doctrine was well on its way to fruition. 'Yank' Levy's *Guerrilla Warfare* was published by Penguin that year, making available to the general public – as well as the services – such matters as mouseholing walls, attacking and defending barricades, urban fieldcraft and house clearance. Levy explicitly acknowledged that his awareness of such techniques was drawn both from Spain and study of more recent events, such as the Siege of Leningrad. *Picture Post* mentioned street-fighting training at the Home Guard Osterley Park Training School in its edition of 21 September 1941, by which time the school had been open over two months and Tom Winteringham claimed that the better part of 6,000 trainees had already attended the school.

Perhaps even more significant were Major Lionel Wigram and his book, *Battle School*, written in October 1941, but not actually published until early the following year, which also built on the experiences of I Corps and the instruction *Tactical Notes for Platoon Commanders*. This aimed at establishing set drills for different circumstances that would provide a system of tactics, easily taught and easily understood, and upon which trained troops would be ready to act as the default method. Variations and orders to suit the precise situation of an engagement could then be overlaid – all concerned knowing the basic steps of the choreography of minor tactics and performing them with confidence. *Battle School* contained drills for clearing a village and for individual house clearance, and these would later form the basic elements of the classic street-fighting manual of the Second World War, *Fighting in Built Up Areas*.

Wigram was certainly not unknown prior to the Norway raids, and had indeed been commander of the first divisional battle school, established at

Chelwood Gate in July 1941. By December of that year – and just prior to the events at Vaagso – Chief of Home Forces had ordered the replication of battle schools in every division. A 'Central Battle School' to train the instructors was set up at Barnard Castle with Wigram as Chief Instructor. Remarkably, it is recorded that Commando leader Mills-Roberts visited Barnard Castle in 1943. Afterwards he corresponded with the then commandant, Brigadier H. W. Houldsworth, who thanked him for his interest in the Central Battle School and remarked that though the school had formerly been the subject of 'a great deal of criticism' much of it 'not unmerited' – the 'wild lines' previously followed had now been changed and the teaching could be regarded as 'fairly sound'. It would be extremely naive to assume that Mills-Roberts was the only Commando officer to take an interest in the development of battle schools, or that officers and some other ranks – being keen enough to go through the gruelling processes required to enter an operational Commando – had not read Levy or other popular works, or were entirely unacquainted with tales of street-fighting from Spain or Russia. It would, therefore, be much more accurate to suggest that the Commandos succeeded in forcing Vaagso against stiff opposition because they had managed to assimilate some of the latest knowledge, and applied it enthusiastically in battle before most other British units.

Beyond tactical and other military training, American observers also noted how non-specific Commando training contributed to morale: sport, for example, being used constructively to create an 'excellent spirit of fellowship', with the officers also participating in athletics; 'current events talks', using material furnished by the Army Bureau of Current Affairs, ABCA; and the bringing in of outside speakers from the Navy, academia, and the general civilian population broadened the soldiers' point of view and kept boredom at bay. Perhaps the most curious thing noted about Commando methods was that billeting in 'various houses', as opposed to barracks, appeared to have the effect of lowering the 'rate of venereal admissions'.

Interestingly, as *Hansard* makes clear, Commando training was discussed in parliament more than once. On 17 March 1942, for example, the Under Secretary of State for War was asked in the House of Commons, 'whether in order to extend training in the newest forms of fighting, a proportion of the Commandos will now be utilised in the capacity of training officers and non-commissioned officers throughout the Army'. Mr Sandys avoided this query in the usual parliamentary manner by saying that 'Training of the Commando variety is already being extended to other types of units.'

A big step in the regularisation and improvement of training was the opening of the new 'Commando Depot' – later known as the 'Commando Basic Training Centre' – at Achnacarry Castle in the western highlands of Scotland, in February 1942. With a name derived from the Gaelic for 'field of the weir', Achnacarry, on the banks of the River Arkaig, was the ancient seat of the chiefs of the Clan Cameron of Lochiel, who had maintained a home there since at least the seventeenth century. The current castle, or perhaps more accurately, Scottish baronial hall, dated from 1802. When Queen Victoria visited in 1873 she described an idyllic spot, low, but surrounded with fine trees and surmounted by rugged hills. The 'lovely' Loch Arkaig with its pier lay just over half a mile from the house.

Seventy years later, Commando trainees were presented with a rather less bucolic scene, and highly unpredictable weather. Most trainees were not in the castle itself but in a hutted camp or tents. Surviving photographs show Nissen huts grouped around a central parade ground, large enough to draw up a complete Commando, on what had once been a lawned area. Comfort was undoubtedly lacking, but the basics of at least a spartan existence were to hand. The huts themselves were generally large enough to house about twenty-five men at a reasonable density of occupation, but in case of necessity could be crowded with forty on wooden planked bunks. The bunks themselves were equipped with rough Army blankets and coir pads as a basic mattress; pot-bellied solid fuel stoves provided rather inadequate heating. A cookhouse made it possible for the would-be Commandos to focus on their training rather than housekeeping. Officers were in for a few surprises. No 'batmen' were allowed: officers were expected to clean their own uniform and equipment, and thereby learn what the men had to do, and the approximate time such chores would take. There was no 'dressing for dinner' as in an ordinary UK officers' mess, and hot water was virtually non-existent. Presiding over 'Castle Commando' was the bulky figure of Lieutenant Colonel Charles Vaughan, a Londoner and former ranker of the Coldstream Guards, latterly with the Buffs and 4 Commando.

An Achnacarry intake was usually divided into three separate training Commandos named: 'Keyes', after Admiral Sir Roger and his VC-winning son; 'Haydon', after Brigadier Haydon; and 'Sturges', after General Sturges. Each of these units was further divided into four troops, each with its own dedicated officer instructor and attendant NCO. A small 'demonstration troop' of seasoned Commandos also operated at Achnacarry. These versatile characters gave shows of camouflage and movement, sniping and various drills, provided the distinctive pipers, acted as a small in-house 'enemy' force, and often did the live firing, which created a genuine sense of realism during exercises. For training purposes, officers would form a section of their own and follow the same syllabus as other ranks, carrying similar loads and firing the same weapons. Instructors were distinguished by Denison camouflage smocks and green berets with regimental badge and a Cameron of Lochiel tartan badge backing. Trainees wore khaki 'denims' – and the soft 'cap comforter'.

The famous green beret, similar in style but different in hue, to that already worn by the Royal Armoured Corps, was mooted as early as May 1942. However, formal approval was not forthcoming until an Army Council Instruction of 24 October 1942. The tradition of awarding the beret on successful conclusion of basic training at Achnacarry was soon in place. Though the beret became standard wear for the trained Commando, the badges of the different parent regiments from which men had come continued to be worn. Occasionally there were other more flamboyant additions. Lance Corporal Morris of 6 Commando recalled that his Sergeant Major 'Lofty' Ray wore not only the distinctive cap badge of the Black Watch, but the red hackle of that regiment on his beret even on the beaches of Normandy. Not long after the adoption of the green beret, the various shoulder titles were standardised to a red on dark-blue cloth pattern with the word 'Commando' prefixed by the unit number. Mountbatten stated that this arrangement, conforming with the colours of the Combined Operations badge, was personally approved by the King in discussion with himself. Another mark that suggested that the Commandos were well on their way to becoming an established corps with its own trappings and traditions was *The Commando March*, composed by Samuel Barber in 1943 and available commercially as sheet music the following year.

The Achnacarry training cohort was rather larger than an operational Commando – allowing for a significant number of failures – and in any case, newly-graduated men were usually sent first to a 'holding Commando' in the UK until required by an active unit. The basic training lasted six weeks, and though the syllabus of Castle Commando altered and was refined over time, certain elements remained much the same.

James Dunning, who transferred from 4 Commando and was soon promoted to Captain and put in charge of the 'Haydon' training Commando, was of the opinion that perhaps nine-tenths of the course remained very similar during 1943 and 1944. The biggest single element was weapons training and firing, absorbing almost a third of the time available. This may have started with a revision of the familiar Bren, rifle, Thompson, antitank weapons, pistols and grenades, but soon became more interesting and creative, going on to cover enemy weapons and US pieces such as the Garand semi-automatic rifle and the M1 Carbine. An introduction was also given on mines and demolitions. The next largest element in terms of the time devoted was fieldcraft, movement and tactics; this took up just a little longer than the physical aspects: PT, unarmed combat and rope work. The remaining subjects between them were left with just under half the syllabus, so effectively a total of three weeks was used to tackle boating, map-reading, speed marches, night training, climbing, drill, training films, first aid and the set-piece 'opposed landing' exercise.

As part of the fieldcraft element came the famous 'crack and thump' demonstration. Members of the instruction troop concealed themselves with a variety of weapons, and the pupils drew up a distance away and were invited to find them with the aid of binoculars. Tips on systematic searching were given during this process. With this complete, the hidden men opened fire, one at a time, aiming their rounds over, or to the flank of the (doubtless concerned) trainees. Trainees were taught to recognise weapons – both friendly and enemy – by sound, and to identify the locations of the firers. Particularly significant was recognising the difference between the 'crack' of a passing bullet, and the 'thump' of a discharge. Remarkably, the crack came first, followed by the thump. The reason for this phenomenon was that, for all but a tiny minority of weapons, the velocity of the round was supersonic: so it was that the bullet passed or struck home before the person on the receiving end heard the round being fired.

From late 1942, Company Sergeant Major Jack Rowley of 6 Commando was charged with Achnacarry small-boat training. His little flotilla was twelve Goatley boats; two 32-foot Naval cutters, a whaler, and a small dinghy. Dories with marine engines were added later. Paddles, sails and other gear were stowed in a stone building, and the trainees appeared in batches. The initial instruction was on the Goatley boats, intended, primarily, for river crossings:

These had wooden bottoms and canvas sides kept up with struts, six of these were quickly erected and after I explained what they were doing for the first lesson, told them to take a paddle each from the boathouse, and ordered them ten men to each boat, one at the bows to jump ashore when landing, four men each side with paddles and one with a paddle at the stern to steer.

Practice with the cutters and whaler followed. Though Commandos often tended to refer to small assault boats indiscriminately as 'Goatleys', it is worth noting that there was more than one type, and the Saunders-Roe, Isle of Wight boat designer, Fred Goatley, created many different products, of which no less than eleven were submitted for service evaluation, and several saw use. These included the two-man canoe used on the 'Frankton' raid, a slightly longer three-man version, and folding assault boats in more than one size. Remarkably, the first of the Goatley designs was produced for the War Office as early as 1937, and Fred had been hauled out of retirement to recommence work for the military after the outbreak of war. His more unusual innovations included a supposedly 'unsinkable boat' with a self-sealing system for bullet damage, a power boat for rescue missions, and a collapsible bridging pontoon.

Once basic water competence was achieved, the students moved on to more realistic practice, involving, for example, paddling or rowing several miles, landing, and then performing a march or other exercise on arrival. In some sessions, the smaller boats were towed or folded up and transported on the larger boats. Though most of the training intake were British, there were also pupils from elsewhere. Due to communication difficulties, the most problematic were a group of Yugoslavs – for whom the only common language for instruction proved to be Arabic. As might be expected, from 1943 the Royal Marines took more of a lead in matters afloat, with the appointment of Jim Keigwin as boating officer, and the 'fleet' was further expanded with landing craft. By this time the introduction to the course included not only a lecture but a training film on the importance of vessels in Combined Operations and water skills.

Sport may not have been at all unique to Achnacarry, but was encouraged to foster both team spirit and competitiveness. Indeed, a formal 'Competition Day' was usually included in the syllabus with rifle-shooting, tug of war, speed march and boat race included on an inter-troop basis. Boxing of a sort was also conducted – the ultimate Commando trainee test of which was 'Milling'. This was no strictly choreographed affair but a team game in which each troop put forward perhaps ten of its best, and these fought their opponents one after another, for just one minute at a time, often flailing madly to land as many blows as possible before a whistle sounded and the next pair waded in. There were no points for style, just a count of the punches that hit a legal target area on the other boxer.

Street-fighting was probably the least realistic aspect of the Achnacarry training regime. This is perhaps unsurprising, since the surrounding area was uncompromisingly rural and devoid of very much worthy of the title 'street'. In an attempt to overcome this difficulty some not-very-convincing-looking rough wooden sheds were constructed, which did at least permit the practice of entry drills and the use of small arms in a confined space. Nevertheless, the best street-fighting training was done elsewhere, as, for example, in bombed-out areas of London, Portsmouth and Plymouth, where the work of the Luftwaffe had created the ideal environment to mimic the towns of the Continent.

Interestingly, trainees from other countries were introduced to Achnacarry at a very early stage. The French were first – being a group of forty (under Muselier Kieffer) whom Brigadier Haydon was particularly keen to include in the ranks of the Commandos due to their knowledge of the European coast. Five had been in detention when first approached by Kieffer but released when they volunteered for service. Initially known as 1st Marine Company, the unit later added the word Commando to its title. Eventually changing their blue berets for green, with the Cross of Lorraine badge, they became No. 1 French Troop of the No. 10 (Inter-Allied) Commando in July 1942. Hot on their heels were forty-eight Dutchmen from the 'Royal Brigade Princess Irene', who arrived on 22 March 1942, and just over half of whom graduated to become the original nucleus of the No. 2 'Dutch Troop'. Belgians, Norwegians, Poles and Yugoslavs followed – as did the unusual and mysterious selection of Central European anti-Nazis, later to be known as No. 3 Troop, 'X-Troop', or 'miscellaneous'. For purposes of cover they were the 'English' Troop, many of whom changed their identities in the hope of avoiding dire retribution in case of capture. US Troops, destined to become the first Rangers, also reached Achnacarry before Dieppe.

These last certainly took their training seriously at Achnacarry, and elsewhere, as was witnessed by Tom Churchill, who joined No. 2 Commando at Largs, in Ayrshire, as one of the replacements for the officers lost at St Nazaire. As he later recalled:

It so happened that No. 2 Commando was at this time about to undertake a series of exercises with American troops, to assist them in the final stages of the training which they had undergone in the British Isles since their arrival from America. The Americans took their training very seriously, and were quick to weed out officers or NCOs who were not up to their job. I remember that at the conclusion of one particular exercise, the brigade commander and the three lieutenant colonels commanding the three regiments in the formation, were all relieved of their appointments, put in a train, and packed off to London, and twenty-four hours later a brand new team arrived.

The opening of Achnacarry, regularisation of courses, and commencement of an almost sausage-machine-like production of Commandos, trained to similar high standards, was timely indeed. For Commandos 7 and 8 suffered heavy casualties in Crete and were later disbanded; the Middle East Commando was disbanded in 1942; and No. 5 Commando, deployed to Madagascar, was later moved on to the Far East. The result was big gaps in the 'Special Force' order of battle, and other parts of the Army were beginning to show distinct unwillingness to keep up a flow of first-rate volunteers. In 1943 Brigadier Haydon would complain that, in fact, other units were now attempting to offload troublemakers with 'bad crime sheets' – and some who were physically below par. Churchill wanted the three 'missing' Army Commandos reformed and the induction of 'good quality' men continued, but in the event, fresh expansion was mainly by dint of conversion of Royal Marine battalions to smaller and leaner Royal Marine Commandos. This move was seen in some quarters as a re-establishment of the Navy's natural purview, but was looked askance by many. The nub of the matter for many Army Commandos, who had been in at the start of the Special Force, was that they had all been volunteers and now their position was being usurped, potentially by less suitable candidates. Indeed, 'real' Marines were often regarded as those who went to sea and stayed there.

Yet distinctions were not always so clear cut: many had volunteered for Marine service from the Navy in general, and the first 'RM' Commando unit – born on Valentine's Day 1942, and later to be called 40 Commando – was formed by a volunteering process. John Forfar, medical officer with 47 RM Commando, recalled a system that was almost a 'reverse' volunteering: Marines from the contributing battalions having the right to 'opt out' of Commando training – and the unfit being similarly weeded away during the process. In 48 RM Commando it is recorded that almost

65 per cent of the potential intake was turned away due to lack of fitness, age, or other grounds. Eventually, nine Royal Marine Commandos were formed: 40 being followed by 41 Commando in October 1942, Commandos 42 to 47 in the summer of 1943 and, finally, 48 Commando in March 1944. Interestingly, though establishments were similar, Royal Marine Commando nomenclature was not always the same as that used by the Army. So it was, for example, that whilst Army Commando troops were numbered or lettered in alphabetical order, Royal Marine troops were lettered, usually 'A, B, X, Y' and 'Z', after the designations of gun turrets on battleships. The Heavy Weapons Troop was 'S'. Though formed later, many Royal Marine Commandos were quickly put to the test – notably at Dieppe, then Salerno and Reggio in Italy, as well as along the Adriatic coast of Yugoslavia.

Perhaps the most obvious question to be asked about the birth of the Royal Marine Commandos in 1942 is: why had this development taken so long? The significance of landing operations in the First World War, and particularly the disastrous adventure at Gallipoli, was not lost on Naval planners. As a result, the Admiralty made explicit statements that the future role of the Royal Marines lay not only in manning ships and guns and protecting fleet installations, but in finding a 'striking force' available 'for amphibious operations'. These would include 'raids on enemy coastline and bases' and the seizure of temporary bases for fleet use. When, in 1924, the Madden Committee revisited these issues, it similarly concluded that the remit should include a strike force for small-scale operations on shore – and assistance in the landing of full-scale armies. Yet, in a post-Versailles Treaty period of reduced military investment, the Marines – like virtually every branch of the armed services – did not get everything they wanted. In 1936 a 'Combined Operations Development Centre' had been formed at Portsmouth, and though this did valuable work with prototype landing craft, it lacked real teeth in the form of any permanently established raiding arm. Only in 1939 was a new 'Marine Brigade' raised, and plans to expand to divisional strength were still unfulfilled at the time of the fall of France. So it was that the Army, through their 'Independent Company' experience and political intervention, had formed the first Commandos.

Like the Army Commandos, the Navy men would be honed at Achnacarry. No. 44 Royal Marine Commando was ordered to its stint at Achnacarry in the latter part of 1943 – an event viewed with distinct foreboding. A number of the officers were worried that, as an essentially conscript outfit, the unit might not live up to the high standards set by the sifted volunteers that made up the original Army Commandos. Obvious deficiencies were the relatively few men in the ranks qualified as marksmen, and concern that the overall standard of fitness was low. As a result, a 'Doubling Week' was ordered prior to arrival at Achnacarry, during which all ranks were required to run, everywhere they went, from eight in the morning to five in the evening, and strenuous efforts were made to turn 'second class' shots into 'first class'.

Like many units that passed through Achnacarry, 44 Commando experienced near continuous rain. There was a string of accidents during the first week, including several on the assault course involving knees and ankles – Captain Farquharson-Roberts broke an ankle and was evacuated to hospital. Later a Marine blew off a hand with a grenade. Speed marches appear to have been accomplished with less incident, Marine Ferguson managing to cover 9 miles in a creditable seventy-one minutes. The worst tragedy struck on 19 September, when an accident with a mortar killed two NCOs. At the end of the month the unit completed its 30-mile endurance march and took part in the 'opposed landing' climax of the course. However, another Marine was killed during an exercise simulating an attack on an enemy strongpoint. Of 555 all ranks who attended the Achnacarry course with 44 Commando in September 1943, no less than 125 failed through one cause or another: many were turned away by the staff as unsuitable, but the injured, and those worked to complete exhaustion, also accounted for a fair few. The 44 Commando experience may have been dangerous and gruelling, but it was not exponentially worse than quite a few others.

Lieutenant W. G. Jenkins was an 'other rank' before becoming a commissioned officer in 43 Royal Marine Commando at the beginning of 1944. By this time the training regime was both extensive and detailed. Following both ordinary basic training and traditional officer training at Deal, he was posted to Dalditch camp at Woodbury Common, where the activities included assault courses, marching and orienteering, use of toggle ropes and bridging, embarkation and landing. Next came a special one-week course at the London District School of Street Fighting, Battersea. Subjects of study included room clearance, with pairs of men covering each other as they broke in and got against the walls, 'beehive' charges for making breaches in walls, and movement along streets and over walls. By way of contrast, one day was taken out of street combat and the pupils divided into two groups: one was taught basic train driving, the other shown how Battersea power station could be destroyed using charges. At Gibraltar Camp, near Tywyn in North Wales, the training moved on to rock-climbing and motorcycling. Only after all this was Jenkins thought fit for the 'basic' Commando training at Achnacarry:

> The introduction to the Commando Basic Training Centre was typical. We formed up in squads with our baggage (myself with a suitcase instead of a kit bag) and were then harried along a fast speed march down the 8 miles to Achnacarry. This was the seat of Donald Cameron of Lochiel, and while we were there we wore a circle of his tartan behind our globe and laurel cap badge. As we doubled along the final stretch towards the entrance to the camp our attention was caught by a line of graves with white crosses alongside the road. Later inspection revealed that they were training aids – 'This man died from skylining himself'. 'This man failed to detect mines at night' – a dramatic way to bring the lessons home. In point of fact, forty men did lose their lives in training over the four years that the CBTC was in operation.

Many accidents involved weapons or explosives, but there were also drownings. One fatality was 33-year-old Scots Guards Sergeant James Hughes, who was plucked from the water several days after an accident in September 1943. CSM Rowley remarked, somewhat philosophically, that the body was well preserved by the coldness of the water. Against the far greater losses in war, and the perceived risk reduction of having exhaustive training, such tragic incidents went relatively unremarked.

The final exercise was an assault crossing of Loch Ailort. Weapons were stowed in the middle of the assault boats, and as the crews paddled, Bren guns fired streams of tracer overhead and off to the side for added realism. According to one account, the most enthusiastic Bren gunner was Company Sergeant Major Robertson, whose realism extended to peppering oars whilst missing trainees. The landing itself was greeted by pyrotechnics and smoke grenades thrown by the instructors, under harassment of which the groups had to find firing positions, knock down metal targets and then launch a bayonet charge against dummies. Once the 'enemy' were cleared, the attackers had to withdraw in their boats – again under a fusillade of fire.

Most of the trainees appear to have finished their courses at this point but Jenkins was now packed off to Cornwall for 'Cliff Assault' training under the tutelage of CSM 'Spider' Leach. Climbs were arranged around

Sennen, Land's End, and Kynance Cove. At the latter, Jenkins was introduced to various forms of grappling iron. Another technique was for the very best climbers to 'free climb' ahead of the sections, carrying wicker baskets of rope on their backs, paying out as they went. Gaining the top, the rope was secured and the remaining climbers now had a way to go up quite rapidly, hand over hand. Complete exercises were commenced with a sea landing from a small boat, from which jumping onto shore required careful judging of surge and swell.

No. 48 RM Commando, formed specifically with the invasion of Europe in mind, did not reach Achnacarry until 12 March 1944. Its recruits were drawn mainly from 7th Royal Marine Battalion and the Mobile Naval Base Defence Organisation (or MNBDO), but its machine-gun teams were from 15 Machine Gun Battalion Royal Marines, and a few seagoing Marines were added. The majority were volunteers but specialisms could not easily be filled so rapidly, and some drivers, for example, were simply redirected from their existing employment. Perhaps unusually, therefore, there were at least some in the ranks who lacked training in recent infantry tactics or the most modern weaponry. To make matters even more difficult, time was running out, so the usual Commando Basic Training was compressed from six weeks to just eighteen days, and overcrowding saw some of the Marines relegated to cold, damp bell tents.

Though Achnacarry is justly remembered as their most significant camp, many others were used at various times by Commandos. These were widely spread geographically and had a variety of different purposes, being adapted for aspects of combined operations, training, and as depots for different kinds of equipment and craft. Among them were Castle Toward (Dunoon), Dorlin House (Acharacle), HMS *Quebec* at Inveraray, two different locations in the vicinity of Largs, and HMS *Rosneath* – a base soon turned over to US forces. One of the most interesting was the Commando Mountain and Snow Warfare Training Camp at Braemar, which opened in December 1942. Its six-week courses taught all manner of mountain warfare skills including skiing, climbing and dealing with living and fighting in cold conditions. During 1943 the chief instructor here was mountaineer Major John Hunt, of Marlborough and Sandhurst, a King's Gold Medal winner, rugger blue, veteran of the Bengal Police and King's Royal Rifle Corps – and later a conqueror of Everest.

Just as mountains required new training, so did new theatres of war and different climates. Combat in the Far East, for example, necessarily

Lord Lovat

Simon Christopher Joseph Fraser, Lord Lovat and Chief of Clan Fraser (1911–1995), was born at Beaufort Castle, Inverness. Interestingly, he was related to David Stirling, later to be founder of the SAS. Lovat's first military experience was at Ampleforth College, in the Officer Training Corps, and he was also in the Oxford University Cavalry Squadron. He was commissioned into the Territorial Lovat Scouts in 1930 (a unit founded by his family and justly famous for its scouting and sniping skills in the Great War) but the following year became a regular officer with the Scots Guards. There he stayed until 1937, when he resigned his commission and passed into the Supplementary Reserve. He rejoined the Lovat Scouts, now ranking as captain, on the eve of war in August 1939. Lovat – known to friends as 'Shimi' – volunteered for the Commandos in 1940, and was on the Lofoten raid in March 1941. Promoted temporary major, he led the small Hardelot raid the following month, for which action he was later awarded the Military Cross. As acting lieutenant colonel, he was appointed to lead No. 4 Commando in 1942, and was arguably the most successful commander in the entire Dieppe Operation, for his part in which he was awarded the Distinguished Service Order. By 1944 Lovat had reached the rank of brigadier and was commanding the 1st Special Service Brigade. This he led on D-Day, joining up with the Airborne on the far left flank of the invasion force, but he was seriously wounded by an enemy shell on 12 June. Though this injury put him out of action for the rest of the war he went into politics in 1945 and eventually sat in the House of Lords. His final years were not the happiest: two of his sons predeceased him, and family fortunes declined. Beaufort Castle was sold in 1994. Bill Millin, Lord Lovat's personal piper, who had also been present with him on D-Day, played at his funeral. Winston Churchill is said to have described Lord Lovat as 'the mildest mannered man that ever scuttled a ship or cut a throat'.

entailed the learning of a whole new range of tactics and techniques – not least those of jungle warfare. The men of 44 (RM) Commando received what was effectively a refresher course over ten days at Londa, in late May 1945. This reiterated the latest small-unit tactical thinking and covered jungle battle drills, field firing exercises, jungle survival, night movement, ambushes, signals, sniping and competitions based on attack and defence scenarios. The standard jungle battle drills were probably based on those to be found in the manuals *Warfare in the Far East* (1944) and *Preparation for Warfare in the Far East* (1945), stressing the importance of 'infiltration' around enemy positions, responses to Japanese sniping, grenade combat and possible programmed responses or 'contact drills'. What was unusual about the prosaic sounding 'field firing exercises' was that 44 Commando had just received supplies of the American M1 Garand rifle, which, though rather long for easy handling in dense vegetation, was both powerful and semi-automatic. The Commandos quickly discovered that a subsection firing just one eight-round clip per man 'could destroy the side of a jungle hut'. Interestingly, at least some of the men also received the versatile US M1 helmet in the last days of the war, which could be worn complete with its steel shell – or out of contact just as a separate fibre liner element.

The competitive element at Londa was based on *Training Memorandum 13*, and was made distinctly more interesting by the award of the prize of a long weekend in Bombay for the winning troop. Approximately three-quarters of the marks in the competition were given for weapons skills and tactical movement. Top of the list came advancing and firing with rifle and Bren, closely followed by similar work with Tommy gun, sniper rifle and pistol, with points awarded specifically for movement, fire control, accuracy, snap shooting and weapons handling. Attracting somewhat fewer marks collectively, but still of crucial importance, were grenade-throwing, and firing the mortar and M9A1 grenade launcher. The remainder of the marks went to items regarded as 'administration', smartness and ceremonial. Though this still included a weapons inspection, it also covered documentation, a parade, drill, and a hut inspection. Crucially, therefore, an extremely smart troop, good at drill and housework but poor at the arts of combat, could never beat one that was slovenly but alert to fieldcraft and shot well. Where two units had equally good battle skills, a good parade and a clean hut might, however, sway the result.

Chapter 6

Close Combat and Lessons Learned

In the minds of many – in the 1940s as now – one of the defining features of the Commando was expertise at close combat. Such work was often interpreted to include both the tactics of small units at close range, and the fighting skills of the individual, armed and unarmed. In this latter sphere the two most famous instructors were William Ewart Fairbairn and Eric Anthony Sykes. Fairbairn's background was humble, being one of many children of a Hertfordshire leather cutter. He left home at an early age, going to serve with the Royal Marines in the Far East. In 1907 he went into the Shanghai Municipal Police, where he rose through the ranks being employed as a training officer specialising in drill, musketry and self-defence, and also studied Jiu-Jitsu. The introduction to *All-in Fighting* states that he was the first foreigner living outside Japan to be awarded a 'Black Belt' by the Kodokan Jiu-Jitsu University, Tokyo, and that he taught 'Chinese boxing' – or Kung Fu – in Peking. The veteran of many street-fights and riots, he finally reached the position of Assistant Commissioner. Fairbairn published the first of several works on self defence as early as 1926, punningly entitling his system 'Defendu'. Few schools of combat are completely original and the roots of some of the Fairbairn methods have been discerned in those of Leopold MacLagen, who also instructed in the SMP at the time of the First World War. Inspiration was also drawn from both pre-existing martial arts and oriental styles of knife-fighting. Yet Fairbairn was always insistent that the object of his scheme was never ritualistic, or aimed at general skill, but fiercely pragmatic – how to win a fight, disarm, disable and often kill an enemy.

Paradoxically enough, Sykes – who served as a sniper on the Western Front in the First World War – was of German descent. Like Fairbairn, he also joined the SMP, where he specialised in firearms. Neither were young men in 1940 – Fairbairn was fifty-five and at the age of retirement from the force, while Sykes, aged fifty-seven, would die of heart failure at the end of the war. Nevertheless, both returned to the UK and were commissioned as captains in the Army for the purposes of instruction. It is believed that Fairbairn and Sykes mounted their first close-combat training sessions as early as mid-1940 with the organisation that soon became SOE ('Special Operations Executive'). A syllabus that included unarmed combat, knife, cane and baton work was certainly in place at Inverailort in July 1940 for fledgling Commandos, and this was later revised in the light of subsequent experience. During training, Major Hall was amazed to see 'two old men' tumble down a set of stairs, arriving at the bottom holding submachine guns at the ready, as a first lesson for their students.

Most of the troops had carried some form of edged weapon or blade from the time of the first formation of Commando units, but these were a motley selection: bayonets, fighting knives from the First World War, and various sheath knives intended mainly as tools for field butchery and other tasks. In November 1940, however, Fairbairn and Sykes put forward an idea for a purpose-designed fighting knife. According to one version of events, they had visited London museums to look for suitable historical inspiration but were disappointed to find many of the displays removed for the duration. This being the case, they decided to build upon types they had already encountered during their service in Shanghai, and for which Fairbairn had already formulated various moves. The general premise received some encouragement so preliminary sketches of a slender-bladed knife with cross guard and checkered grip were taken to John Wilkinson-Latham of Wilkinson Sword for the making and testing of a prototype. This was successful, and so in January 1941 the first small production order was made. These were delivered to the War Office at the (then fairly hefty) cost of 13s 6d each. Following minor modifications a second pattern was manufactured, so that by the end of the year over 2,000 had been made. Within a couple of years there were over 100,000 equipping not only Commandos but also other personnel, including some Dutch and Norwegians. A knife of a similar design was also produced by Case Cutlery for the American OSS.

During 1941 both Fairbairn and Sykes gave numerous demonstrations and training sessions in knife, pistol and unarmed combat to Commandos. They also worked in many non-Commando units and introduced a 'Specialist' two-week close-combat course designed to turn out instructors to spread their methods as widely as possible. These also encompassed the submachine gun, boxing, 'point and shoot' snap firing, and bayonet work. Trainees were expected to pass an exam before returning to their units as instructors. Some demonstrations, such as that to No. 6 Commando on 16 June 1941, were recorded in the Commando unit *War Diaries*, others have been recalled by veterans. Lieutenant Milton of No. 7 Commando remembered meeting them during intensive instruction at Lochailort:

> The course was on demolition and sabotage and the instructors were the best I had come across since Sandhurst. Among them were Lord Lovat, later of 4 Commando, Spencer Chapman, who raided behind Japanese lines in Malaya, one of the Stirling brothers of SAS fame, and Fairbairn and Sykes, who had been in the Shanghai police. The course involved 'survival', as it would now be called, but which was then known as fieldcraft. It consisted of stalking deer, unarmed combat from Fairbairn and Sykes, and weapon training under a colonel who handled a rifle in a way I would not have thought possible.

Whilst all this was going on, Fairbairn and Sykes were also working up writing projects, at least one of which was begun before they left Shanghai. These efforts led to the publication of no less than three books during 1942. Fairbairn's *Self Defence for Women and Girls*, which became *Hands Off!* in an American edition, is of curiosity value, but the other two committed to paper, in polished form with line drawings, many of the techniques taught to Commandos. These works were *Shooting to Live*, co-authored by Fairbairn and Sykes, and the classic, and much better remembered, *All-in Fighting* – also known by the American edition as *Get Tough!*

Shooting to Live – essentially a manual of combat pistol-shooting, is illustrated with police and civilian figures, and is substantially based on experience in the Far East. It also carried remarks on choosing a pistol, and circumstances in which antagonists face each other at close range before weapons are drawn. All these factors argue that a good part of the volume had been completed even before the commencement of Commando training. Its key aims had nothing to do with target shooting, and everything to do with the pistol as a weapon of combat – the two being as different as 'chalk from cheese'. The three main things identified as required of the combat pistol user were: extreme speed in both drawing and firing, instinctive as opposed to deliberate aim, and practice under as near as possible to actual fighting conditions. The need for speed was obvious in that the person who fired first might live to shoot again. *Shooting to Live* suggested that anything slower than one-third of a second to fire a first shot was too sluggish. The idea of 'instinctive aim' needed a little explanation but was

> an entirely logical consequence of the extreme speed to which we attach so much importance. That is so for the simple reason that there is no time for any of the customary aids to accuracy. If reliance on these aids has become habitual, so much the worse for you if you are shooting to live. There is no time, for instance, to put yourself into some special stance or to align the sights of the pistol, and any attempt to do so puts you at the mercy of a quicker opponent. In any case sights would be of little use if the light were bad, and none at all if it were dark, as might easily happen.

In order to achieve 'instinctive aim', pupils were taught to keep their eyes on the target and simply raise the gun in line with the vertical centre line of their own bodies until it appeared to be 'surrounded by the target' – the trigger being pulled 'immediately the aiming mark is covered'. This type of shot was best achieved with a fairly firm grip and increasing the pressure of the whole hand, rather than a 'violent pressure of the forefinger alone'. The best sort of target for initial practice was large, white, having a full-size outline of a man, and placed quite literally at a 'point blank range' of no more than 2 yards away from the shooter. The advantage of this almost ridiculously short distance was that even the most awkward trainees would find it difficult to miss, whilst the instructor would be able to see easily, and correct faults simply, before proceeding to more demanding shots. Moreover, the fact that almost every round would hit home from the start would lend satisfaction and confidence, so that even novice shooters were unlikely to be discouraged. Part of the practice involved firing two shots in rapid succession.

Subsequent sessions gradually introduced problems and realistic novelties; as, for example, a dummy round in the pistol load, which the shooter was required to treat as a misfire and clear as rapidly as possible. 'Bursts' were then increased so that a whole magazine was discharged as a series of double shots. Next came 'advanced methods' – these included firing from a 'three-quarter hip' and other positions, moving targets, a 'pursuit' course with running and traversing obstacles as well as shooting, rapid loading and emptying of the weapon, shooting prone and from cover. The main weapon chosen by way of illustration for all these exercises was a Colt automatic but, explaining by means of a number of real-life law and order examples, the authors conclude that there is no such thing as a 'perfect' pistol – the best attainable being one which combines maximum stopping power, speed and volume of fire with a form that the user finds 'easy to carry and convenient to use'. Trainees passed the courses described by getting half of their shots safely onto target in time: there was no extra credit for more exact shooting, nor was any 'marksman' distinction given.

Whilst these methods sound remarkably modern, it should perhaps be asked how much of a departure they were from current Army practice. Perhaps the closest comparator is the generally issued training pamphlet *Pistol .38-inch*, produced in 1937, reprinted in 1940 and appearing in a new edition in 1941. In fact, as early as the 1937 recruits were being taught that the pistol was a weapon 'unsuitable for firing by deliberate aim' but that it was useful in shooting at 'surprise and moving targets'. Indeed, though pistols were rarely used, it was vital that 'shots should be delivered accurately and very quickly'. In recommended drills options were presented for either deliberate shots, using the sights, or for 'service shooting', in which firing would be 'instinctive' and there would be 'no aiming'. Shots were to be taken as soon as the pistol was raised, and firing was by a 'squeeze of the whole hand'. The 'elementary' training test demanded six shots within six seconds, five of which were to hit a target. Only very moderate accuracy was required to pass the basic test – even at a target just 2 yards away.

By June 1941 the basic Army instructions had moved even further in the direction of snap shooting, and had dropped what was considered sensible maximum pistol range from 25 yards to 20. Under battle conditions quickness was always to be considered 'more important than the close grouping of the shots'. Lesson five in the new version of the instructions included the direction that 'two shots will always be fired in quick succession at every target to inculcate the habit that, on engaging an adversary on service two quick shots should always be made to make certain of a killing'. It is difficult to escape the conclusion that the Army as a whole – which included conscripts on the borderline of mental capacity – was not very much worse served in its basic pistol training than were the Commandos, a crack band of volunteers, self-selected and kept at a peak of physical efficiency. Where Fairbairn and Sykes seem to have scored real advantages was in the imagination of the advanced training methods, and the fact that they had relatively recent experience of pistols in combat situations they could use to bring realism to their lectures. It was also the case that where most of the Army had to make do with revolvers, the basic design of which was already antiquated, Commandos were soon making use of automatics, including the Colt.

All-in Fighting appears to be quite a neat summation of the many knife and unarmed combat techniques Fairbairn applied to his Commando trainees. Unlike *Shooting to Live* its line drawings are of the moment and feature British soldiers in both steel helmets and cap comforters doing battle with German infantrymen, parachutists, and immaculately attired officers who are roundly slapped, kicked, kneed, stamped upon, thrown, stabbed and bound. Yet, for Fairbairn, this is the nature of the war against Nazism:

> Some readers may be appalled at the suggestion that it should be necessary for human beings of the twentieth century to revert to the grim brutality of the stone age in order to live. But it must be realised that, when dealing with an utterly ruthless enemy who has clearly expressed his intention of wiping this nation out of existence, there is no room for any scruple or compunction about the methods to be employed in preventing him. The reader is requested to imagine that he himself has been wantonly attacked by a thug who has put the heel of his hand under his nose and pushed hard. Let him be quite honest and realise what his feelings would be. His one violent desire would be to do the thug the utmost damage – regardless of rules.

The basis of success in this enterprise was to be able to respond automatically – for 'he who hesitates is lost'. In war the attack could have only two possible objectives: to kill or capture the opponent, and even to capture would usually require some disabling blow. Significantly, and despite the plethora of moves Fairbairn presents us, he recommends that it is better that a student should select 'about ten', and thoroughly master them, rather than try to learn all. For some build, fitness, strength or other factors might make some moves natural, whilst others could be difficult to apply. Those seeking to perfect the techniques were encouraged to start by practising each step 'slowly and smoothly', increasing speed later. Throughout *All-in Fighting* the treatment is spare – there is nothing ornamental, everything is designed to incapacitate an opponent or prevent him from incapacitating you. Wrestling is specifically omitted because it takes so long to learn and, in war, when one is likely to be set upon by more than one opponent, useless.

The original 1942 *All-in Fighting* is put together as a compendium to cover several different aspects of close combat in one volume. Fairbairn later defined 'close' as all combat at anything from physical contact out to about 20 yards. The parts attributable to Fairbairn himself form the bulk, being chapters on blows, releases, holds, throws, miscellaneous advice and disarming. Fairbairn's 'disarming' moves taught a double lesson, for not only did they show how an opponent could be separated from his weapon, but they also demonstrated the fallacy of getting too close to a captive and the mistake of actually jabbing him with the muzzle of a gun. The last part of the work, covering the use of the rifle in close combat, was contributed by Captain P. N. Walbridge – another officer of the Special Training Centre. This not only increases the value of the book as an authentic account of Commando training, but further highlights the fact that Fairbairn with his Marine and police background was less involved with the use of the rifle as a combat weapon than some of his fellow trainers. Walbridge's credentials in this area included not only close-combat skills, but traditional rifle trophies including various triumphs at Bisley and membership of the Army shooting team from 1935 to 1939.

In recent years it has become regarded as axiomatic to state that Fairbairn's methods owe little to the oriental martial arts that are mentioned in his *Curriculum Vitae*, and it is certainly true that he says that what he teaches is practical – not a sport, fitness regime, or philosophical mental preparation. Yet there is more than this to be said, since Fairbairn does include things like the use of the edge of the hand to the throat, which would be quite unthinkable in traditional English pugilism. It is also the case that *All-in Fighting* is distinctly 'unBritish' in its disregard for any rules or sense of fair play. In this sense, at least, it uses an oriental stereotype as a device to get over to its students the idea that they have to get 'English' concepts – like cricket and 'fair play' – out of their minds before they can properly engage in Fairbairn's world of 'gutter' fighting. This may appear odd until one considers that many of the people who had to be convinced of the necessity of Fairbairn's 'rough house' methods were steeped in the traditions of the public school, boxing with gloves and contact sports that were governed by strict rules and codes of conduct.

Whilst the sections on blows, holds, releases and throws have become tolerably familiar through repetition and subsequent use, some of the most interesting parts of *All-in Fighting* are contained in the miscellaneous advice and Walbridge's rifle combat notes. 'Miscellaneous', for example, covers the use of the knife:

The knife in close-quarter fighting is the most deadly weapon to have to contend with. It is admitted by recognised authorities that for an entirely unarmed man there is no certain defence against a knife. With this we are in entire agreement. We are also aware of the psychological effect that the sudden flashing of a knife will have on the majority of persons. It has been proved that the British bayonet is still feared, and it is not very difficult to visualise the many occasions, such as on a night raid, house to house fighting, or even a boarding party, when a knife or short broadsword would have been a far more effective weapon.

Though some methods of carrying a knife are more effective than others, Fairbairn concedes that what is convenient for one physique or condition is not necessarily ideal for the next. For Fairbairn, the best way to carry a knife was in a concealed position, using the left hand – this making for the greatest element of surprise, 'the main factor' of success in close-quarter fighting. Nevertheless, students were reminded that 'no matter how good a position or the manner in which a knife is carried, a really quick draw cannot be accomplished unless the sheath is firmly secured to the clothing or equipment'. In this respect the F–S knife was near perfect, since its scabbard was supplied with four leather tabs, by means of which it could be sewn onto, or into, virtually any part of the uniform or equipment.

The remainder of the advice on the Commando dagger is not for the squeamish as, for Fairbairn, one of the most effective knife attacks is the severing of an artery. This is not just any cutting, since a tear or jagged wound to an artery may be survivable, but a complete and clean cut through a main artery that leads to rapid unconsciousness and usually death. If correctly attacked an opponent with a severed artery can be rendered insensible in anything from two to thirty seconds. *All-in Fighting* gives diagrams showing how, by means of stabs or slashes, this may be accomplished. Next to the biggest arteries, the heart or stomach, when not protected by equipment, are determined good points of attack.

Interestingly, the 'F-S' knife is not the only edged weapon addressed. The other is the fearsome 'Smatchet' – a massive broad-bladed dagger sometimes seen in use by Commandos, and perhaps the sort of thing that Fairbairn had in mind when he spoke of 'short broadswords'. It has a leaf-shaped blade, like something out of Africa or the Bronze Age, a large industrial-looking pommel, and a disc-shaped crossguard. A leather thong could be used to secure it to the wrist, like the sword knot of old. It may not, in fact, have been that practical a weapon in an age of machine guns and tanks, but as Fairbairn observes:

The psychological reaction of any man, when he first takes a smatchet in his hand, is full justification for its recommendation as a fighting weapon. He will immediately register all the essential qualities of a good soldier – confidence, determination, and aggressiveness. Its balance weight and killing power, with the point, edge or pommel, combined with the extremely simple training necessary to become efficient in its use, make it the ideal weapon for those not armed with the rifle and bayonet.

The recommended method of carriage was in a scabbard on the left-hand side of the belt. Only a few techniques were described. These included a drive to the stomach, 'sabre cuts' to the neck, wrists and arms, and pommel 'smashes' to the face and under the chin.

Also mentioned under Fairbairn's miscellaneous section are some unusual party pieces such as: fending off an enemy using a chair ('most lion tamers consider a small chair to be sufficient to keep a lion from attacking them'); getting up quickly from the ground; the use of a matchbox to reinforce a punch; attacks with a cane; and the double-ear smack. This last was expected to burst one or both ear drums if performed smartly enough and lead to a 'mild form of concussion'. Perhaps most controversial were the methods described for 'securing a prisoner', since manacling prisoners of war was often regarded as contrary to the proper usages of war. This gave rise to an extremely delicate dilemma, since it would often be difficult for a raiding party to take prisoners and treat them in the normal way; though, conversely, failure to take prisoners was tantamount to inviting one's men to slaughter those attempting to surrender. The taking of prisoners to discover what units were present, or for propaganda purposes, might also be a significant objective of an operation.

Walbridge's remarks on the rifle in close combat begin by reminding the student that the rifle and bayonet are not obsolete, but that many of the teaching practices used with it of late have been suited mainly to 'peace time conditions and slow shooting'. Following some basic remarks on general accuracy, sights, and the importance of the prone position, he passes on to 'quick handling' and close combat. For Walbridge, the secret of rapid shooting is essentially that of quick opening and closing of the breech. Remarkably, it is assumed that, with a few days of practice, twenty-five aimed shots per minute can be squeezed out of the bolt action Lee Enfield for very short periods – this being not quite double the famed 'fifteen rounds a minute' of the action at Mons in 1914.

In close quarters work, Walbridge imagines that it is likely that the rifleman will be engaged in street-fighting, clearing woods or similar, and that, in doing so, he will probably be in motion or standing when a rapid response is demanded. Quick shots from the shoulder or hip are therefore crucial: 'In firing from the hip, you must be very close to your target if you are to obtain a hit, whereas from the shoulder, firing is much quicker and accuracy is not so much sacrificed.' When approaching an area where targets were likely to appear suddenly, as, for example, in stalking a mortar post or machine-gun nest, students were advised to advance with the weapon held at roughly waist height and the right hand ready at the small of the butt. From this position they would be able to lift the rifle very quickly to the shoulder. The most advanced practitioners could obtain a rate of fire 'previously imagined unobtainable' by pressing the trigger with the first or second digit, still retaining a hold on the bolt – not an easy thing to describe, let alone achieve successfully, but Walbridge himself claimed to be able to get off five shots in four seconds in such a manner. The technique was described as invaluable for crossing gaps in cover or very close work.

Walbridge was clearly not as keen on the bayonet as some of his contemporaries, seeing it as useful mainly when a man was out of ammunition or had no time to reload. In action, the soldier was best carrying the bayonet point low, as there was less chance of a thrust being parried:

> to make a point, lunge forward on either foot and drive the bayonet point into the pit of your opponent's stomach. Most of the upper part of the body will be covered by equipment. To withdraw take a short pace to the rear as you wrench out the bayonet. You are then in a good position to deliver a second point, should this become necessary. If you are close to your opponent and unable to deliver a point, smash him on the side of his head with the butt and follow up with the bayonet or any other method previously described.

It was not without significance that the work of Fairbairn and Sykes played well to a home audience: the appeal to 'cold steel' being definitely something of a morale booster. Perhaps typical were Gordon Holman's remarks in the popular book, *Commando Attack* of 1942:

> Commandos know all about the use of knives – not in the approved film villain fashion, but scientifically, with wrist work playing an

important part and little more than an inch of the stiletto-like blade needed to kill a man. These Commando knives are strong, all metal weapons with a blade about 6 inches long. They mostly carry them slipped into a slit pocket in the leg of their trousers so that their hand is always near the hilt. It is curious that, in these days when so many high-grade weapons have been perfected for killing at close range or otherwise, cold steel, one of the oldest of weapons, should remain so menacing. I hope I never have to make a choice but I think I should rather meet a Commando soldier with a Tommy gun than one of those knives!

Some of Fairbairn's work was recorded on film, for both instructional and publicity purposes, including some rather camp footage of a tutorial with American OSS trainees in which Fairbairn and his pupils all wear Lone Ranger-style eye masks to disguise their identity. In the latter part of the war, Fairbairn and Sykes no longer worked together, due, apparently, to personal differences. Now 60, Sykes may already have been suffering from the illness that killed him, but it is also thought that he had come to regard Fairbairn as something of a prima donna – something which, in fairness, the propaganda aspect of the work demanded him to be. As Fairbairn had so many engagements, with other units and in the US, it was natural that other unarmed combat trainers would be required for the continual round of Commandos passing through Achnacarry. Just one of these was Stanley Bissell – Olympic wrestler, martial artist and former Metropolitan Policeman. It was reported that Bissell was amongst those on an intake from the police to Achnacarry and that his talents had been quickly spotted so he was asked to stay on. Fairbairn and Sykes thus had a number of competitors and imitators in the fields of unarmed combat and knife-fighting, and in some ways the rise and popularity of such 'no holds barred' methods was symbolic of the whole desperate resistance to Nazism. In the UK, other disciples of unarmed combat included James Hipkiss, 'British Jiu-Jitsu Champion', who published his manual *Unarmed Combat*, subtitled 'Your Answer to Invasion: Jiu-Jitsu', as early as February 1941. It was reprinted twice within five months. The claims contained in this volume were by no means modest:

Should invasion come, the part which Unarmed Combat must play in the overthrow of the invader is rapidly being realised by the public. Members of His Majesty's Forces are being officially instructed in this new phase of warfare. The Home Guard may find it one of the greatest factors in their part of the struggle, and it is by no means unlikely that the average civilian – man or woman – who has learned Unarmed Combat would find it a potent means in repelling the intruder from their own homestead. With a knowledge of Unarmed Combat, even the unprepared citizens of Holland and Belgium could have frustrated the designs of Hitler's vital link in his plans – the Parachutists.

In Bernard's *Manual of Commando and Guerrilla Warfare*, which appears to have been printed very shortly after *All-in Fighting* – and traded explicitly on the Commando name – are simplified versions of many of the Fairbairn techniques, including not only various disarmings of opponents but the 'matchbox attack' and simultaneous smacking of the ears.

On the other side of the Atlantic, an official US Army manual of *Unarmed Defence for the American Soldier* was produced by June 1942. Its object was not only self-protection, but building confidence and rapid reflexes. Again, it was inspired by oriental martial arts and stipulated that it was intended to eliminate all stigma of the 'foul tactic', for, 'in hand-to-hand combat there are no referees, no judges, and no timekeeper. You are on your own. No measure of defence is too extreme when your life is in danger.' It was illustrated by photographs of an aggressor – larger, sometimes armed, and clad in a dark shirt – being soundly defeated by a defender in a light coloured shirt. *All-in Fighting* was itself produced in American editions as *Get Tough*. Similar ideas were also promulgated by US Army Colonel Rex Applegate, who had worked with Fairbairn and Sykes, in *Kill or Get Killed*.

Perhaps the most extraordinary of the North American unarmed combat systems to claim Commando connections was the Canadian 'Awrology', promoted by Gordon E. Perrigard MD in his 1943 book, *Awrology: All Out Hand to Hand Fighting for Commandos, Military, and Civilians*. This vicious catalogue of throws, hold breaks, toe-stampings, testicle-grabbing and eye-poking, claimed jokingly that its title was actually derived from Welsh. Its inspirations were purportedly callisthenics and medical principles. X-rays of fractures illustrated the perils of not being able to fall correctly. The instructions in *Awrology* included: methods for avoiding grenade explosions by dropping away to one side and breaking the fall with a forearm and shooting back in the direction from which the bomb was thrown; tactical crawling; 'the deadly natural weapon' that was the edge of the hand; kicking the head of a prone opponent; 'death locks' and dagger play. Also mentioned were different ways to use the steel helmet:

> If you have your steel helmet on, use the top for butting and the front rim for cutting down blows into your opponent's face. If your enemy has a strap under his chin holding his helmet on his head, from behind you can jerk the helmet off the back off his head so the strap catches him across the front of his neck.

In short, it was suggested that, 'in Commando work especially, Awrology could work like an arrow in the dark'.

That Perrigard drew some of his inspiration from Fairbairn is strongly suggested by, not only the circumstantial evidence of the date of his book's publication, but that it contained a substantial section on the use of the 'Commando dagger'. Interestingly, the specific 'sturdy dagger' illustrated was not the familiar 'F–S' knife but a very similar weapon with a somewhat fatter grip, recently designed, so it was claimed,

> by the Society of Arwrologists for All Out Hand to Hand Fighting. It features a steel knob at the end of its long handle, which projects behind the gripping hand, and which can crush a skull with a back-hand blow. The wide handle permits a firm, powerful grip, and the knife rides snugly in the hand. It has a 7½-inch blade, hollow ground, with two cutting edges, the lower two thirds being razor sharp, the proximal third has an edge designed for rough hewing. It has a tapering needle point, which is not brittle. It is balanced for throwing. It may be concealed.

How much of the unarmed combat fad was genuinely useful, and how much morale raiser or propaganda, is difficult to judge with exactitude. It certainly sold books that encouraged a healthy spirit of resistance. Nevertheless, Commandos were one of the few groups to use such techniques in earnest on any sort of regular basis. Yet, even in raids, casualties inflicted by Bren gun, Naval gunfire, mortar, grenades and other weapons must have outnumbered stab wounds and neck breakings by a factor of dozens, if not hundreds, to one. Remarkably, it seems there is at least some evidence that the enemy took the stealthy threat of knife and unarmed combat seriously, for it appears that, in 1942, the German

Army Command in Norway published its own riposte. This was entitled *Abwehr Englischer Gangster-Methoden – Stilles Töten*: or *Defence Against English Gangster Methods – Silent Killing*.

This little booklet contains a series of photographs and drawings by means of which German soldiers may protect themselves against attack by knife-wielding, throttling, spine-breaking, or Judo-posturing British soldiers. The text suggests that its publication was inspired by the capture of instructions from 'English sabotage schools' and notes how the British have descended to the 'lowest instincts of the savage' in their use of dirty gangster techniques. Even so, *Abwehr Englischer Gangster-Methoden* is an odd pamphlet, partly because some of the attacking methods shown were not usually taught in British unarmed combat, and partly because Commando and SOE documents on such matters were rarely if ever taken into the field. Also strange is the lack of a reference number on the booklet, and its limitation to Norway. Several possible explanations have been put forward, including that of an attempt by Nazi propagandists to gain the moral high ground over unsporting British 'gangsters'.

Another extraordinary, but far from impossible, interpretation is that the booklet is not really German at all but a work of the British 'Political Warfare Executive', which produced many bogus German documents designed to undermine enemy morale. Since at least some of the contents were not taught in the UK, and that no actual invasion of Norway was planned for the foreseeable future, there was little to be lost by encouraging armed German sentries there to respond to an unlikely type of assault with their bare hands. It was also the case that the contents of the booklet could not really be construed as secret. By 1942 Fairbairn and Sykes had taught not only Commandos and SOE, but many regular formations and other instructors. Moreover, spreading the impression that the British were tough, completely ruthless, and highly trained gangsters who might assault at any moment using 'silent death' was not calculated to make the German garrison of Norway – already stretched over a vast inhospitable area – any the happier. In the context of other 'black propaganda' efforts intended to incite desertion onto Swedish territory, and the promotion of the idea of an all-out Allied invasion of Norway seemingly demanding the diversion of more German troops to Scandinavia, a British provenance for *Abwehr Englischer Gangster-Methoden* suddenly becomes plausible.

* * *

Derek Mills-Roberts

Derek Mills-Roberts (1908–1980) was educated at Liverpool College and Oxford University, and trained as a solicitor in the 1930s whilst working for his father's firm. In 1936 he joined the Supplementary Reserve of officers of the Irish Guards, and accompanied 1st Battalion to Norway in April 1940, where he fell sick with pneumonia. Not long after his return to the UK he joined the Commandos, and initially served as second-in-command to Lord Lovat in No. 4 Commando, but after his outstanding performance at Dieppe was promoted to lieutenant colonel and given command of No. 6. He led this unit in North Africa during 1943, where he was awarded the Distinguished Service Order for his efforts in combat against a superior German force. In June 1944 he commanded No. 6 Commando in the D-Day landings and, as brigadier, went on to lead 1st Commando Brigade, gaining a bar to his DSO. In May 1945 Mills-Roberts took the surrender of German Field Marshal Erhard Milch, and in a fit of anger over evidence of the 'Final Solution' that he had so recently witnessed, broke the German general's baton of office over his head. This incident later become a subject of heated discussion, with the controversial David Irving claiming it as an incident of brutality, and others empathising with a dramatic gesture all too natural under the circumstances. Though Mills-Roberts retired from regular service at the end of the war, he remained with the Territorial Army and commanded 125th Infantry Brigade from 1947 to 1951. His Commando memoir, *Clash by Night*, was published in 1956. A manuscript of this, plus many other Mills-Roberts papers, including material on the Milch incident, letters from Eisenhower and Major General Laycock, and an account of the operations in North West Europe, are preserved in the Liddell Hart Archive at King's College. Mills-Roberts died in 1980, and his ashes were laid by a small memorial at Bavent near Caen in Normandy.

As we have seen, early Commando small-unit battle tactics were often taught directly by the Commanding Officer and his troop leaders, and amongst these characters Robert Dawson (a former officer of the Loyal Regiment) and Peter Young (previously of the Bedfordshire and

Hertfordshire Regiment) featured as keen proponents of improved tactics and battle skills. Yet there was no 'magic formula', nor were the basics of Commando infantry combat radically different to what was taught elsewhere. Arguably, what was distinctive was the remarkable ability of the Commando sections and 'half sections' to operate in even smaller groups than the standard infantry establishments, the willingness to build on the basic strokes of existing 'Battle Drills', and the grafting on of new drills to fit specific circumstances and equipment.

In learning, and in formulating improved methods, the Commandos had four great advantages. The first was that virtually everybody had already undergone basic training well before they became a Commando: so dropping into skirmish lines, going prone, use of weapons, dividing into 'fire groups' and 'rifle groups', fieldcraft and movement, camouflage, patrol and arrow formations and other basics were already common currency. The second was that, as volunteers who had been further sifted through selection, those remaining were either troops to whom tactical considerations were second nature, or men with the aptitude to assimilate skills very quickly. Third, Commando tactics were tested operation by operation: after contact was broken off there was opportunity for methods to be minutely re-examined before being retried. Where this did not happen – as was sometimes the case in the Mediterranean and Middle East – the advantages of the Commando were compromised. The final boost was that, though equipment of all sorts was in short supply in 1940, new or scarce items were often in the hands of the Commandos before permeating to other units. This process may have begun with fighting knives, Tommy guns, toggle ropes, and priority access to field engineering stores, but was continued with canoes and assault boats, rucksacks, assault jerkins, various types of special explosives, additional machine weapons and ultimately, later in the war, specialist gear for different climatic conditions, 'Buffalo' and 'Weasel' tracked carriers, and other novelties.

At the core of most small-unit tactics of the period lay 'fire and movement' – the basic idea of engaging a target with one fire element, allowing another the opportunity to move. This could be successfully performed with the fire of single light machine gun, a subsection or a whole unit, provided only that the force applied was sufficient to suppress, or at least attract, the full attention of the enemy. Arguably, the principle was even more important to the Commando than to other troops because rarely were the original Commandos supposed to remain on the defensive in one place. They did not exist to deny an area to an enemy, still less to permanently shift a prepared defence by set-piece attack and hold the ground gained. Initially, of course, heavy weapons – such as Vickers machine guns and mortars – were lacking and without these, assaulting an enemy who was alert and prepared, or, conversely for Commandos to hold a position in any protracted manner would have been difficult if not impossible.

Nevertheless, the concept of 'fire and movement' was developed with experience. *Infantry Section Leading* of 1938 had expected that 'covering fire' during an attack would be given primarily by the artillery, machine guns, mortars and carrier platoons – although, even without any of these, infantry platoons and sections would be expected to continue making use of cover as they advanced and rush across any gaps in concealment. 'Attacking platoons will be able to help themselves forward by using ground to give them cover from view and enable them to surprise the enemy, and by using their own fire to cover their advance.' By such methods, attacking platoons would make progress 'using their fire when necessary'. *Training in Fieldcraft and Elementary Tactics*, 1940, uses the term 'fire and manoeuvre' to describe a situation in which the section commander divides his men into 'covering and assaulting parties', with the Bren being used 'to protect the assaulting party as it moves from cover to cover, until it is close enough to bomb or rush the enemy post'. By 1942 the message in the *Instructor's Handbook on Fieldcraft and Battle Drill* was completely unambiguous, and positively shouted: 'No advance is possible in modern war unless the enemy's heads are kept down by weight of metal – COVERING FIRE is essential to any advance.'

Perhaps surprisingly, Commando small-unit tactics were taught by means of the 'Battle Drill' system championed for the Army in general by Major Wigram early in the war. The trainees were usually the finest material, the trainers probably the most imaginative, and the basics were fitted to Commando establishments or a particular mission – but the method of learning, and key ingredients of the system, were the same. What was taught much of the time as the basis of Commando combat was, in various forms, the contents of the *Instructors' Handbook*, and later that of *Infantry Training*, 1944. Also included were 'Individual Battle Practices', five of which were issued in a handy manual form in March 1943. These practices were officially defined as a step between the firing range and the full-blown 'field exercise', and were:

1) 'Firing and Observing'. To be exercised using 'falling iron plates', tiles or bricks, with one man of a pair shooting, the other observing at 200 to 300 yards. Added realism was provided by concealing the target with foliage which could be momentarily pulled aside.

2) 'Endurance and Quick Firing'. Intended to stimulate concentration and quick accurate shooting, this consisted of showing a target for a few seconds at a time over a period of five minutes. The targets could appear at different places on a small piece of ground.

3) 'Attack'. Using four human figures exposed at various ranges from 200 to 400 yards the firer had three minutes in which to engage them. When hit the targets were dropped.

4) 'The stalker'. The trainee was given a time limit to advance stealthily about 100 yards, before engaging a target in a 'battle position'. Realism was added by an instructor or marker observing from a pit using a periscope. Whenever the trainee was seen a round of 'ball or blank' was fired.

5) 'LMG'. A Bren team is given three widely spaced targets to fire at and these are exposed in turn as each is hit. During the exercise the instructor tells the Bren firer that he has been hit and the Bren No. 2 must take over, moving and engaging from an alternative position.

One tactical weapon drill appears to have been adopted directly from the Brigade of Guards, a diagram and notes on the method of which appear amongst Brigadier Haydon's papers, under the date of February 1942. This exercise was performed on a range, but one especially laid out to allow the trainees plenty of space to practise their advance towards the butts. The diagram shows a trench below the 'target' area and in this stood seven soldiers acting as markers – not to point out where rounds strike, as in a more conventional arrangement, but to walk along the trench each with a figure-shaped target held above their head. These 'moving targets' provided the objective. The trainees started 285 yards away with empty rifles and began the drill by loading whilst prone. They then sprang up, ran 45 yards to cover, and halted for ten seconds prone, before again springing up and running another 45 yards and going to cover to fire off ten rounds at the target figures. Having discharged their weapons, they retired speedily to the first cover again, where their weapons would be checked as clear before results were determined.

Often, as in the infantry, the idea of progression from basic weapons competence, through 'individual battle practice' and small units to full exercise, was followed. No. 48 RM Commando, whose detailed tactical training had to be squeezed in between Achnacarry in March 1944 and D-Day, undertook most of its practice in north Kent. As the official history records, ordinary weapons training at Achnacarry was followed by specific drills:

> The next step was individual battle practices on Cliffe Cooling Marsh ranges; then Bren and rifle group, subsection and finally Troop field firing with fire support from the Vickers and 3-inch mortars of the Heavy Weapons Troop were practised. Practically all the training was done with ball ammunition, thanks to our enormous field firing range area. The countryside favoured intensive training. The Cliffe Cooling Marshes were a large uninhabited area, 5 miles long by 1 mile deep.

The summation of wartime tactics, *Commando Battle Drill* (Royal Marine Training Pamphlet No. 2, 1945), shows clear connections with its *Infantry Training* cousin, albeit slightly modified to take account of the Commando establishment of section and half-sections. Just as in the general *Instructors Handbook* of October 1942, Commando battle drill began with parade ground instruction – with a wall diagram of unit organisation and even, where possible, 'labels for hanging round necks' so that the members of subsections could be readily identified. The object of this apparently pedestrian approach was, 'to ensure uniformity in elementary movements of open warfare. To cut down orders in the field – each man knowing what he has to do without being told. To ensure speed in getting into action.' The subsection comprised twelve individuals, plus a commander. This could be further divided into Assault Group 'A', Assault Group 'B', and the 'Bren Group'. Each group had its own NCO to lead the three or four men in the team. If under fire, the parts of the subsection could be moved alternately, being either running or 'down', so as to provide effective 'fire and movement'. About 5 yards spacing was left between each man, and full-scale attacks usually comprised entire sections, so doubling the numbers firing and moving. Chillingly, the advance to contact was often prefixed with the command, 'We will kill all enemy'. Additional details could be filled in from *Infantry Training*. The building and village clearance drill included in *Commando Battle Drill* was likewise a polished and slightly modified version of the tactics spelt out in *Fighting in Built Up Areas*, in which the subsection split down into parts with the Bren group, 'flank men' and sniper covering the structure, whilst the 'door men' and 'assault party' crept up on a door with bayonets fixed and a Sten gun to the fore. Following a grenade, the assault party entered. Anybody leaving the house as the attackers entered would be forced to cross a 'killing ground' and 'must be killed'.

*   *   *

Probably the key feature in the advancement of Commando tactics in general was the concept of 'lessons learned' – the now-familiar idea of a planned operation or exercise being performed, a 'debrief' undertaken, and reports written. Importantly, debrief was not merely for the benefit of those who had directed the operation, to inform of success or otherwise, but also aimed at a detailed analysis by means of which specific techniques could be advanced. The broad idea of learning empirically – or 'by experience' – was not new. The military had had various 'institutions', staff, and training colleges that had used similar methods for over the course of at least a century, with papers being written in the light of a campaign or operation, digested and integrated into experience. In the First World War the whole Army had used such a learning cycle. What was arguably different about the Commandos was how quickly this process was expected to work, the level of detail regarding what were often micro operations, and the modernity and novelty of the subject matter in the minutiae of the many co-operative aspects of the 'Combined Operation'. A significant advantage of the raiding force over either the BEF of 1914 or 1939 was that, until much later, it was not in continuous contact with the enemy and the debrief and post-operative study could therefore be made in a relatively measured manner, with all those who had survived at hand to answer questions. Individual techniques could then be tested out of range of the enemy. Interestingly, at least one contemporary document refers to the Channel as being essentially a very wide version of 'No Man's Land'.

The Vaagso raid report, also subsequently circulated in the US, adopted a completely multi-service approach and contained a specific 'Lessons Learned' divided into eight sections under 'weather', 'air support', 'treatment of German merchant ships', 'bombardment charges', 'floating reserve', 'smoke', 'arming of landing craft', and 'maintenance of communications'. A separate note towards the end of the document contained 'Notes for Lessons' by a boarding party commander. The main observations on weather were that bad weather around the target would have made the chance of success 'remote' and that precise navigation and timing were indispensable. In a similar vein, situations could easily arise in which surface forces could sail whilst aircraft were grounded. The floating reserve was determined 'essential' – without such a force the military commander would be 'at a very serious disadvantage'. The behaviour of enemy merchant ships had come as something of a surprise – they appeared to have orders to 'render useless or destroy their ship' at any cost in the event of threatened capture. Therefore, 'nothing short of complete ruthlessness is likely to be understood': the best way to achieve a capture was to force the crew 'to abandon ship in a panic'. This could be achieved by 'plastering' the bridge and upper deck with Oerlikon, machine-gun, and rifle fire. British vessels would ideally have two snipers on their decks whenever a fjord was entered, in addition to what other weapons were deployed. Likewise, the arming of landing craft with Bren guns and mortars was recommended to become standard. Remarkably, street-fighting – so often cited as the defining feature of this operation – did not merit its own separate 'lessons learned' comments. Nevertheless, opinion was offered that the activities of the Commandos were hampered by 'orders which had been issued to avoid damage to Norwegian property' and the limitations imposed both by the time taken up by street-fighting against determined opposition, and the conflicting claims on time, which was strictly limited.

One of the most comprehensive set of Commando 'lessons learned' was published by US Military Intelligence as the chapter 'Summary of Lessons' in the volume *British Commandos* of 1942, though its contents suggest it was most relevant to 1941. This effectively provided a complete list of how to execute a Commando raid, from choice of target, through to exploitation of the post-mission publicity. According to *British Commandos*, the choice of target was not deemed important, since it would be extremely difficult for any raid 'to do really substantial material damage'. In fact, the likely object of any assault was to 'inflict casualties and gain information', the targets being identified mainly 'as guides on which to focus attacks'. A simple way to choose a target was to select a length of coast about which there was good intelligence, then select a point where it was possible to land from the sea without detection, and then list whatever targets lay within a mile of the landing point. Any places that had too many, or possibly no, defenders, were to be discarded as unfruitful. Finally, the field would be narrowed to objectives that were easy to find, within range of the attack, and on the fringe of an area of enemy troop concentration. Other things being equal, 'pick one which is nearest the sea'.

Another document, in the Mills-Roberts collection, post-dating Dieppe but predating D-Day, is entitled *Lessons Learned in Combined Operations*. This looks specifically at Commando experience but again is arranged as a series of salient points regarding raids. This blueprint or checklist is arranged under the headings of 'planning', 'training', 'sea voyage', 'operations', 'equipment', 'intelligence', 'administration', 'medical', 'morale' and 'communications'. Importantly, it suggests that multiple planning agencies are a recipe for disaster – Army, Navy and any other planners should be merged into one agency only. Training should be on terrain similar to that to be encountered during the actual operation, and alternative beaches for use in case of a change of plan should be identified. Assaults were to aim for surprise, but if this was impossible, Naval and air support had to be adequate. Light or self-propelled artillery was to accompany any strike inland, but where Commandos lacked heavy weapons, intelligent and generous use of smoke became indispensable. Air support was extremely useful but not suitable where the target was small or within 1,000 yards of friendly troops. Enemy fortifications could only be successfully attacked by night or where surprise was achieved in daylight, and the Commandos were to be used for special and specific purposes, not dissipated on unsuitable tasks.

When it came to preparation for the landing, stores were to be organised on vessels with three major points in mind. The first of these was that different types of item were to be split between a number of craft, forming several consignments, so that if a beach was cut off, every individual group had the maximum chance of survival. The materials themselves were to be loaded in reverse order of priority, so that the last in and first off were the really crucial pieces for immediate use. Finally, even where they were due to be used on the same landing ground, vital classes of equipment were to be divided between vessels. The loss of one would not therefore jeopardise the whole operation. Interestingly, this point had been learned in the Crimea, where the loss of a ship full of boots had taught a painful lesson – clearly it was relearned again during the Second World War but forgotten by 1982, the time of the Falklands and the loss of *Atlantic Conveyor*.

On the detail of the raiders themselves, the bulk of the troops were to wear 'a light variation of fighting order', but some consideration was to be given to using some men 'practically without equipment to act as skirmishers'. On small raids in particular, the men should have no webbing, equipment, steel helmets or bayonet scabbards, but have blackened bayonets. Mae Wests were to be worn inflated on the run in, but deflated on reaching the beach. Bangalores were to be carried for the demolition of beach obstacles. Though German stick grenades were 'better in the hands of an unskilled thrower', the Mills was ideal in its lethality. In street-fighting situations, identification signs were to be worn. Whilst Commando units had not hitherto taken transport with them into action, it was now proposed that movement in tracked carriers was the ideal. When proper transport was lacking, the provision of handcarts for the movement of heavier items was 'better than nothing'. For the purposes of junior leaders, reconnaissance and despatches, motorcycles or bicycles should be used.

Some 'lessons learned', circulated in Combined Operations and Commando brigade HQ, became the subject matter of raid reports and of specific improvements to Commando training; but much also found its way into the mainstream as the war progressed, by means of a series of printed Combined Operations pamphlets. These covered specific points encountered when amphibious or co-operative ventures between arms were undertaken. The series had begun by 1941, and many were successively replaced and updated in the light of operations and new information. The series reached '35A' by the time of D-Day, so several dozen were in circulation, covering both very large and significant subject areas, as well as those that were quite detailed. At one end of the scale were pamphlets dealing with the myriad duties of the Royal Engineers, at the other a volume covering *Driving Instructions for Combined Operations*.

Eventually, most aspects were covered, up to that of full-scale invasion. Just one interesting example from the middle war period was number 34, *Combined Operations: RA*, of April 1943, giving methods of artillery co-operation with a landing. The crucial point was that supporting fire fell into two distinct phases during such an operation, the first of which was delivered by Naval bombardment and aircraft 'in accordance with a pre arranged plan'. The second phase would see support garnered from both the assets deployed during the first phase, and 'an increasing proportion of Army weapons as they become available'. The artillery would be expected to land, then fire in support of infantry and tanks, and engage in anti-aircraft work.

For the artillery, the main limiting factor was that all materials had to be channelled through vessels and beachheads, restricting what could be achieved. As had been noted in raids, supplies had to be carefully chosen, with loads meeting predetermined parameters, and ordered in reverse priority. Units would not be at 'full war establishment' during the initial phases of landing, as this would mean taking up space with inessential items. Gunners were therefore to go in on an 'assault scale' or a 'light scale' of equipment – enough to allow them to fight for either forty-eight hours or for three weeks at a distance of up to 30 miles from the beach. So were applied the theories of 'light equipment' for amphibious assaults that had been pioneered in early raids, but were later improved on increasingly large operations in North Africa and the Mediterranean.

The corollary of both cumulative 'lessons learned' and the increasing use of Commandos as part of invasions, rather than as raiders, was the growing realisation that the special force would have to adapt or die. So it was that Brigadier Robert Laycock, previously commander of the 'Layforce' and now officer commanding Special Service Brigade, put forward a series of options to Mountbatten on the possible future of the Commandos. One possibility was that, having passed on many of their skills and fulfilled much of their original purpose, they now lacked a clear tactical niche and should be disbanded. A second was that they should be kept small and discrete and used only for minor raids. The third was that they should be thoroughly revised, restructured, and equipped in such a way that they could participate in both the assault phase of an operation and the fighting that followed. Since small raids now tended to fall within the province of the 'small scale raiding force' or SSRF, the SAS, 10 Commando and others, and disbandment was viewed as extremely counter-productive, the only real possibility was a comprehensive review and re-equipment.

From April through to September 1943 this reorganisation would be carried into effect, creating five 'fighting' troops and one 'heavy weapons' troop, while adding a somewhat larger permanent establishment of vehicles for the carrying of heavy equipment and reconnaissance duties. As of late 1943 these included jeeps and trailers for the heavy weapons and command elements, as well as eight 15-cwt trucks, three 3-ton lorries and some motorcycles. By early 1945 the transport element was considerable. That listed in the RM Commando 'war establishment' totalled more than seventy vehicles: being thirty-five bicycles, nine motorcycles, a 'General Service' car and eighteen Jeeps plus the eleven trucks and lorries aforementioned.

Chapter 7

D–Day: Assault Infantry

D–Day would see Commandos deployed in a way in which could never have been envisaged early in the war: *en masse*, often using brute force, in daylight – and sometimes frontally – to overcome enemy defences, performing systematic acts of clearance and breakthrough. As part of the 21st Army Group plan for 'Operation Overlord', the Commandos would operate as a 'Special Service Group', under the overall command of Major General R. G. Sturges, with Brigadier Durnford-Slater, former Commanding Officer of No. 3 Commando, as his second-in-command. Two brigades, the 1st and 4th 'Special Service', with a total of eight full Commandos, were available. The 1st Special Service, under Lord Lovat, comprised 3, 4, 6 and 45 RM Commandos; and 4th Special Service, under Brigadier 'Jumbo' Leicester of the Royal Marines, 41 RM, 46 RM, 47 RM and 48 RM. Nor was this all, for there were also smaller special detachments for particular purposes.

'No. 30 Assault Unit' (or '30 Commando') was to be used for the 'capture of enemy documents and secret equipment in the assault area'. One detachment was destined for 'Juno' on D-Day; the other for the 'Utah' area four days later. No. 30 proved its worth, sending back to the UK a wide variety of documents and special equipment, including charts showing swept channels through mines, signalling apparatus, code books, information on radar, a night sight, and samples of a new type of mine. This was all deemed of 'very high grade intelligence value'. Towards the end of June, Captain Hargreaves-Heap of 30 Assault Unit would also be instrumental in the surrender of the German Naval Headquarters at Cherbourg. Nevertheless, according to the *Battle Summary*, the work of the unit was 'hampered by the ruthless way in which captured equipment was looted for souvenirs or mishandled from sheer destructiveness'.

Also part of the Normandy landings were the 'Royal Naval Commandos' – not to be confused with the Royal Marine Commandos. The 'RN' Commandos had first been created as 'Beach Commandos' at the end of 1942 after experience in Madagascar, using what were then

'Naval Beach Parties' during 'Operation Ironclad'. Their job would be to secure and control landing beaches, acting under the 'Beach Masters', moving traffic off the potentially confused and crowded landing grounds. The RN Beach Commandos were lettered, not numbered, and arranged into subunits – each subunit being sufficient to handle the craft required to land a battalion. As the Admiralty had decreed in 1943, they formed a 'buffer between the Naval and Military aspects' and were consequently trained in aspects of both. Though some did basic training at Achnacarry, the main centre for teaching the RN Commandos was HMS *Armadillo* at Ardentinny, on the shore of Loch Long. D-Day would be the biggest deployment of the RN Commandos with nine units – eight British and one Canadian – on the beaches. In some instances heavy casualties were taken and the Commandos had to dig in to hang onto their European toe-hold. Their residence in the vicinity of the Normandy beaches would last some weeks, as they not only marshalled the potential chaos, but also did valuable service in helping to moor the Mulberry harbours.

Though not present as a complete unit, No. 10 (inter-Allied) Commando also played a significant role. The two French troops, led by Commandant Kieffer, acted under Lieutenant Colonel Dawson of No. 4 Commando as a special force within a special force. Though relations between the British and French Commandos were cordial, and Dawson himself spoke French, he was wary of mixing his two contingents too closely for fear they would fail to understand each other quickly enough in heat of battle. He therefore allotted Kieffer's men their own specific objectives. Another troop, 3 or 'X' Troop, would see service in Normandy spread out amongst the other Commandos. Altogether, one officer and forty-three other ranks would be deployed on 6 June. Split into small patrols, they acted as scouts for the Commando brigade, using their linguistic ability to pass where others could not. To scout the enemy meant being close to him – and speaking to him closer still – so it was not surprising that this little detachment would suffer particularly heavy losses.

The Army and RM Commandos were task force of choice all along the British and Canadian landing grounds. Perhaps curiously, the arrival of the Commandos was timed just after the first wave of tanks and infantry on the main beaches, when they would flow into gaps and around enemy flanks, so unhinging the defenders and allowing beachheads and parachute landings to be joined. Not all were happy with this arrangement: Lieutenant Colonel Moulton, Commander of 48 RM

Commando, was just one of several who felt that the tried-and-tested technique of arriving early and attempting to flank batteries and seize vital points by stealthy movement would have been better.

The biggest Commando attack was by Lovat's brigade, coming in through 'Sword' beach at La Brèche, on the eastern end of the landing grounds. Here, 4 and 6 Commando were to come in close behind the first assault of the 8th Infantry Brigade. No. 4 was to immediately wheel sharp left to assault the battery at Ouistreham from the rear, whilst the Tunisian veterans of No. 6 Commando were to make inland for the Bénouville bridges over the Canal de Caen and River Orne, and rendezvous with the parachutists of Sixth Airborne, whose landing was planned to have taken place during the early hours. These bridges were code-named 'Euston 1' and 'Euston 2', but the best known would soon find fame as 'Pegasus Bridge'. All being well, Commandos and Parachutists would link at about one in the afternoon, and 6 Commando and the Paras could clear the village of La Plein together. Ninety minutes after the first landings would come No. 3 and No. 45 RM Commando. These were to follow the path first beaten by No. 6, cross the bridges, and No. 3 could now clear the area of Bas de Ranville. No. 45 Commando was to carry on north-east, via Sallenelles and, if it was not already in the hands of the Airborne, take Merville Battery with its four 100mm guns and Franceville Plage from the rear. By this method, the Commandos would help secure the flank of the whole 'Overlord' operation: though, in the event, and as might be expected, not everything happened in the time and order planned.

Leicester's brigade, entirely of RM Commandos, was to be deployed further west at points along 'Gold', 'Juno' and 'Sword', seizing specific villages and moving laterally to link the divisions of the Allied invasion forces. No. 41 RM Commando was tasked with a two-pronged assault at Lion-sur-Mer on 'Sword' beach, before moving inland to seize Douvres and its radar station. No. 48 RM Commando, 'last to be formed but first to land', was supposed to make shore at 'Nan Red' on 'Juno' beach near Aubin-sur-Mer, and pass through the Canadians, turn east towards Langrune, and attack the coast defences from the rear, finally moving in support of No. 41. Landing furthest west, No. 47 RM Commando would come ashore near Le Hamel on 'Gold' beach and undertake a fairly lengthy march around the back of Arromanches, via La Rosière, and attack Port en Bessin from the rear: here they would be right up against the US forces on 'Omaha' beach. No. 46 RM Commando was initially held back as a floating reserve and actually came in on D-Day +1 (or 7 June).

With Leicester's Brigade things would go much further awry than they did with their Army colleagues to the east.

By the time of D-Day, Commando weaponry had long since expanded to a point commensurate with taking and holding ground in the face of determined opposition. Indeed, as early as 1941, equipment included mortars as a matter of course, and by mid-1943 each Commando had formed a dedicated 'Heavy Weapons' or support troop. In this unit were carried two Vickers Medium Machine Guns, and two 3-inch mortars. Whilst jeeps had now been provided to shift the heavy weapons over distance on land, wheeled transport would not be included in the Commando first waves and the equipment would have to be manhandled onto the beaches. The 3-inch mortars were rapid-fire weapons when handled well, but as each bomb weighed 10 lb, taking enough ammunition to where it really mattered was something of a logistical problem. This was solved, for the most part, by giving individual soldiers one or two bombs to be deposited with the mortar teams as needed. The larger mortars did not replace the little 2-inch mortars: on the contrary these were increased to twenty-seven per Commando – enough for one in every subsection plus a substantial reserve. The PIAT or 'Projector Infantry Anti Tank', which fired a hollow charge bomb, had also replaced the old antitank rifles in 1943 on a scale of one per troop with another five kept in the reserve. This was fairly heavy firepower, but for the jobs that D-Day demanded, yet more was required.

No. 4 Commando, which was expected to face serious and entrenched opposition at the German battery on the western flank of the invasion beaches at Ouistreham, received additional armament in the shape of Vickers 'K' guns. These were not new but had previously been issued in small numbers to give Commandos extra ability to hold positions after disasters in North Africa, where lack of firepower had become apparent in static missions. In No. 4, eight of these machine guns were grouped in one troop to tackle the battery – surprise being out of the question as Naval and air activity would have already made it completely obvious that a major assault was under way. A further four guns went to the French detachments, with a section of two guns in each of their landing craft. The 'K' guns were useful but, as Private Alex Morris recalled, had less than adequate sights. Accordingly, they were loaded with one round of tracer to every four of ordinary 'ball': this not only allowed the gunner to see exactly where his shots were going, but created a demoralisingly visible stream of fire.

Bren guns had long since been increased in number, so that there were usually forty or more in each Commando, a dozen of which were held as a reserve with the HQ. Nevertheless, the weapon was popular, powerful, not as heavy as many light machine guns, and often formed the base of fire around which small-unit tactics worked, so there was a widespread demand for more. On D-Day it would appear that quite a few were forthcoming, as Peter Young now commanding No. 3 Commando explained:

In the Commandos we were supposed to have five Brens in a troop; an infantry company, which had about twice the number of men as a rifle troop, had nine Brens. It seemed to me that we should increase our firepower so that at a pinch one of our troops could do much the same job as an infantry company. We worked this out and decided that eight was the ideal number. We then indented for the extra guns, through the usual channels, and, lo and behold, they quickly appeared. Things happened very fast in the early months of 1944. The office and administrative staffs were going down the ramps on D-Day at the same time as everyone else. Every fourth man in Headquarters carried a Bren, and so we were really going into action with seven troops, all with teeth, as opposed to six troops and a long and harmless tail.

This was doubtless an extremely sensible precaution – particularly given the enemy penchant for rapid-firing machine guns such as the MG 34 and MG 42, but there was a penalty to be paid in that Bren guns used ammunition more quickly than bolt-action rifles, so extra rounds would also have to be carried. According to Sergeant J. Kite, some even greater liberties were taken with formal establishments. His own half-section was equipped mainly with Sten guns, with each man carrying six magazines of 9mm ammunition for his own weapon and an extra fifty rounds of .303-inch for the Bren gun.

More firepower was just part of the extra equipment – indeed, most Commandos would go ashore carrying heavy rucksacks weighing over 60 lb. According to Mills-Roberts, though in short supply, 'these had been provided by Sir Raymond Quilter Bt'. Bangalores and other explosives were also included to deal with obstacles and fortifications, as P. Pritchard recalled:

Our packs were of the Bergen type. As our supply lines were uncertain, we had been issued with the rucksack type so that we could carry a greater load than normal infantry. This was intended to give us a measure of self sufficiency until our supplies caught up. My Bergen, which I weighed on a railway station weighing machine, together with my belt and bren pouches, came to 96 lb. In addition, I carried a rifle – Lee Enfield Mk 4 [i.e. No. 4] and bayonet which would put the average weight carried by any Commando soldier in 1st Brigade at well over 100 lb [...] On the late afternoon of 4 June we made a final check of our kit and were issued with our combat rations. Each soldier received two twenty-four hour ration packs, which had been specially formulated for the invasion. The pack consisted of dehydrated meat with boiled sweets, chewing gum and blocks of sweetened oatmeal, together with a ration of 'compo' tea. Included was a round paper cylinder of eight hexamine (solid fuel) tablets and a small stove, the first I had ever seen. In addition to the two ration packs was the usual iron ration [...] I should mention that none of us carried the useless entrenching tool, and in lieu we carried the general service shovel with one man in three carrying the general service pick.

Some backpack flamethrowers, and folding bicycles, for one troop of each Commando, completed the impedimenta.

This was not only a very far cry from 'lightly equipped' raids of yesteryear, but an impractical amount for any advance requiring swift movement. Accordingly, orders were given to many of the Commando units that their loads were to be dumped prior to undertaking specific assaults, and wherever possible retrieved again afterwards. Steel helmets remained a vexed question, and one in which some units allowed the men a fair degree of latitude. Some veterans of former actions continued to hold that the helmet was too much of an encumbrance in action: others heeded warnings that a daylight assault against entrenched positions was a very different proposition, requiring any sort of protection that was available. So it is that photographs of 6 June show the HQ of 4th Special Service Brigade landing in berets, and odd mixtures of headgear on several other units – indeed, in the latter part of the war it would appear that quite frequently Commandos wore the famous beret when not actually being shelled, changing to a helmet at vital moments.

It is worthy of note that the different Commandos employed on D-Day did not all arrive at the beaches by the same method. Some transferred from larger ships to the familiar little 'Landing Craft Assault', others were in the 'Landing Craft Infantry (Small)' – or LCI (S) – all the way across the Channel. On balance, though it was obviously inconvenient – and sometimes dangerous – to change from one vessel to another at sea, LCAs were probably better for the task in hand. Small vessels were more manoeuvrable, a less obvious target, and if disaster struck, fewer troops were at risk. Getting off them was also quicker. The LCI (S), by contrast, was 104 feet long with two troop decks like large open cabins, one each fore and aft. These provided no protection from shells, could not be evacuated instantaneously, and tended to trap fumes. The vessels themselves, though perfectly seaworthy, also pitched and wallowed most disconcertingly. Lacking hinged drop ramps, the Commandos were forced to use gangplanks with transverse battens to provide a modicum of grip on the way down. In an emergency, the only other way off was to throw oneself over the side – a hazardous venture, particularly if one was laden with kit. Each LCI (S) could accommodate a full troop, and at a pinch a Commando was fitted into six vessels – one 'fighting' troop in each of five, and the HQ in the sixth. The heavy weapons troop was distributed between the others – an awkward arrangement at first sight, but one that ensured all the support weapons would not be lost in one go.

During the run-in, the experiences of the Commandos were virtually indistinguishable from those of thousands of other Allied servicemen. Corporal Andrews of 47 RM Commando found his journey uneventful until within a few hundred yards of the shore:

> then it was clear they did not want us to land, and the shells started to come down with great accuracy, many hitting the water with instant explosions. Captain O'Hare was in the front of the craft by the ramp, and kept saying 'Piece of cake. Piece of cake.' We bumped, then the ramp went down, we all got ashore without getting our feet wet really, due to the consideration of the Coxwain.

With the same unit, J. B. Wetjen had an opportunity to shave 'indifferently' – but found that the 'pitching and tossing' disagreed with an earlier breakfast of fried eggs and bread, bacon and tea. Major Flunder of 48 RM Commando described conditions aboard his wooden Landing Craft Infantry (Small) as 'abominable' – an experience more like bouncing on the water rather than floating on it. Commander Kieffer saw a shell tear off the ramp off a Commando landing craft in 'a scream of metal and wood' – but the survivors knew that to stay still was a greater peril than to move, and immediately jumped into 6 feet of water. Bryan Samian,

Intelligence Officer of No. 45 RM Commando, left a graphic impression of the landing on 'Queen' beach:

> Everyone looked to their weapons and ammunition, to their rifles and Tommy guns, to the bombs on their belts, and the fighting knives strapped to their hips. We checked our rucksacks, too, those heavy packs which held everything we needed to fight for three days without supplies from anyone, and which totalled up to eighty pounds in weight [...] The bottoms of our craft scraped ominously over treacherous underwater obstacles of wire and concrete as we covered the last 50 yards. Suddenly a German battery of antitank guns opened up on us from a flank. Through the haze of thick smoke and the deafening roar of the battery – firing at almost point blank range – someone was trying to shout orders. Men were scrambling furiously to obey, but no sooner had they leapt to their feet than they seemed to crumple visibly, fumbling with dazed, frightened hands for tender wounds. There was a thunderous splash as the craft beached on the edge of the wreckage-filled water, in most cases still with 4 or 5 feet of water forward.

For Harry Timmins of 48 RM Commando the most impressive thing was the sound:

> As we got nearer the beach the noise was more than you could possibly imagine. There were explosions all around us in the sea and the shells and mortars were kicking up sand all over the beach. A couple of buildings were on fire and, to add the tumult, the Oerlikon guns on our boat also joined in the barrage and deafened us. As we were getting closer, I was looking at the boat alongside when a shell hit it, falling among the lads who were waiting to get off. I saw one fellow completely cut in half, his waist and legs went one way in to the sea and the top half followed an instant later.

In theory, Commandos usually disembarked from landing craft in the following manner. Within the craft were three columns of men, and to get through an exit, or down a plank, the centre column ran off first, then the left, finally the right. The snake-like file then moved as rapidly as possible to a predetermined point, deploying on the way or on arrival.

Where landings were unopposed, or circumstances allowed, this was adhered to, but on D-Day this was often not the case. Lord Lovat's Piper,

Bill Millin, simply jumped into the sea – to suffer the indignity of his kilt billowing up and the shock of cold water. Samian saw the men of 45 Commando 'pile out' – a 'desperate collection of men in green berets, white teeth grinning viciously across blackened faces. Holding their precious weapons high above their heads' as they waded ashore, before running, 'boots squelching' with sea water and uniforms sodden under heavy rucksacks, up the beach. Not all were so lucky. As the official post-war *Battle Summary* put it:

> No. 47 Commando landed on 'Jig' sector at 0930 and in doing so lost all but two of their LCA and much equipment including all their wireless sets. This did not deter them from achieving their object – the capture of Port en Bessin – but all contact was lost with them till the afternoon of the following day.

This was true, but the full picture was much more complex. The Commando had arrived off the correct area of beach to find it still under fire, and one landing craft was promptly hit by a shell and sunk. The main body was therefore turned to the east, to land in a rather scattered manner over a mile of the strand. No less than four landing craft hit beach obstacles with mines attached, and seven suffered other damage. Such was the confusion where 47 RM Commando landed, near Le Hamel, that the commanding officer lost contact with his men. Major O'Donnell was therefore forced to gather 'the very disorganised unit together, under fire', and bring it to the prearranged rendezvous just east of Buhot. At this point five officers and seventy-three other ranks were missing. Of the Troops, 'B' was almost unscathed but 'Q' was at half strength; 'A' had few missing but had lost most of its weapons. Eventually, the mortars would be recovered but without their sights, at least one of which was lost when the landing craft was hit and the man holding it had to jump out into 8 feet of water. In Troops 'X' and 'Y' most of the men were in tolerable shape, though the officers of the latter were hard hit.

Nevertheless, much delayed, 47 RM Commando set off for its objective, some of its men rearming themselves with enemy weapons dropped around the beach. As they made their way to La Rosière they repeatedly came under sporadic fire, suffering further casualties. Eventually they dug in for the night, but were disturbed more than once by patrols. The following day the attack on Port en Bessin took the form of a set-piece action, commencing with Naval bombardment and attack by

Typhoon aircraft, plus artillery fire. Medical Officer John Forfar was with 47 RM Commando:

> The defensive position on the Bayeux road was quickly charged and overcome and its occupants captured. One troop was then detailed to attack the Western Feature. As the Marines moved up the open slope of the Feature, rifle and machinegun fire was directed at them and grenades thrown down on them. The slope was also mined and had hidden flamethrowers. Using their fieldcraft to good effect, the Marines had advanced more than halfway up the slope when disaster struck. The intelligence given to the Commando was that the harbour was empty of any armed ships, but just before D-Day, unknown to the Commando, two FLAK [ships] had moved into the harbour. They had a direct view of the Marines on the slope. Opening fire they killed twelve and wounded seventeen – more than half the Troop within a few minutes. The Troop had to withdraw.

Even so, the Commandos kept trying – and the enemy kept counter-attacking, at one point forcing their way across the Escurès to Port en Bessin road, isolating the men defending Escurès. Worse, the Commando HQ was overrun, taking casualties. Eventually, however, the Marines began to gain the upper hand, painstakingly working their way around the harbour, taking one building at a time. Finally, Captain Cousins led an assault on the Eastern Feature, leading a group of about thirty Commandos, and assisted by some covering fire from a machine gun. A mortar, which still continued to function, if less accurately without its sight, attempted to cover the attacking Commandos with smoke – a worthy action that was prematurely terminated by lack of ammunition. The Captain rushed one of the concrete bunkers with a handful of men only to be killed by a grenade, but the remainder continued to climb, gaining the top before the evening was out. As Fred Wildman would later recall:

> the Germans had had enough and started to surrender. 'Q' Troop wheeled to the right on reaching the ridge top and charged along the top firing from the hip, and very soon began taking prisoners. It was by now about 23.00 and the Eastern Feature was effectively ours.

The Western Feature was finally conquered a day later, by which time 47 RM Commando had sustained 116 casualties, forty-eight of which were fatalities. Port en Bessin was now open, and would soon become the French terminal of PLUTO – the 'Pipe Line Under the Ocean' supplying fuel to the invasion forces. Brave and undoubtedly remarkable as the capture of the little port had been, it was far more a work of extreme tenacity, and well-rehearsed infantry skills, than anything resembling Special Forces tactics.

No. 48 RM Commando also had an extraordinarily difficult time coming in on their 'Landing Craft Infantry' in the wake of the Canadians. Disembarking via gangplanks under fire required considerable agility and there were many mishaps. Two craft hit obstacles and tore holes in their hulls. To make matters worse, some of the troops were landed almost directly in front of fortifications not yet suppressed. Given the noise of shelling, the Commanding Officer did not realise they were under fire 'until I saw two men collapse and fall over the starboard side. By then it was too late to beat a retreat, and I later found three bullet holes in my map case.' Hurrying onto the treacherous wooden plank, Moulton mistimed a wave, which overthrew him and rolled him in the surf, costing him much of his equipment but leaving him clutching his walking stick. Looking back from the beach, a man of the North Shore regiment saw Commandos hit by machine-gun fire fall 'overboard as though they were a row of wheat sheaves tumbling into the water. Those men who had not been hit jumped into the water to swim ashore.' Troop Sergeant Major Travers also fell off a ramp and was dragged right to the bottom by his heavy rucksack, but fortunately was bobbed up again, face upward, by dint of his properly inflated and adjusted life belt. Two officers of 'Z' Troop were drowned, as was Lieutenant Yates of 'Y' Troop. In 'B' Troop Marine Cusack was hit even as he stood waiting to lower the gangplank, and knocked back into the well of the landing craft.

Perhaps those who had the most difficult exit were the most heavily laden: despatch rider Marine Mathieson attempted to get his motorbike down the gangplank but it was hit, and both man and machine fell into the water. Others struggled with wireless sets and mortar bombs. Douglas Gray of 'B' Troop came down the ramp,

> with a full pack on my back, spare bags, ammunition, grenades, a rifle in one hand and a Bangalore Torpedo in the other [...] When I got off the ramp and into the water it came almost up to my neck. I was immediately hit by the strong undertow, which nearly swept me off my feet. The Bangalore Torpedo was wrenched from my hand, but I hung on tightly to my rifle. I managed to get a good grip with my feet and

struggled up the beach, but many others round me were in real trouble. Once they had gone over in the water it was a hell of a job for them to get back on their feet with the heavy packs on their backs.

Sergeant Ian Mair of 'S' Troop was attempting to carry three mortar bombs, as well as rifle and equipment, when a shell landed nearby and wounded him. He would be left at the top of the beach for the rest of the day before being evacuated.

James L. Moulton

James L. Moulton (1906–1993) joined the Marines in 1924 and first served on the battleship HMS *Rodney*, but moved to the Fleet Air Arm in 1930. As a flying officer he flew in both the Mediterranean and the China seas, before going on to staff college in 1938. Appointed to the headquarters of the British Expeditionary Force, he was evacuated from Dunkirk in 1940. Under Major General Robert Sturges, he took part in both the seizure of Diego Suarez and the subsequent occupation of Madagascar. In 1944 Lieutenant Colonel Moulton was appointed to command the new No. 48 Royal Marine Commando, which took considerable exertions to get ready for D-Day. Even more skill was required to get the unit off 'Juno' beach: Moulton was awarded a Distinguished Service Order. After Normandy, Moulton led 48 Commando through France and Belgium, and in the Walcheren operation. In March 1945 he took over 4th Commando Brigade. After the war, Moulton commanded first the Small Arms School at Browndown, and then the Commando School at Bickleigh. In 1952 he took command of 3rd Commando Brigade in Malta, and two years later was promoted to Major General. He campaigned extensively for the retention of a significant amphibious ability, and was appointed Chief of Amphibious Operations in 1957. Some of the vessels whose construction he sponsored in the early 1960s were still active in the 1982 Falklands War. In retirement, Moulton was an active writer and historian, and served on the Council of the Royal United Services Institution from 1964 to 1971. He was Colonel Commandant, Royal Marines, from 1969 to 1972. His papers are preserved at the Churchill Archives Centre.

As the Canadians were temporarily blocked, the beach was getting so crowded that a couple of tanks – coming up in support and battened down against enemy fire – actually ran over some of the wounded. Next, 48's Commanding Officer was injured by a mortar bomb – although he was able to continue and to take stock of the situation. The main problem was that, long after the initial landings, enemy strongpoint (*Widerstandnest*) 27 remained operative, and other weapons were still able to sweep the landing ground. It was later discovered that this position contained a 50mm gun, seven machine guns, mortars and trenches, within a mined and wired enclosure, the whole being set at an angle, so as to enfilade the shore. For a while, most of the Commandos were pinned on the beach, sheltering behind the sea wall with Canadians and Naval personnel who had survived the first wave. Some, like Lance Corporal Appleyard, tried to return fire – but to see enemy positions meant exposure. Appleyard was shot through the head by a sniper. In all, the 'disaster' of St Aubin accounted for almost a third of the Commando, including wounded and missing, though a virtually complete troop were rescued when their craft began to sink and were taken back to the UK on a vessel already bound for home. Particularly problematic was the plight of the heavy weapons troop, temporarily reduced to a single mortar – and Marine Thornton, who did his best to gather ammunition for the piece. Understandably, it took a while before the unit could be rallied and headed off the beach exit headed for Langrune-sur-Mer, being sniped as they went.

Just a couple of hundred yards off the beach the Commando gained the assembly point, and from there headed east along the road behind St Aubin, joined, happily, by their attached Royal Artillery 'forward observer', and jeeps that had come ashore from an LCT. On the way, Mike Reynolds, commander of 'A' Troop, was discovered to be badly wounded and had lost the use of both arms, despite which he had been continuing with his men until ordered to the rear. As they neared the rear of Langrune, enemy opposition stiffened, the Commando having to work its way around another machine-gun post with 'B' and 'X' Troops leapfrogging each other as they advanced. Strongpoint 26 on the sea front was well fortified with mines and wire, and though the approach was from the rear, it was discovered that a whole block of houses had been incorporated into this mini fortress, with windows bricked up and machine guns and wire protecting the perimeter.

The two leading troops took parallel streets to move in against either end of the strongpoint. Then the fighting degenerated into a bloody attempt at village clearance, as Lieutenant Colonel Moulton recorded:

On the far side and inland side of Langrune we found the strong old walled farmhouse and garden, which I had selected from the air photographs to hold as a firm base for our house clearing operations. I ordered 'Z' Troop to organise its defence and 'X' Troop to start their sector of house clearing [...] Apart from this 'B' and 'X' Troops had met with nothing but snipers and patrols, which then withdrew before their advance.

As 'X' Troop prepared to attack, its leader, Captain Perry, was killed by a sniper: immediately afterwards two of its sergeants were wounded by a mortar bomb. Fortuitously, a pair of Centaur tanks now appeared on the scene and were able to offer 'B' Troop assistance to get forward. The additional firepower worked well for a while, but one of the vehicles hit a mine and was immobilised, blocking the road.

A handful of 'B' Troop, led by Lieutenant Rubenstein, now dashed across the road to plant an improvised charge that went off with a satisfying bang but failed to penetrate the strongpoint, which had been reinforced with concrete. Whilst sheltering behind a wall, the Commandos were showered with stick grenades, only avoiding them at extreme peril, before running back. As Rubenstein recalled:

By then my section and I were immediately under the wall and the Jerries behind the wall were slinging over stick grenades. They were not very effective for they seemed to be made out of thin metal like cocoa tins. They were, however, tying them in bunches to make them more deadly. One bunch landed behind me and one of my section yelled out [...] I turned my back on it in a natural reaction and it went off, spattering me and one of my men with shrapnel. The amount of blood on my tunic led me to believe that I had a bad wound. We were by now in serious difficulties ...

Clearly, Langrune was not going to be taken in short order, and 48 RM Commando was enervating itself in the attempt. Five of six troop commanders, and roughly two-thirds of all the officers, were now *hors de combat*; the whole unit was at half strength, and there were reports that enemy armour was closing on the beachhead. Brigadier Leicester ordered a halt for the night and a 'defensive posture', until more tanks could come up to help the following morning.

Though some elements of 192 Grenadier Regiment did get as far as the coast, luckily nothing actually got within striking distance of 48 RM

Commando during the night, and with the arrival of two M10 tank destroyers and a Sherman, it proved possible to take the offensive again, with the armour battering the village in earnest. As Lieutenant Colonel Moulton recalled:

> The Brigadier came up and confirmed that we were free from threat of counter-attack and that our job was to finish off the strongpoint. I realised our duty, both to the military world at large and to our own self respect, to capture it ourselves and not to leave it to someone else; it would make a great deal of difference to the Commando's future morale to finish the job – and we all, by now, had a personal score to settle. But then weakness: the strongpoint was beginning to seem impregnable; and it would be nice to stop and lick our wounds, without the prospect of more casualties, more danger and perhaps more failure. Jumbo Leicester's matter of fact order was just what I needed.

Now 'A' Troop of 48 RM Commando went forward, using its remaining Bangalores in order to explode gaps in the minefield. Some of the men quickly occupied houses, and used their weapons to cover the open space created for the advance of an M10.

In this way the attack leapfrogged forward, the small arms of the Commandos being used as a guard against German antitank teams, whilst the tank destroyer was able to use its heavy armament on the strongpoint. It appeared improvised but was, in fact, a known tactic, as US training literature of 1944 explained:

> Tanks assist the attack of infantry by destroying or neutralising hostile automatic weapons, reserves, counter-attacking troops, artillery [...] Infantry assists tanks by destroying or neutralising hostile antitank weapons, and tank hunting teams, locating and removing mines and other obstacles, seizing ground from which tanks may attack, locating defiladed routes of advance for tanks, or taking over an objective which tanks have captured or are dominating.

At 13.30 the final attack went in, with the Commandos blowing holes in the walls of the houses, and where necessary enlarging apertures with pick and shovel. Eventually, the Sherman burst its way over the last antitank barrier, and Commandos who had been advancing in its wake were able to spread out, lobbing grenades into houses and firing into trenches. A total of thirty-one German defenders survived to surrender.

No. 41 RM Commando had a bitter experience at Lion-sur-Mer from the start – and would get nowhere near completing their first day's objectives. Trouble began even before landing because the craft came ashore a couple of hundred yards west of the appointed spot – where the beach was still unsecured and swept by fire. As Company Sergeant Major Tilney recalled:

> I remember a line of detached houses, seen through smoke, two or three tanks burning, troops on the beach, and some bodies in the water. There was a lot of shelling and machinegun fire, not aimed specifically against our craft, but a nasty pause before we got off the ship, and I had to wade a bit. I have vivid memories of the burning tanks, and many of the assault battalions were still on the beach. We lost quite a few men on the beach. I remember standing up because I thought I was just as good a target lying down …

Remarkably, and despite some early casualties, many of the Commandos were able to clear the beach and get over the sea wall, aided by tanks. One of these was driven by N. D. Marshall:

> the Troop Lieutenant gave a troop order for individual rapid fire at our own selected targets. Within five minutes of sustained 75mm HE fire the situation was well under control, and with the advancing Commandos firing from the hip, white flags soon started to flutter.

The twin attacks were now put into action. The first, against the strongpoint, was anti-climatic, as it was completely deserted. The second, aimed at an enemy-occupied château, found it so strongly defended that three officers were killed in the assault, which failed, and the building had to be left for subsequent waves. It was 'Y' Troop that bore the brunt, according to Troop Sergeant Major Fawcett, progress being abruptly arrested by a shower of mortar bombs, and enemy, in numbers, ensconced in houses, overlooking the route:

> The Bren gunners of the sub section on the left of the road were killed instantly, and several others were badly wounded, including one from [...] troop HQ, which was ahead of and on the right of the stricken section. Meanwhile captain Howes-Dufton at the head of the leading section pushed on undaunted, but regrettably was killed by machinegun fire during the attack on an enemy strongpoint.

Again, the battle tended to become a deliberate slogging match. As Captain T. M. P. Stevens, who won an MC during the action, observed, they had run into 'a lot of Germans', including a halftrack, on the main street, and were forced onto the defensive:

> In street fighting it is extremely difficult to see what is going on. I got separated from the rest of the troop with about seven others. The Germans tried a rush, with one running down the centre of the road firing a Schmeisser. I shot at him and so did the rest [...] he fell in the road outside and died. We withdrew for a while then came back, getting close to the half track which was still firing. I threw a grenade into it, then beat it back into cover as fast as I could.

As a result of the severe resistance encountered, and threat of enemy armour interposing between beaches, 41 RM Commando did not get to the Douvres radar station, nor indeed did anybody, until 17 June. In fact, the site was bypassed and finally taken by Commandos acting in concert with 26th Royal Engineers Assault Squadron, when flail tanks were used to clear the minefield and heavy charges used to blow in its bunkers.

It was 7 June when No. 46 RM Commando, under Lieutenant Colonel Campbell Hardy, were finally landed on 'Juno', and by this time their actions bore no relation to the original plan, which had been that they would be deployed against batteries east of the Orne. For, in fact, they now attacked the strongpoint at Petit Enfer, and managed to secure sixty-five prisoners. They were then put under the command of 3rd Canadian Division and took part in the clearance of the valley of the Mue. In an attack described as 'wearing their enemy down', they fought alongside French Canadians supported by tanks and artillery for the villages of Rots and Le Hamel. At the latter, the Commando lost fifty killed, wounded and missing, in a hard battle. Major General Keller was delighted with their performance nonetheless, writing his warm congratulations to Jumbo Leicester – but observing that the Commandos left behind 122 of the enemy for his men to bury.

As we have seen, 45 RM Commando came ashore at La Beche on 'Sword' beach as part of Lovat's 1st Special Service Brigade, and being two hours behind the first wave, had a better experience on the beach than some. It was also the case that No. 6 Commando had managed to knock out some enemy positions before the arrival of the Marine Commandos. Nevertheless, two of the unit's landing craft were hit by shells, and the troops still had to wade the last few yards before doubling up the beach as best they were able, towards the rallying point at a wood, half a mile inland. There were some casualties, and the moaning of enemy *Nebelwerfer* rocket launchers was heard and projectiles exploded nearby – but luckily these did not hit the Commando:

> We sorted ourselves out into single file, to become a long winding snake of men, each of us carrying heavy equipment of some sort or another. Some trudged with mortars or PIATs on their backs, others carried stretchers and extra heavy medical rucksacks. A few men even pushed bicycles. Of all things to go to war with, perhaps a bicycle was the worst.

Amongst other impedimenta were small dinghies, carried against the possibility that the bridges over the Orne might have been blown by the enemy.

With brief pauses to avoid enemy shelling and mortars, No. 45 made pretty good progress, crossing the bridges at about 1 p.m. – but not without incident, as there was still harassing fire from machine guns and some particularly accurate sniper fire. One of the victims was the commanding officer, Lieutenant Colonel Ries, who was disabled by a shot to the leg. From the crossing point, 45 RM Commando was directed on towards the Merville Battery. They passed through Sallenelles without incident but, emerging on the far side, were amazed to see Germans running across the road a few hundred yards ahead of them:

> Both the enemy and ourselves seemed to see each other at precisely the same time, opening fire with everything; but the former had the advantage. They had the road well and truly covered with numerous machineguns, making all movement impossible. As a result Major Grey's headquarter party [...] was completely 'pinned down' in a ditch at the side of the road, unable either to advance or retire. After twenty minutes Major Grey finally decided to make a run for it, and rejoin the rest of the unit hidden in Sallenelles. All those of his party who could move without being unduly exposed were ordered to crawl along the ditch leading to the village.

This check forced the commencement of a circuitous attack, so while the mortars fired on enemy positions the Commando skirted round the opposition to manoeuvre into place for an assault on the battery. No sooner had they arrived on some fairly open ground, however, than the battery began to fire upon them. An order was soon received from the brigade commander not to launch a potentially suicidal assault, but to take and consolidate on Merville village, which was to be held for the night. This was duly achieved, but not without resistance, since the village was still occupied by some of the enemy, who attempted to conceal themselves, and had to be 'winkled out' from the 'oddest places'. HQ was established in a pair of cottages and the men then quickly dug slit trenches. The day had cost the Commando twenty killed and wounded, but a further twenty-nine were still missing.

For 45 RM Commando, action on 7 June began early as, at 3 a.m., orders were received to abandon Merville and fall back on Le Plein, only held the previous day with the greatest of difficulty. The route took them back through Sallenelles, and since there was a danger the enemy had managed to reoccupy the village, it had to be cleared systematically, with the Commandos fanning out in two columns either side of the road, going cautiously from door to door. At Le Plein, the Commando dug in again and some of the missing who had been held up by contacts now managed to rejoin the ranks. A new plan was now hatched, by means of which 45 RM Commando would take Franceville-Plage by set-piece attack, whilst No. 3 Commando dealt with Merville Battery. Preparations for the attack began under desultory enemy mortar fire, although, on the plus side, jeeps bearing fresh ammunition and other supplies arrived, and on their return trip to the beaches, were able to ferry away the wounded. Sadly, one of the jeeps was hit and exploded, and two men carrying mortar barrels were also killed.

With an area of flat ground ahead of them, the Commando attack on Franceville-Plage had to be something of a set piece, with two troops advancing under covering fire from a third. One of the troops then cleared a wood near the village, which was found to be full of slit trenches, dugouts and other defences. Most were empty but some Germans had to be dealt with using grenades. With the preliminaries complete, two troops entered the village, one advancing down either side of 'Piccadilly', as the main street became known. Efforts were aided by a forward observer, who took post in a tree and was able to direct Naval gunfire. The most serious problem was a pillbox dominating the street. With the Commando stopped in its tracks and falling into cover, Major Beadle decided to go forward and silence the obstruction with three men and the PIAT. The enemy immediately opened fire with mortars and machine guns and one man was killed, another wounded. 'A minor battle commenced almost immediately, with everyone on both sides blazing away at each other furiously.' During this action, Major Grey attempted to bring his HQ forward, but was quickly fired on by an antitank gun, which killed the RSM and a corporal.

As this unfolded, other German positions – hitherto silent – opened fire and the action was continued only by the Commandos 'leapfrogging' from house to house against a determined enemy. As Fred Harris recalled, it was 'chaotic', with enemy fire apparently coming from everywhere. At one point Private Arnold, on attachment from No. 10 Commando, attempted to bluff the enemy into surrender, telling them that they were massively outnumbered. This did not work, however, and things went from bad to worse as more enemy reinforcements arrived and began to attempt to force 45 RM Commando out of the village and onto the beach. Here they would have been back in the open, and very probably under the guns of other, as yet untackled, defences. Major Grey had no option but to order a fighting retreat, back up Piccadilly: this was accomplished, essentially by placing holding parties giving covering fire for the remainder as they made their escape.

By nightfall, the Commando had dug in on a sandy knoll outside the village, but this position was precarious so, under cover of darkness, they withdrew again on Merville, where a much-reduced unit, again low on ammunition, was able to form a more solid defensive perimeter. Here they would be attacked the following day, with the enemy coming in from two separate directions, and getting so close that Major Grey was able to shoot both members of a machine-gun team with his pistol. By this time it was reckoned that roughly a quarter of the Commando had become casualties. Nevertheless, there would be no respite throughout the afternoon:

> They mortared our positions and sniped us continually. Just before three o'clock a small party of the enemy succeeded in working their way into Merville from the east bringing up extra machinegun teams and snipers. However two Sergeants attached to us from 10 Commando – Sergeants Shelley and Stewart – put a stop to this ruse. Unknown to the enemy, they succeeded in crawling up to the side of a barn, on the other side of which the newly arrived party of Germans was setting up a machinegun post, and lobbed grenades over the roof. These fell right amongst them, wounding two (who were captured) and putting the remainder to flight.

There would be a third attack before the Commando was driven out of Merville and back on Le Plein – a tricky manoeuvre covered by fire from the fleet. By the end of 8 June, total losses to the Commando were 184 killed, wounded and missing.

Like 45 RM Commando, No. 3 Commando was in the second wave of the 1st Brigade attack. Even so, it came under fire about 1,000 yards from shore and three of its craft were hit. In the 6 Troop boat, mortar bombs were detonated by the primary explosion, causing devastating damage. Another ran aground onto a false beach some way out, and troops dropped off into neck-deep water: everybody was subjected to sporadic mortar fire. Nevertheless, casualties were not as bad as might have been expected, and only No. 6 Troop was seriously damaged with more than twenty out of action. The Commandos succeeded in picking their way through or around wire and obstacles, and having first assembled between some houses and the road, headed off to the rendezvous 1,000 yards inland. Progress was not particularly swift, as the way was impeded by a minefield through which they had to pass in single file, using this track in the wake of No. 6 Commando. On the way to Bénouville, they broke into the double, intending to make up lost time, having already sent their cycle troop ahead. Contact was made with the Airborne near to the River Orne, where it was discovered that the parachutists were more widely spread than anticipated, and the plan was altered so that No. 3 Commando would secure Bas de Ranville and Le Plein instead of going on to Cabourg.

Lord Lovat soon arrived on a bicycle and promptly ordered No. 3 Troop to attack Amfreville without delay, led by two officers, but this move met with concentrated fire – as was reported by Lieutenant Colonel Young:

> At once Westly was hit in the arm; Abbott, who had been my Bren gunner at Dieppe and Agnone, and two other men were wounded. Sergeant Hill, Troopers Osborne, Barnes and Jennings returned the fire and the casualties got away. As they withdrew a bullet made a neat parting down the Sergeant's scalp!

Having got some idea of where the enemy were, the troop was reorganised and a covered approach located. Then, using one of the sections and the 2-inch mortars to give some low-angle covering fire, the Commandos attacked again and succeeded in seizing the school, which was a key feature of the village. With the arrival of No. 6 Commando at the southern end, the position was consolidated and posts established on the enemy side. Though there was shelling, the position was held, and in the evening more gliders arrived and the Commando was relieved by infantry.

The next afternoon two troops were used to attack Merville Battery in support of the 45 RM Commando action at Franceville Plage. This detachment had discovered that their path was blocked by a minefield, but rather than fail in their task, No. 4 Troop gave covering fire whilst No. 5 went straight through – luckily suffering only three casualties in the process. However, the few Germans still around the battery put up a fight, and soon after the main resistance had ceased, Major John Pooley was killed. As Young recalled:

There had been a few shots, but all serious fighting seemed to be at an end. However in one of the heavily concreted gun positions one lone German with a Spandau had hung on, and when John was a few yards from him he had opened fire. I found Alan Pollock, a small dark young Subaltern of 5 Troop, attacking this position on his own, a Gammon bomb in his hand. Angry and distressed, as we all were, at the death of John, he was exposing himself fearlessly. Getting up close to the gun, he hurled his bomb. Still uncertain whether the defender was dead, some of us got on top of the grass covered casemate and dropped Mills bombs down the air vent.

Unfortunately, the weakened detachment now found itself isolated and vulnerable to counter-attack. This fact was tragically illustrated when a fighting reconnaissance patrol ran into trouble and the enemy brought up two self-propelled guns. Under heavy fire, the remains of 4 and 5 Troops withdrew, some of their wounded falling prisoner. In Young's opinion the whole episode had been doomed from the start – no explosives had been to hand for the destruction of the guns in the battery, and in any case there was no direct evidence that they were still in working order: 'Not since Dieppe had the Commando met with such a misfortune.' Back at Amfreville, No. 3 and No. 6 Commandos formed a defensive line, digging two-man weapons pits at roughly 15-yard intervals. This position, on high ground the Germans might have used as an observation point to overlook the landings, was held for several days in the face of counter-attacks.

When No. 6 Commando came ashore from their LCIs at about 8.40, there were still plenty of enemy-occupied fortifications in their path. Nevertheless, most got out of the landing craft fairly cleanly, with Captain Robinson's bicycle troop, for example, wading through knee-deep water, carrying their machines. The inexperienced Sidney Dann described the scene:

We were on the starboard ramp and Colonel Mills-Roberts and half of
the HQ section were on the port ramp. The beach was covered in
smoke with mortar bombs and 88mm shells dropping in. From a
concrete blockhouse an MG 34 was spraying the area and buzzing
noises were zipping past. Burning tanks, flails and other weird
armoured vehicles lay at all angles [...] Most of us had never seen a
dead body before, so it was somewhat of a shock to see bodies floating
in the water and others, minus head, limbs, etc., lying on the beach.

The defence had been systematically organised, as Lord Lovat explained:

Each Pillbox was a citadel of reinforced concrete, sunk hull down and
half buried in the ridges of the dunes. Walls 2 feet thick stood 6 feet
above ground level, their height made up by a very solid roof giving
further feet of concrete head cover. They were certainly bomb – if not
blast – proof and made equivalent precautions at home appear
inadequate. Positions sited in depth, 100 to 150 yards apart, were
surrounded with barbed wire, with minefields in between. No Pillbox
faced directly to the front but each was at an angle to either side, sited
to enfilade the wire and deal effectively with approach from the flanks.
Each was manned by a crew of half a dozen men firing 75mm cannon
and light automatics.

Lance Corporal C. Morris, a Bren gunner of 6 Commando, jumped into
waist-deep water on landing but got up the beach unscathed. Soon he was
into the thick of the action against pillboxes, the drills for which had been
practised at length by individual teams:

The box I was on was listed as number one and the attack on it was to
be led by the skipper, Captain Pyman and the Sergeant Major, Lofty
Ray. Method of attack was, position the Bren on a ridge 100 yards from
the box, then open up with rapid but careful fire endeavouring to shoot
through the slits in the concrete, then whilst our Bren section was
drawing the fire and attention the PIAT [Projector Infantry Anti Tank]
men and assault section would start creeping forward till they were in
position to blast the box with the PIAT then the assault section would
rush in and kill them off. If they got pinned down by heavy fire, the
Bren group would charge the box keeping up heavy fire, thereby
switching the fire from the other group and enabling them to get

moving again. Each box was timed to be wiped out at the same time, and by now the rest of the Commando would have spread out and be preparing to pass through this area.

The technique was a classic straight out of *Infantry Training* 1944: such was the theory – reality was more difficult.

The assault team reached the ridge, and a couple of men began to snipe at the pillbox, with the Bren initially silent so as not to divulge its position. A Commando called Adams raised his head over the ridge and promptly fell back – shot through the neck. Next, Morris attempted to open fire but found the Bren still waterlogged: he and a comrade then had to strip the gun under the curses of his comrades. Under cover of the rifles alone, the Captain and Sergeant Major began to creep closer to the box. Perhaps realising the threat the Germans chose this moment to make a run for it: 'so we whipped our Bren round and started giving it to them as they made a dash for it'. Three prisoners and a 'bomb happy' dog were secured.

The delays were minor and the Commando was able to press on across marshland. At the outskirts of Bénouville, the cycle troop was in the lead, and alone at their head was Lance Corporal Masters, a German speaker on attachment from 10 Commando. At this point he felt he was essentially a stooge – to draw enemy fire – and thereby reveal the positions of the enemy to the rest of the troops. Advancing beside a hedge, he called on the enemy to surrender:

A man popped up from behind the parapet and shot at me with a Schmeisser. He missed because he fired too quickly and perhaps he was a bad shot anyway. I didn't see where the bullets went but assumed they went right high because that's how a Schmeisser fires. Then he ducked back and as he ducked I went down on one knee and fired. My Tommy gun fired one round and jammed [...] But then I heard a noise behind me and saw the rest of the Troop charging down the road with fixed bayonets. One of them was firing a Bren from the shoulder – most unusual – and it was he who shot the machinegunners, who had retreated a little way down the Ouistreham road. Then some of our tanks turned up and put some shells into the village.

Luckily, casualties were not high on the beaches and surrounding area, and No. 6 was soon able to reach the Orne, where, not long after the appointed time, they were able to link with the paratroops. Lord Lovat recorded that he ran across the canal bridge,

> with piper Millin and a handful of fighting men. There was a fair amount of mortaring and a machinegun up the water pinging bullets off the steel struts, but no one noticed and brave fellows from the gliders were cheering from their fox holes at the other end.

Nevertheless, stiff opposition had greeted No. 6 Commando at Bénouville, where 3 Troop in particular were heavily hit by artillery and mortars, suffering about twenty casualties. By now, all Troops had taken losses. Also down were Major Coade, the second-in-command, and Captain Pyman, who had been hit by machine-gun fire whilst attempting to identify nearby troops. So it was that the leading element was pulled back, carrying its wounded, plus a captured machine gun, and dug in around Saulnier's Farm at Le Plein. Here they took part in the defence against German counter-attacks, which came to a crescendo on the night of 9 and 10 June.

The bulk of 4 Commando came ashore from small assault landing craft – but the two French troops, seconded from 10 Commando, made do with two of the larger LCI, with all the usual difficulties attendant on getting off them. One smashed through the obstacle belt and beached, the other suffered a hit that damaged its gangplanks, forcing the Commandos to resort to scaling nets to get them down its sides. In theory, the enemy should already have been neutralised: in fact, the Germans were still extremely lively and the landing ground was littered with dead and wounded, mainly of the East Yorkshires. Commandant Kieffer was soon injured in the leg by a mortar fragment, and one of the Troop commanders was put out of action. Others were killed or wounded.

Nevertheless, the Frenchmen were ordered briskly up the beach by Lieutenant Colonel Dawson, dumped their rucksacks as planned, and, with more than a third of their men missing, swung into the attack. Lofi's Troop was first into action against a blockhouse not far from the Casino, crossing a minefield, and taking several empty machine-gun nests *en route*:

> Bagot placed his section carefully for the assault. Hulot, with exemplary courage, rejoined the Troop despite his wound. I put him in reserve with Chausse's section on the left of the blockhouse but with

exemplary courage he managed to reach within grenade throwing distance of the trenches. Chausse, well installed on the left flank, opened fire with everything he had, but though it was effective – as were Hulot's grenades – the blockhouse remained intact.

Amazingly, Germans now appeared from the defences and attempted to surround the Commandos attacking them. The 'K' guns, which until now had been giving useful covering fire, both jammed and had to be withdrawn to be stripped and cleaned. The blockhouse would only be taken later, by follow-up troops.

In the meantime, the other French Troop had taken the lead into Ouistreham, then turned off to cross the little seaside suburb of Riva Bella to attack the main Casino strongpoint from the rear. Here they discovered their path blocked by a substantial antitank wall, but luckily the small gap through it was not consistently covered by fire and the Commandos managed to creep up to the passage by circuitous routes. They then rushed through, and dispersed quickly to either flank once inside the defensive perimeter. Then the Troop advanced down either side of the street with two Brens, four Tommy guns, and a flamethrower at the head of each column, intent on the strongpoint embrasures which were now little more than 40 yards away.

Now they were close, two PIAT teams were sent to the upper floor of a villa, taking with them four projectiles – all that could be managed, given depleted numbers of men and the amount of other equipment. Despite shortage of ammunition, the effect was devastating: the first two rounds, fired simultaneously, knocked out the anti-aircraft guns atop the strongpoint. The second two hit home on weapons embrasures, creating a disabling blast effect inside the bunker – leaving survivors momentarily senseless. The PIAT crews then quickly withdrew before other guns could be focused on their position. With the aid of a local man, the Commandos also located communication cables to the strongpoint, and these were soon severed. Nevertheless, some of the enemy were still shooting and Kieffer believed that he lacked the strength for all-out close assault, so hobbled off, soon to return on top of a Sherman tank that he had managed to commandeer to complete the attack. This proved decisive – shells from the tank finally silenced the defenders long enough to allow the Commandos to go in and mop up. A number of prisoners were taken. Kieffer would be awarded the Military Cross for the 'final liquidation' of enemy strongpoints. The French Troops would later move on with the rest of No. 4 Commando to Sallenelles and Le Plein, where they continued to do good service: but the cost was very high. Eventually, nine of the eleven French officers were casualties, and of the entire contingent of 177 only seventy remained four days after the landings.

Most of the rest of No. 4 Commando had managed to get up the beach in better style than the French, being able to pour off their small assault craft more quickly – 'sharpish' as one of them recalled – and move through the dunes to the assembly area. Nevertheless, there were quite a few casualties, and Lieutenant Colonel Dawson was wounded in the face, so command devolved to Major Menday. Captain Carr performed particularly valuable service by working his way through the wire and lobbing a grenade into a machine-gun post that might otherwise have held up movement off the beach and led to greater loss. This was all the more remarkable since Carr was a skinny character – nicknamed 'Muscles' by his teasing peers – but now Lord Lovat was of the opinion that, under other circumstances, he would have won a VC. Carr was modest about his achievement:

> As I moved across the beach I was hit three times, twice on my hand and wrist by small splinters and once on my rucksack, but not seriously. As I came up to the strongpoint a German soldier behind it threw two stick grenades into the air which exploded harmlessly behind me. He was immediately shot, and the strongpoint was captured.

The battery at Ouistreham was the main target of No. 4, and the *modus operandi* was again to offload rucksacks and advance the lead Troops under covering fire towards the rear of the target. The 'K' guns were then worked into good positions in buildings, from whence they could pour in close fire, allowing the Troops tasked with the actual assault to go in with maximum chance of success. Again, a passing tank was commandeered, and this lent considerable punch to the Commandos' efforts. The men advanced in bounds and were soon able to get snipers and PIATs close enough to play on the defenders. It was soon apparent, however, that the antitank ditch around the battery would be a serious obstacle, particularly since those Commandos responsible for bringing up ladders had already fallen casualty. It was therefore extremely lucky that the defenders had placed planks across the ditch for their own convenience of access, and had either forgotten, or been unable, to remove them before they were attacked.

Nevertheless, the concrete battery tower still seemed impervious to assault, and the defenders threw showers of grenades at anybody close enough. Eventually, Captain Porteous got his men across the ditch and into the weapons pits, which were protecting the gun emplacements proper. Having established themselves and taken several prisoners, they were now leapfrogged by Burt's and Coulson's Troops, which fought their way into the battery only to discover there were no heavy guns. The Germans had placed telegraph poles inside the emplacements, and withdrawn the actual weapons to a position much further back.

With this much accomplished, No. 4 set off to join the other Commandos of 1st Brigade across the Orne. With their jeeps not due to arrive until the following day, manpower was key to getting all the heavy equipment where it had to go. An exception was the mortars, as one of the team succeeded in commandeering a farm cart. Evidence of the progress of No. 6 Commando lay along the way in the form of dead bodies, British and German, beside the road. Compared to the resistance encountered by others, the passage of No. 4 Commando was relatively straightforward, at least until the bridge when Lieutenant Mercer-Wilson was sniped and killed. On reaching their defensive position around the château of Hauger, they dug in. This was accomplished with pick and shovel, many of the pits being of the normal two-man type described in *Infantry Training*. The 'K' guns were also dug in, to bolster the defence, and some of the outer walls of the château were loopholed for weapons. In text-book fashion, one man in each team was to remain awake, alert against possibility of attack, but that night no attack came.

Not until the night of D+2 did the counter-attacks begin in earnest, and it was then that the 'K' guns really came into their own. In the morning – and probably under cover of darkness – the enemy managed to creep close to the No. 4 Commando position, attempting to envelop it on three sides. It was then that everything that could be fired was unleashed. As Private W. Bidmead recalled:

> Taff Isherwood picked up his 'K' gun and emptied a full magazine into them [...] The rest of the Troop added their firepower. The screams and cries of the dying and wounded Germans on that June morning were terrible.

Yet, in return, the enemy continued to mortar and shell the position, and casualties gradually increased. Against this debilitating harassment the

Commandos began to use tactics that would not have appeared out of place in 1915 – overhead cover for their pits and trenches, and a whistle to be blown whenever the telltale sound of mortar bombs leaving the barrel of the weapon could be heard. No. 4 Commando would still be defending more or less the same location weeks later.

Few would be churlish enough to deny that the Commandos put up a characteristically brave and resourceful performance on D-Day, frequently tackling and subduing fortifications, batteries, and machine-gun posts that might otherwise have remained significant obstacles to the success of 'Overlord'. The way in which this was done – by manoeuvring around and behind defences using a flexible mix of small-unit tactics was exemplary. Individual acts of heroism were legion, and perhaps less than adequately reflected in the sixty-odd gallantry awards to Commandos in Normandy. Lovat was of the opinion that the landings were a 'soldier's battle' – confusion that favoured 'spirited assault'. However, this should not obscure the fact that a good number of the objectives were not achieved on the first day – and that casualties were significant.

Key to these specific failures was the order in which the invasion troops landed, with the Commandos behind, rather than in front of the first assault wave. This gave the enemy clear warning, in broad daylight, of what might be coming. They would have to be overcome more by force and persistence than by surprise. More than one commentator has observed that more might have been achieved if the special force had been deployed first, and possibly under cover of darkness. Nevertheless, this was not a simple error on the part of the planners, for the use of Commandos as part of a large invasion force posed problems that were not apparent in a raiding or small landing context. Had the Commandos been landed some hours in advance, like the parachutists, this would almost certainly have alerted the enemy to the main landing beaches more quickly, perhaps to the jeopardy of the main invasion. Landing the Commandos further away and marching them towards their targets might not have worked either, since the area was so densely occupied by the enemy, and a need for significant amounts of equipment had been foreseen. Moreover, it had already been decided, probably wisely, that several of the Commando targets would benefit from softening by air or Naval bombardment, which of itself would be a wake-up call to the enemy had he somehow missed other obvious signs of invasion. Quite possibly some of the objectives may simply have been over-ambitious, given the size of the Commandos and the strength of the opposition. Like everybody else, the special force dug in and defended its gains when this became necessary. So it was that the Commando brigades were used less like a swift rapier, than as a deliberately wielded can opener, often with the full panoply of support weapons, smoke, and even armour.

Chapter 8

Conclusion

The first Commandos were independent, usually clandestine, 'task forces' in miniature. More than once, official literature referred to this initial incarnation as 'Guerrilla'. Their job was to cause consternation here, destroy a dock facility or battery there, capture prisoners, assist in the gathering of intelligence, or delay the enemy in achieving one of his designs – and depart before retaliation by a superior force could do them serious damage. This activity stung and nibbled the enemy, and brought hope to the occupied. Thus they began as an improvised light striking force of the 'hit and run' variety, pioneered by the original Boer mounted Commando and the trench raiders of the Great War. Their tactics owed more to the conception of the underground force devised by Colonel Gubbins than that of the elite regular. At first, they lacked heavy weapons. In this form they were not, nor indeed intended to be, a force for pitched battle. As Gordon Holman put it, writing in early 1942:

> The Commando is not intended to engage in long drawn out operations. Speed is the watchword. Compact and mobile, its whole construction suggests rapier-like thrusts at the enemy with speed as one of its main defences [...] It is clear, however, that the tactics to achieve success must be to go in and come out at our own time. The Commandos operate not under the nose of the enemy but right inside his jaws. Having pulled a tooth here and there, there is no call for them to wait until the jaws shut. They are obviously constituted to deliver blows but not to trade blows with a foe who, as far as they are concerned, must always carry the knock-out – if they wait for it!

The early Commandos were supposed to strike terror into the enemy, be ruthless in their methods, encourage the British people with their exploits – judiciously manipulated for public consumption through the media – but, on the other hand, be soldiers in uniform entitled to proper treatment if captured. This was indeed a desperate force for the darkest hour of war, and a difficult path to tread.

As the Luftwaffe lost air superiority in the west, and later the Wehrmacht plunged east into Russia, the general situation gradually improved. The Commandos became – perhaps unwittingly at first – the experimental test bed of the 'Combined Operation', and by extension, the guinea pigs of the large-scale invasion. Metamorphosis was marked internally by new structures and new weapons, and later confirmed at the surface by the

---

Peter Young

Peter Young (1915–1988) was commissioned into the Bedfordshire and Hertfordshire Regiment and served in France in 1940, but volunteered for special service after evacuation from Dunkirk, becoming one of the founders of No. 3 Commando. His raiding career encompassed Guernsey, the Lofoten Islands, Vaagso (where he won his first Military Cross), and Dieppe, where his extraordinary persistence and 'gallant and distinguished service' won him a Distinguished Service Order. In 1943 he was at the forefront of the invasion of Sicily, where he gained the first bar to his MC, and it was for service in Italy that he was awarded a second. Young led No. 3 on D-Day, but in the autumn of 1944 was appointed second-in-command to 3rd Commando Brigade in Burma, where he was in the thick of the action against the Japanese at Kangaw in early 1945. In June of that year he returned to the UK, where he took over command of 1st Commando Brigade from Mills-Roberts. Young was instrumental in the erection of the Commando memorial at Westminster Abbey, unveiled by Winston Churchill in May 1948. Amongst his diverse post-war activities, Young commanded 9th Regiment of the Arab Legion, helped to establish the Department of War Studies at Sandhurst and the National Army Museum, and was founder of the Sealed Knot re-enactment society. Arguably the most scholarly of all the Commando leaders, Young wrote a book about his Arab Legion service, several on the English Civil War, a number of works of more general military history, and one of the best Commando memoirs, *Storm From the Sea*. He died in September 1988. The present author was honoured to be called upon to give one of his memorial lectures. Alison Michelli's biography, *Commando to Captain General*, was published in 2007.

departure of Admiral Keyes and the appointment of Lord Mountbatten. 'Lessons Learned' documents percolated from the Commando to the staffs, and subsequently informed not only D-Day but many other operations that were carried out by all arms of 'ordinary' troops. This change in direction of Commando tactics and purpose was inexorably linked with the change in the direction of the war – moving from a situation in which Britain was 'backs to the wall' and welcoming any opportunity to strike out against occupied Europe, to one in which her forces prepared to take part in permanent seizure of large swathes of territory, first in Africa, then Europe.

Arguably, 1942 and the 'end of the beginning' marked a watershed in the change of role between raiders who might be called upon to perform as highly-trained assault troops, and highly-trained assault troops who might, under special circumstances, perform as raiders. Other symbols of this period of change and increasing professionalism included the permanent establishment of the Achnacarry centre, and the first co-operative training with US forces. Unfortunately, the fateful year of 1942 included not only Alamein but Dieppe, which, perhaps, showed up more forcefully than any other engagement that a 'raid' and a 'reconnaissance in force' were very different beasts, and neither was much akin to a full-scale invasion of Europe. It was a clear signal to all concerned that much had to be rethought, and, successful as they might be, Commandos had to be prepared to take on new roles and skills.

In their later guise, the main Commando formations became more akin to elite assault infantry, capturing and holding beachheads, taking villages or parts of towns, seizing and maintaining strategic points. For this they needed more, and better, specialised equipment, transport and methods. They had to learn to co-operate more closely with other ground troops, and be prepared to operate for extended periods of time. The tactics and *raison d'être* of the Commando thus evolved as the war progressed, and as the Allies gradually gained or regained territory around the world. If the Commando was to survive as part of the order of battle, this transformation was not only desirable but essential and inevitable. For what the Commandos were, was a function of the job they had to do, and the tactics that they had to perform their tasks. This change was apparent at the time, not least to Robert Laycock and many other Commandos. Perhaps one of the best witnesses was Captain Denis O'Flaherty. After being badly wounded and winning a DSO at Vaagso at the end of 1941, he spent two years in hospital and convalescence. When he returned, everything was different:

One thing that is quite clear to me is that 1 Commando Brigade, by 1944, was a very fine professional set up, with command, control and tactical know-how far ahead of the ordinary infantry, and far advanced from the good old days of 1941. At the same time, and quite rightly, they had lost the blind dash that I thought was remarkable in the minority who were actually engaged at close quarters at Vaagso. I have never seen that equalled in any Army since.

How the Commandos evolved as an instrument of war is explained by their very different tactics in battle from the mid-war period, and their increasingly 'regular' training literature. *Commando Training Instruction No. 1* and *Commando Battle Drill* were rather less than five years apart – but under other circumstances could easily have been from different conflicts in different decades. The main use of the Commandos in Europe in the latter part of the war was as a spearhead, to take strategic points, or to link rapidly with other units – such as parachutists, tanks, or infantry – and to ensure that the gains they had made were maintained. In the abstract, there was nothing very novel about any of this, except that it was expected to be performed better, and that establishments were expected to remain 'flexible'. However, added to this were the sea skills of a Marine, those of the camouflage and movement expert, some demolitions, and at least the basics of as many vehicles and enemy weapons as could be obtained at the time. Swimming and riding a bicycle were taken as given.

Nevertheless, it is arguable the most extraordinary thing about the Commandos was that the evolution of different tactics – alongside developing use of novel technology – so rapidly gave birth to a succession of types of 'special force'. Much of this approach, and the gamut these new forces covered would still be relevant half a century later. Raiding and the evolution of modern 'Combined Operations' was clearly the main thrust, and the key aspect we have followed here – but there were many others, each with their own distinctive tactical niches. 'Beach Commandos' were a natural marriage of the beach masters' duties and Commando training. The Parachute Regiment began as a Commando, and the Special Air Service was grafted onto the same root; the Special Boat Service grew essentially out of Commando operations in 'Folbots', 101 Troop, and 6 and 8 Commandos; the Special Operations Executive was intimately linked through the fertile imaginings of Colonel Gubbins, the Small Scale Raiding Force, (also known as 62 Commando), and the 'behind the lines' work of 10 Commando. No. 30 Commando pioneered aspects of intelligence-gathering. The shortlived 14 Commando of the middle war period was at the cutting edge of the development of Arctic warfare in the use of small boats and cross-country skiing. It would be little exaggeration to say that the Commandos were both the parent of, and the test bed for, all of Britain's modern Special Forces. They also influenced the formation and training of the US Rangers, Australian Commandos and, indirectly, many other Special Forces units around the world.

Commandos were not just a military tool for a fast-evolving and ever-spreading conflict – but also a valuable bolster for the national will: this much is beyond dispute. They were both a new 'special' force for their times and a conscious match for the admitted prowess of a determined and successful enemy. Significantly, they were also both 'British' and 'Allied' in a way that other corps and regiments found difficult to equal. From their first formation they drew on units around the nation in a manner that both maximised recruitment potential, and allowed the public to identify widely with their achievements. Almost every cap badge in the Army was represented, as was almost every locality in the Kingdom. As the blatantly triumphalist – and somewhat stereotypically inaccurate – Gordon Holman remarked about the men on operation Claymore:

> The Commando engaged in this operation was a particularly representative one as it had such a fine mixture of Englishmen, Welshmen, Scots and Irish. The Irish, indeed, both from North and South were predominant. And how they wanted to fight! The Welsh were as tough as any in a very tough party. The Scots were dour, as usual, and the English, the least conspicuous, linked up the whole collection [...] Of course the irrepressible cockney was present among the English.

With the formation of the Royal Marine Commandos, the Commandos also came to represent the 'Senior Service' ashore at a time when 'old-fashioned' combat between named capital ships was becoming increasingly rare. After the formation of the 'Inter-Allied' Commando, they similarly came to stand for the determination of other nations to resist tyranny and oppression in the most active and dramatic way – even when those very countries were occupied. Though the Commando force was never 'political' in a partisan sense, its anti-Nazi inclusivity was extended to Jews and even Austrians and Germans. In this way, they could be regarded as 'freedom fighters' and, conversely, Hitler came to dub them 'guerrillas' – in a sense that was defined by the enemy as 'terrorist'.

That the Commandos had been brought into existence largely at the behest of Winston Churchill certainly served to heighten this significance – and antipathies – being further strengthened when the Prime Minister's own son, Randolph, served with No. 8 Commando. As George Jellicoe remarked, observing this unit on Arran: 'Evelyn Waugh did not really fit in [...] He did extremely well in Crete and was extremely brave. He wasn't really suited to this type of thing. Neither was Randolph, but it was a great help having him in the Commando because it meant that views were received at a very high level.' The personal backing of Churchill doubtless raised profile, but support was not unequivocal and at times the Prime Minister could be mercurial and impulsive, if not capricious. Whilst his public favour was plain for all to see, there were moments – in the depth of the winter of 1940, and at the time of the departure of Admiral Keyes, for example – when, in private, he could be surprisingly dismissive of Commando achievements. At an early stage, and perhaps in the grip of one of his famous depressions, he is reported to have referred to the Commandos of one raid as 'cut throats' – unworthy of the British Empire. At the same time, he clearly promoted the 'medium'-scale raids, almost certain to be costly and of dubious military usefulness, at least in part on the diplomatic and political grounds that this would do something to placate the Soviets, who were desperate to see the Western Allies taking a bigger share of the horrendous bloodshed of late 1941 and 1942.

To this extent, the Commandos were a sacrifice atoning for Churchill's all-too-understandable unwillingness to entertain the possibility of a Western Front in any way resembling that of the Great War. Moreover, perhaps this was indeed to the greater good: British military deaths in the Second World War were scarcely half those of the First. Even for the Commandos themselves, raids may have been less costly than a conventional stand-up fight in France commencing in 1942 or 1943. Total Commando fatalities over the period of conflict were about 1,700 – set against roughly 25,000 who passed through Achnacarry. This was undoubtedly high, undoubtedly painful, and worthy of signal respect: but in terms of bald percentages it was still a 'butcher's bill' smaller than the price paid by their fathers in the infantry in 1914–1918.

Though operational secrecy remained paramount, the existence of Commandos was never denied, and a good deal of morale-raising material relating to their exploits was produced even as the war progressed. One of the first publications dedicated to a raid was the 1941 *Epic of the Lofotens*, credited to Dr G. Mikes, 'famous Hungarian Journalist'. The racy dust jacket showed Commandos, blazing oil, Norwegian mountains, and cover blurb promising, 'the full thrilling story of the Lofoten islanders' resistance to the Nazis and the dramatic swoop on the Islands by British forces'. Priced at 1s it was illustrated with eight photographs. War correspondent A. B. Austin published the book *We Landed at Dawn*, containing a dramatic 'full eyewitness' – and highly optimistic – account of the Dieppe raid in January 1943. The same year Lord Louis Mountbatten turned out the officially sponsored *Combined Operations* volume, which dealt with the development of Commandos and associated troops from the outbreak of war to the end of 1942. In the middle war period the Commandos were also the subject of an eponymous and blatantly propagandist official booklet. Its rear cover showed a map of Europe skewered with bayonets at the locations of Boulogne, St Nazaire, Spitzbergen, Lofoten and Vaagso, and the menacing legend 'Where Next?' It described the Commando as 'the crack guerrilla fighters of Britain and they come from every unit of the British Army – cavalry, infantry, artillery and sappers. Their first qualification is fine physique. They must be alert, quick-thinking and resourceful.' These men had 'little' training of the barrack square type of discipline, but an emphasis on field training, hunting, trapping, woodcraft and fieldcraft. More questionably, *Commando* claimed these supermen could march 60 miles a day, that each was 'a boxer', 'has knowledge of Jiu-Jitsu', and that all the operations to date were either 'a success' or 'unqualified success'. On the other side of the Atlantic, in 1944, there was direct appeal to the youth market with a volume by Victor Lawson entitled *Ranger-Commando Junior*, promising 'special features for Rangerettes and Commandettes'.

One of the most self-consciously propagandistic books produced during the war was Gordon Holman's *Commando Attack* of May 1942:

> It must not be thought that the newspapers, and news agencies which work for them, are entirely self-centred in their desire to get good stories about Commandos or any other interesting departures of the services. Propaganda (that much overworked word) is one consideration, and the good effect on the morale of our people is another. Newspapers and periodicals, news agencies and all other branches connected with the great business of the printed word, have served and are serving, their country well in this war. They have a

proper understanding of their responsibilities: they also have a proper understanding of their powers, which they are anxious to use to the utmost in the interests of their country.

Amongst Holman's most misleading claims was that British tank columns in North Africa were organised 'as Commandos', and perhaps most surprisingly of all, that 'Commando units, which included Indian troops, operated in Malaya during the retreat to Singapore'. Given the disastrous outcome of the latter campaign, this can hardly have been the most morale-raising reference. Elsewhere, Holman's prose was illuminated by stirring quotations from suitably elevating parts of British history and literature: William Blake and the 'spirit of liberty', Rudyard Kipling and 'sacrifice', Nelson on the *Victory*, Wordsworth, Shakespeare, Tennyson and others.

An interesting side light on the value placed on the raids of the first half of the war is the relative number of gallantry medals and other plaudits awarded to participants. For the admittedly extremely risky – if not completely suicidal (but relatively small) – assault on St Nazaire, twice as many awards were made as for the total participation of more than eight complete Commandos throughout their time in Normandy. Indeed, it has been claimed that, with 135 awards amongst 611 participants (of whom more than a quarter were killed), the ratio was one of the highest of the entire war. At Vaagso – a one-day action – the number of deaths was similar to the number of awards. The Commando contribution to Dieppe, which shone against an otherwise dreadful background, resulted in quite a number of awards, though both VCs were won by Canadians. These statistics would seem to confirm the maxim that the more disastrous the operation – and the more difficult the period of war – the better the bravery of individuals was acknowledged. In this respect the Commandos were the genuine heirs of both the 24th Foot at Rorke's Drift and the Lancashire Fusiliers at Gallipoli.

Nevertheless, it is arguable that the propaganda value of the Commando had its most effective popular exploitation through film and pictures. Several Commando missions were filmed, and clearly the intention of doing so was more to lift the spirits of the public, and to impress US or Russian audiences, than for purely operational reasons. The montage of footage of the Vaagso raid is a particularly good case in point. One surviving clip shows 'Mad Jack' Churchill playing the bagpipes onboard ship, a warship on the horizon at sunset, and footage of a barrage.

Naturally, Gordon Holman's write-up in *Commando Attack* would assume that the enemy heard the 'skirl of the bagpipes [...] above the roar of the guns'. Drama is heightened by a ticking clock as the Commandos wait to attack. In another segment we see an advance towards the burning town, German prisoners, and patriotic posing with captured flag and helmets. The plot line is much the same as that used in official film of 1916 to 1918: the enemy and the props are much the same – the locations and the uniforms a little different. Some of the now rather tame-looking footage of training and of W. E. Fairbairn and his famous unarmed combat was made to fulfil a similar function. That US observers picked up on these points in reference to their own development of the Ranger ethos and *modus operandi* is beyond question. As the US Military Intelligence Service publication *British Commandos* of August 1942 explained:

> Publicity will play a very big part in exploiting the moral value of a raid. Although this publicity should stick to true facts, it should exploit the results of a raid as much as possible. It is essential to make an announcement early, before the enemy has time to issue a communiqué. The opponent who gives the story first is more likely to be believed, as he automatically forces the other side to take the defensive. The communiqué can be drafted in general terms before the operation, and completed and issued immediately after receipt of a telephone message from the commander of the expedition. This telephone call should be the commander's first job on landing, after assuring himself that all his boats are in. It is difficult to exaggerate the importance of good publicity. It may easily extract great moral effect from a raid which achieves few concrete military results.

One is tempted to believe that this was, indeed, one of Churchill's prime objectives when he first called for the rapid establishment of a raiding force in 1940. In times before radio and cinema, events on the battlefield were reported, usually belatedly and sometimes following extensive censorship, in the printed press. The results could be influential, but though sometimes dramatic, were certainly not immediate. With radio reports now reaching much of the nation daily, and news 'picture shows' to challenge and even overawe the drama of the main feature, things could be otherwise – and much of Britain's press – and most especially the BBC – had a level of international credibility that Dr Goebbels could only dream of. Interestingly, mythologising was not limited to works of fact and information or 'white' propaganda. Perhaps most famously, Captain W. E. Johns, author of the celebrated 'Biggles' books, invented a new fictional character, Captain Lorrington King – otherwise known as 'King of the Commandos'. The dashing Lorrington King was in action before the war ended, and was probably more successful in his operations than the real soldiers that inspired his creation. Very quickly, 'Commando' became a form of brand in its own right, and the name was applied far beyond the original definition of Army or Marine raider. In the British forces it was applied to Beach Master units, intelligence-gatherers, the strike force of SOE, and much later to Royal Artillery and RAF units. Australian Commandos were similarly formed at an early stage. The press used the term ever more widely as, for example, in references to 'Russian Commandos'. In a weirdly circular twist of events, there were also mentions of Commando troops being trained in South Africa: this time to fight alongside, rather than against, British forces.

What may not have been immediately apparent was that engaging with the press so directly would set a precedent with which western armies still struggle to this day. For whilst coverage of the Commandos was almost universally successful from the viewpoint of morale, it was not always popular with those being studied by a lens under the already almost intolerable pressures of combat. It could also have very negative impacts, as Vietnam and other more recent conflicts have made clear. How significant, and how tragically intrusive, the demands of the media could become even during the Second World War is illustrated by events during the abortive raid on Floro, Norway, during 'Operation Kitbag', in early December 1941. During the voyage a tableau was staged for the cameras on the assault ship *Prince Charles*. The outcome was witnessed by C. L. G. Bryen:

We had with us several Press cameramen whose aim was to obtain a record of the expedition. They had filmed the usual scenes – Commandos exercising, chaps in their hammocks, or writing a last letter home – and it was suggested that they should shoot a close up of the final weapon overhaul and grenade priming on one of the troop decks below and the cameras began to roll on a scene of intense activity. A hundred men were cleaning all types of weapons, while at a table six men were busy cleaning the Mills type '36' grenades, passing them to the end man, who put the detonator in. One enterprising cameraman, anxious to get the grenades in focus, pulled a handful of grenades nearer, unnoticed by the men busy with their tasks, and so mixed up the primed and unprimed grenades. The number one man picked up a grenade, thinking it unprimed, and removed the safety pin and striking lever to clean it. To his horror, a small bang denoted that it was primed and the fuse was burning. He shouted and made a desperate effort to hurl the grenade through the hatch onto the empty deck above. It hit the hatchway and fell back. A Norwegian standing below the hatch caught it and hurled it again. It exploded just opposite his chest and killed six men outright, injuring eleven others.

Bryen was one of those hurt. Following problems with navigation the entire raid was abandoned. An official report blamed the mixing of primed and unprimed grenades, but apparently not the involvement of the film crew.

Just a few weeks later, in what may have been something of a distasteful postscript, there was an altercation between officers of 12 Commando and the British Gaumont film crew aboard ship returning from 'Operation Anklet'. Captain Pinckney and another officer heaved film belonging to the pressmen over the side in what has since been described as a 'bizarre and emotional incident'. The two officers were placed under arrest. Pinckney later explained that they were upset about the reprisals they discovered the Germans had wreaked upon Norwegian civilians after 'Operation Claymore' in the Lofotens earlier in the year. Now there was every possibility they would suffer more. To make matters worse, departing from the Lofotens again, and so quickly, was a betrayal of those who had welcomed them. In short,

> We felt that there was every danger of films and photographs being made public which, apart from its complete deception of the British people, would seriously increase damage already done to Anglo-Norwegian relations by what one Norwegian so rightly described as a 'very cheap demonstration'.

Unease was not limited to the principled Captain Pinckney and some other relatively junior officers. Senior Commando leaders were all too aware of the overblown and sometimes misleading picture that was painted of them. It was said that Charles Vaughan, Commandant at Achnacarry, was upset about the media circus from the start, finding the whole thing unconducive to successful training. Certainly more than one of those who went through the Commando Basic Training Centre remembered that his favourite introductory lecture included the well turned phrase 'tough but not toughs'. Interestingly, Vaughan may well have taken matters further, for he appears to have been the source of a story that appeared in *The Times* on 15 January 1943 under the heading, *The Commando Soldier – Severe Training – Life at a Highland Depot*. The article, credited to 'Our special Correspondent with the British Army', went to some pains to refute the idea that the Commando was a gangster:

> The original idea of a Commando – a Commando is a unit, and not an individual – held by the majority of people was too often that he was a desperado, a gangster, a 'smash and grab' raider or a 'tough', rather than merely a tough man. There was some reason for that widely held belief. There is no longer any such reason. There were a number of members of unpleasant 'gangs' in the first Commandos. They were found to be useless. Of five such cowardly thugs two jumped overboard from their ship early on the voyage and either swam ashore or were drowned; the other three went sick before anything exciting happened. There was not, and indeed never was, any real reason why housewives should lock up their houses and their daughters when members of a Commando are drafted to their villages or towns. A Commando soldier is, as I can vouch after a long weekend, a normal healthy youth. He volunteers for service with the Commandos. He is sent to a depot in the far North where he is hardened physically and quickened mentally. The discipline is strict; there is no 'spit and polish' which the men like; there is little or no spare time from dawn to dusk, or later, and the food is ordinary Army rations. Twenty percent of the volunteers fall by the wayside, not willingly, but because they just cannot stand it.

What we do not know for sure is whether Vaughan went to the press of his own volition, or whether the idea that a reporter should write a story with his assistance came from above. In any case, it would appear highly unlikely that a pressman could attend Achnacarry for several days without the Commandant's knowledge, if not explicit permission. If Vaughan was not the sole instigator this leaves open some intriguing possibilities as, for example, that some decision had been taken at the highest levels that the wild image of the Commando – once cultivated – was now counter-productive. Equally, the timing of this disclaimer is interesting, following by just a couple of months the Hitler 'Commando Order'.

Long after the war, Brigadier Mills-Roberts, former commanding officer of 6 Commando, remained annoyed that the media had taken the Commando idea and given it the treatment of a 'theatrical stunt'. Truth had been obscured 'by the insidious and now popular propaganda which the press put over'. The 'angle' so played upon was toughness, indiscipline and lawlessness – whereas most Commando soldiers had been highly disciplined, albeit that this was often self-discipline. His conception was that, though Commandos had dash, they were highly trained, not least in 'marksmanship and the use of automatic weapons', and Achnacarry in particular had been 'run with care and discipline'. Brigadier Peter Young countered talk of 'gangster' image by pointing out that many of the replacements received by No. 3 Commando in late 1942 were policemen who had volunteered to join the Army and, incidentally, this had also been noted in *The Times* piece of January 1943. A similar theme was also raised later in the book *The Green Beret*.

More than one writer on Special Forces, and the Commandos in particular, has concluded that their worth should be calculated in terms of 'investment' and 'return'. The investment being the drain on manpower, time, effort and research, and the diversion of resources such as ships, aircraft and other units necessary to make operations work. In such a model, 'return' is portrayed as the strategic, operational and tactical effect on battle, enemy forces, and the war. Clearly this is part of the story, but only part of the story. Much of what the Commandos achieved was less tangible in its impact upon the enemy than upon friends – and more psychological than the physical. The Commandos buoyed up morale at home and were one of the factors demonstrating to the US that Britain was serious in continuing the war after Dunkirk. They were also something Churchill could show Stalin as evidence of British commitment to an eventual – but not immediate – 'Second Front' on mainland Europe. Within the armed forces, Commandos quickly became not just a practical demonstration of the possibilities of the Combined Operation, but a new competitor against whom the existing services strove to demonstrate their own worth. There was duplication and inefficiency, and the Navy eventually subsumed the upstarts but, arguably, the Commandos were one of the catalysts – along with the enemy – that convinced both Army and Navy to improve their game and think in new ways. It has also been argued that the advent of the Combined Operation was ultimately one of the forces that finally helped to push together the various pre-existing bureaucracies into the Ministry of Defence. Interestingly, the conclusion that the Americans took away from the raiding experience of the Commandos had little to do with the material, and everything to do with the moral – as explained in *British Commandos*:

> The moral effect of a raid usually counts far more than any material success it may achieve. If the material effect is important, the moral value will rise sharply; but even if no material success is gained, the moral value will still be high. Unless a raid is undertaken for reconnaissance purposes only, the most important object should be to assure contact with enemy troops, and the target chosen should be of sufficient importance to make this a reasonable certainty. On the other hand, there must be no risk of a complete failure. The moral effect of one fiasco will outweigh that of several successful raids. Therefore, the target must not be one guarded by a formidable enemy force.

A widely held belief is that Commando service retarded, if not actually blighted, the careers of officers. However, the statistical work required to justify this contention would not appear to have been done; and in broad terms the idea that they were actively discriminated against as a group when it came to promotions is difficult, if not impossible, to substantiate. The Commandos were a very small part of the fighting forces – and each Commando was smaller than a normal infantry battalion. They were eventually numbered in 'Brigades' but never 'Divisions'. The number of generals and brigadiers that such a force might require, with the structure that it had, was therefore extremely limited. Nevertheless, several Commando officers – only subalterns or lieutenants in June 1940 – were colonels and brigadiers by 1944 or 1945. This equates to rising a rank a year – and in one or two cases even faster. Some, like Durnford-Slater, jumped a tier when the Commandos were formed. In the early 1950s, Lord Lovat was able to point out that no less than eight of No. 4 Commando had already risen to the rank of Lieutenant Colonel or above. Casualties, and the relatively large proportion of NCOs and officers to each 'other rank' would seem to point to promotions coming faster rather than slower, and at least a few officers were commissioned from the ranks. To reach much more of an opinion than this would be unsafe: the papers on officers serving in and after the Second World War are not yet public records, and without them any study is incomplete.

For one unit a fairly comprehensive list of officer movements has been published, and the work of Tony Mackenzie on 44 RM Commando makes interesting reading – though it covers but the last eighteen months or so of the war. Of twenty-one officers in June 1944, just three were still with the unit a year later: two of the three had received promotion in rank and the third had taken up duties as battalion adjutant. Perhaps surprisingly, officers present in December 1945 – after the war had ended – now included five who had been with 44 Commando in June 1944. There were four Commanding Officers in eighteen months, suggesting an average wartime tenure of fewer than twenty weeks. Looking at the picture from mid-1944 to the end of the war, a total of forty-seven officers were drafted into 44 Commando and somewhat fewer out. Some came in, went out, and were cycled back in again later. There were three fatalities in action, including the padre. Given that the unit served in the Far East, malaria is likely to have been one of the prime causes of officer mobility: but Achnacarry saw a total of six pack their bags, and training, postings, wounds and other illnesses doubtless all played their part. Just to make matters doubly confusing, 44 Commando was renumbered in 1947 as 40 RM Commando.

It is difficult to draw any clear conclusion regarding career prospects from such an extremely volatile situation, but it can be observed that the number of officers who served with 44 RM Commando during the latter stages of the war – however briefly – was at least three times the notional establishment, and death was perhaps the least likely thing to cause an officer to move on. We can also be fairly sure that the picture varied between the different Commandos: some, such as Numbers 2 and 8, suffered short-term catastrophic losses. Some, like 12 Commando, escaped such devastating single events but dwindled in number and were disbanded. No. 3 Commando saw pretty much the entire spread of British involvement in the war in Europe, and like No. 4, contained many vibrant personalities who eventually found a species of celebrity in their own right. Sweeping statements about Commandos are therefore dangerous: they were, and remained, more individual than blanket generalisations can define.

For Commandos, or would-be Commandos, who were 'returned to unit', doubtless there was stigma – self-flagellation for perceived failure – and unease amongst colleagues that the party concerned could go off and leave his colleagues in the lurch, whether through extreme fervour or by a level of personal ambition that was not quite accounted normal. We also need to take some notice of the fact that Commando officers were, as a group, more keen, more individualist, and sometimes more outspoken than the norm. This was, essentially, a result of a selection process that so valued initiative, extreme fitness and mental flexibility. As we have noted, there were few other units in which a reporter or camera crew was so frequently attached at such low, and intimate, levels in the establishment. We also need to be aware that a sense of anticlimax, and unfulfilled expectation, was probably the norm rather than the exception amongst officers in 1945 and 1946. Even with National Service and imperial commitments, there were no longer enough troops to justify an inflated senior officer corps. Suddenly, the civilian world was also teeming with those who had been leaders of men in the most extreme circumstances, and there were not enough challenging roles at what appeared to be a consummate level to absorb them all.

Nevertheless, given their international reputation – and probable strategic and tactical relevance to future actions – it is still surprising to many that the Army Commandos were disbanded so rapidly at the end of hostilities. The haste with which the first Commandos passed into history verged on the indecent. The Emperor of Japan declared the end of resistance on 15 August 1945: before October was out it was announced that the Army Commandos would disbanded, in early 1946, along with all surplus Royal Marine Commandos. The whole force shrank abruptly to just three Commandos in one Brigade. There was naturally the justification that, being a 'special force' raised for a specific purpose, the Army Commandos had only ever been temporary in the first place. Everybody was now 'returned to unit' if not to civilian life. Nevertheless, there were other considerations lurking in the background. With the exception of the two World Wars, the UK had never been a 'big Army' power; the Navy was of more relevance to the far-flung colonies and trade of an island nation and therefore the natural home of amphibious force. Short 'National Service' and a defensive role on the Continent was not likely to be fruitful background to a miniature volunteer army-within-an-army. Perhaps even more importantly, the Army Commandos now lacked that friend in high places that had so often treated them as his private army, and protected them from the winds of change and the all-in fighting of inter-service rivalry. The electorate had already cast off Winston Churchill: his brave 'Leopards' soon followed.

Appendices

Appendix I: British Commando Clothing and Equipment, European Theatre
According to US *Tactical and Technical Trends*, 18 June 1942:

Normal clothing is 'battle dress', a two-piece woollen garment, stout shoes and anklets (short leggings). In colder weather a sleeveless button up leather jacket which reaches the hips is worn over or under the battle dress. A two piece denim dungaree is also provided for wear over battle dress in damp or rainy weather [denims could of course be worn alone in warm weather]. In addition to the ordinary hobnailed shoes ['boots' in British English], a rubber soled shoe and a rope soled shoe are provided for missions that require stealthy movements over paved roads, through village streets, for cliff climbing and so forth. A heavy ribbed wool cardigan with long sleeves and turtle neck and a woollen undervest are also available for cold weather wear. No overcoats are worn at any time during training or operations even in severe weather. All clothing is designed and worn with the sole purpose in view of comfort and utility under actual operating conditions. No leather belts are worn either by officers or enlisted men. A fabric belt is provided for wear when deemed appropriate.

Basically, every officer and man is provided with standard Army field equipment similar to our own. In addition, certain special equipment is available in Commando stores and is issued to individuals or troops as the occasion requires. Principal items are listed below:

Fighting Knife; Tommy (individual) cooker; field ration; skis and poles; individual waist life belt (Mae West); Primus stoves; one gallon thermal food containers; gas cape; wristlets; two man rubber boat; plywood (sectionalised) canoe; collapsible canvas canoe; bamboo and canvas stretchers; 2-inch scaling ropes; 1-inch mesh heavy wire (6' x 24') in rolls for crossing entanglements; toggle ropes; transportation equipment (administrative) consisting of: six Hillman pick-ups (four seats), three 1,500 lb trucks, one three-ton truck, ten motorcycles. Communication equipment: ten radio sets (018 portable voice and key type, weight 36 lb, voice range 5 miles) semaphore flags, blinker guns, Very pistols and flares.

Appendix II: 43 RM Clothing and Equipment, Yugoslav Theatre

From a Movement Order of 9 October 1944:

Dress and Packing of Equipment

On the men –

'Second best' Battle Dress, face veils worn around necks in 'scarf position'.

Berets

Boots and gaiters

Mae Wests

Weapons and Ammunition to normal scale

2-inch Mortars; PIATS; Bren magazines in boxes to go with Troop

In 'Marching Order' to include –

Entrenching tools, water bottles worn on right side, gas cape rolled around leather jerkin and stowed above large pack.

In large pack: ground sheet; blanket; change of underwear; spare socks; laces; pair of Denims.

In small pack: Mess tin, knife, fork, and spoon; washing and shaving gear; cleaning gear; pullover; cap comforter.

In ST Kitbag: to go to rear stores (not readily available)

Steel helmet; 'Best' Battle Dress; Slippers; personal effects.

In AP Kitbag: to be brought up as required or taken with Commando

Greatcoat; felt soled boots; remaining underwear and socks; spare boots and denims

Additional blankets to be stored or carried in '3 man rolls' i.e. 9 blankets.

All 'Khaki Drill' clothing to be returned to Quartermaster for winter.

Appendix III: Establishment and Armament of a Royal Marine Commando Troop

As extracted from *Commando Battle Drill*, and its amendment of 20 June 1945:

Personnel

3 Officers; Captain and two subalterns
1 Troop Sergeant Major
6 Sergeants
4 Corporals
8 Lance Corporals
43 Marines
65

Arranged as One Troop HQ: Captain and TSM, plus three Marines and the PIAT
Two sections: Subaltern, 9 NCOs and 20 Marines each.

Weapons

15 Colt .45 semi auto pistols
3 Signal pistols
38 No. 4 Rifles
3 No. 3 Mk 1 Sniper Rifles
5 Bren guns
9 Thompson (or Sten) machine carbines
2 2-inch mortars
1 PIAT (Projector Infantry Anti Tank)

Grenades: mainly No. 36 Mills with four and seven second fuses for hand or rifle use, plus a selection of numbers 68, 69, 75, 77 and 79 as required by the operation. A reserve of 'EY' rifles for projecting rifle grenades kept by Commando HQ.

Appendix IV: Commando Battle Drill 1945

ROYAL MARINE TRAINING PAMPHLET. No. 2
(R.M.T.P.   (2))

COMMANDO
BATTLE   DRILL

1945

INDEX

	Page
FOREWORD	3
PARADE GROUND BATTLE DRILL—PRELIMINARY	4
SUB-SECTION AND SECTION PARADE GROUND BATTLE DRILLS ...	6
BATTLE DRILL FOR CLEARING A BUILDING	10
BATTLE DRILL FOR CLEARING A SMALL VILLAGE	11
BATTLE DRILL FOR CLEARING STREETS OF A CONGESTED TOWN	12
BATTLE DRILL FOR WOOD CLEARING	14
APPENDIX " A."—ORGANISATION OF A COMMANDO	17
APPENDIX " B."—SET PIECE ATTACK ON SMALL DEFENDED LOCALITY. THE COMMANDO IN THE ATTACK	22

2

FOREWORD

This pamphlet on Commando Battle Drill has been produced in order to help Royal Marine Establishments and Royal Marine Detachments to carry out preliminary and advanced training on Commando lines.

The drills laid down in this pamphlet supersede previous Royal Marine pamphlets on Battle Drill.   It should be noted that the establishment used is flexible and should be taken as a guide only.

PARADE GROUND BATTLE DRILL—PRELIMINARY

LESSON 1.

Stores required :—Wall diagram of outline of commando down to sections, sub-section in detail, as Appendix " A," page 17.
If possible, labels for hanging round necks, showing names of all sub-sections.

1. Introduction.

Barrack square drill is Battle Drill of 150 years ago, used now to inculcate discipline, esprit de corps. Foundation of modern drill. Battle Drill is Barrack square drill for modern war. Modern war demands same qualities that Barrack square drill teaches, therefore, must be carried out with the same attention to smartness, etc.

2. Objects of Battle Drill.

To ensure uniformity in elementary movements of open Warfare. To cut down orders in the field—each man knowing what he has to do without being told. To ensure speed in getting into action.

3. Group 1—Parade Battle Drill.

Elementary movements only. Tactical aspect left until Group 2. In Group 1 must learn sub-section organisation and thoroughly know basic drill.

4. Organisation of Commando.

Go through Wall diagram. Men must understand, but need not learn larger organisation.

5. Sub-Section Organisation.

Go into in detail. Demonstrate with squad using labels. Practice throughout squad.

LESSON 2.

Squad is divided into groups of 13, representing a sub-section. Any men left over are attached evenly throughout the sub-sections.

Order.	Action
1. For Battle Drill Fall in ...	Sub-sections fall in at 5 paces interval between men, 10 paces distance. Surplus men 10 paces on left of sub-sections. Dress and stand at ease from right to left.
2. Right turn	Attention. Turn right. Stand at ease.
3. Sub-sections prove	Tell off by tasks from front to rear as in diagram 1, coming to attention and standing at ease in turn.
4. Fall out one	Sub-section Commander doubles round and joins up in rear. Remainder take 5 paces forward, all stand at ease. Sub-section prove again on completion without further orders.

Note.—The use of labels may be of help to recruits in remembering titles. They should be placed on the ground at each position—otherwise too much time is taken changing them, with loss of precision.

4

Diagram 1.

Sub-section Commander	...		Rifle.
No. 1 Assault Group	...	A Assault Commander—Sten.	
No. 2 Assault Group	...		Rifle.
No. 3 Assault Group	...		Rifle.
Assault Group Commander	...		Rifle.
No. 4 Assault Group	...	B Assault Commander—Sten.	
No. 4 Assault Group	...		Rifle.
No. 6 Assault Group	...		Rifle.
No. 7 Assault Group	...		Rifle.
Bren Group Commander	...		Rifle.
No. 1 Bren Group	...	...	Bren Gun and Pistol.
No. 2 Bren Group	...	...	Spare parts wallet—Rifle.
No. 3 Bren Group	...	...	Rifle.

Diagram 2.

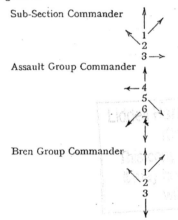

Sub-Section Commander

Assault Group Commander

Bren Group Commander

LESSONS 3 and 4.

Repeat Lesson 2. Sub-section is then in single file facing right.

Order.				*Action*
5. Observe	...	...	...	Each man turns to positions as shown in Diagram 2.
6. Prepare to move	...	...		Turn back to face flank of sub-section commander.

Instructor explains reason for observing :—

Modern war enemy may be all round, must watch for enemy movement in any quarter. Touch must be kept with other units moving with sub-section—watch must be kept for signals from HQ and elsewhere. Therefore, observation must be all round.

Repeat whole lesson until all ranks thoroughly understand organisation of sub-section and positions and observations.

5

Group 2—Parade Battle Drill.

LESSON 5. Introduction—So far drills have covered the forming up of a sub-section ready to move off in single file.

The next phase covers the approach of the sub-section to the enemy, and the drill for opening fire.

Fire is represented on the parade by coming to attention, rifle at the order. Cease fire by standing at ease.

During this phase rifles will be trailed while on the move.

Explain " Run—cover—observe."

Orders	*Action*
As for lessons 1-4 up to Prepare to move.	As lessons 1-4.
7. Follow me ... ... Enemy right or left	Step off in quick time—trail arms. Cautionary.
8. Sub-section run	Halt, turn towards the enemy. Stand at ease. All shout " Run—cover—observe."
9. Sub-section " Sights." Target—Fire.	Attention.
10. Stop	Stand at ease.
11. Assault Groups or Bren Groups " Sights "—Target—Fire.	Group designated up to attention.
12. Assault Groups or Bren Groups Stop.	Group designated stand at ease.

13. Repeat drills 11 and 12 as necessary.

LESSON 6 and 7.

In this lesson the Assault and Bren Groups are split and fire can be brought down in the direction of advance.

Orders	*Action*
Repeat drills up to 13.	
14. Follow me. On command run form line—Bren Group right or left.	Turn to flank of sub-section commander and step off, arms trailed. Cautionary.
15. Sub-section run	Sub-section commander halts and Assault Groups come up to extended line on flank opposite that indicated for Bren Group. Bren Group come up on indicated flank, stand at ease. All shout " Run—cover—observe."

16. Repeat drills 11 and 12 as necessary.

SUB-SECTION AND SECTION PARADE GROUND BATTLE DRILLS

Introduction.

1. The object of this drill is to show the marine diagramatically how the sub-section and section fight and exactly what each man in the sub-section team has to do. It also relates the discipline of the parade ground to that required in the field.

6

The sooner the man understands the tactical application of this drill, the greater the value he will obtain from it.

2. For recruits these drills will be taught after completion of Table B and elementary field training. The squad should know how to give fire orders, handle their weapons and the elementary field formations. Members of the squad should provide the sub-section commanders and Bren Group Commanders, drawn from " section leaders " and prospective candidates. Rear rank instructors may be required to assist in taking these tasks initially.

For trained men, their own NCO's and candidates should take the leaders.

3. Parade ground Battle Drill must not be divorced from the drill on the field, but considered as a pattern where the essential elements of field craft and marksmanship have been temporarily removed in order the better to understand the tactics. By this means, when actually in the field, the actions of each individual in regard to drill become automatic, so that fieldcraft and marksmanship can be applied to the individual circumstances.

4. Points to note :—

(a) All movements are carried out at the double, once under effective SA fire.

(b) Rifles will be carried at the trail until under fire, when they will be canted in the left hand, ready to bring to the shoulder immediately.

(c) " Enemy " is represented by a flag in the middle of the parade ground. It is assumed that the position is located as soon as the sub-section comes under effective fire. Men should be told, however, that in the field this will only come as a result of good training.

(d) The distance between men is 5 yards throughout, and this must be insisted on.

THE DRILL FOR A SUB-SECTION.

Drill No.	Ordered by	Order	Action
1	Instructor	Battle Drill. Fall in. Prove. Observe. Prepare to Advance.	As for Preliminary.
2	Sub Sec Comd	Follow me. On the order " Run " form line, Bren Group right or left.	Step off. Cautionary Order.
3	Instructor	Under effective SA fire.	
4	Sub Sec Comd	Sub-section run.	Sub-section Commander halts Sub-section form line, stand at ease, Run—Cover— Observe. " Sights "—Target—Fire.
		Sub-section STOP.	Stand at ease.
5	Sub Sec Comd	Enemy 400. Indication. We will kill all enemy. Right or Left flanking. Bren Group there. Assault Group that way. " Sights "—tar- get—fire. Bren Group move.	Rifle Group attention.
6	Bren Gp Comd	Bren Group prepare to move. Bren Group follow me. Bren Group down. " Sights "—target—fire.	Move to position. Attention.

7

7	Sub Sec Comd	Assault Groups Stop. Prepare to move. Follow me.	Stand at ease. Move to assault position as indicated in orders.
8	Sub Sec Comd	Down. We will assault from here. Fix bayonets.	Halt.
9	Sub Sec Comd	Prepare to Assault— Assault.	Groups run forward in line. Rifles in " On Guard " position.
10	Bren Gp Comd	Bren. Group switch.	
11	Sub Sec Comd	Bullets—bullets. Charge.	Lower and raise rifles, returning to " On Guard."
12	Bren Gp Comd	Bren Group Stop. Prepare to move. Follow me.	Group move off to reorganising position same flank as the movement, i.e., right flank Bren Group right.
13	Sub Sec Comd	Assault Groups reorganise. Follow me.	Groups wheel to original axis. Groups turn towards sub-section commander on command " Me."
14	Sub Sec Comd	Arrowhead, Bren Group right or left, Assault Groups down unfix bayonets.	Assault Groups go down on opposite flank to Bren. Bren Group move to flank indicated if not already there.

(N.B.—For arrowhead and direction of observation see diagram 5.)

15	Bren Gp Comd	Bren Group down.	
16	Sub Sec Comd	Ammunition Prove. Ammunition and Casualties, Sir (to Instructor).	Section proves. as usual.
17	Instructor	Advance will continue there. (Points in direction.) Prepare to move.	
18	Sub Sec Comd	Follow me.	

Note.—When these drills have been mastered and the men reached a stage in their training when further explanation will not muddle them, the following should be pointed out :—

It will never occur that a sub-section alone carries out an attack such as the above. The section attack, however, will follow the identical lines to the above, except that each Group will have another similar group with it. The orders given above by Sub Sec Comd and Bren Group Commander would be given by the Section Commander and Section Sgt respectively).

THE DRILL FOR A SECTION.

1. This drill is a guide only and can be much expanded as training develops. Further points can be adapted from I.T. Pt. VIII, p. 69 *et seq.*

2. The section falls in in the following formation :—

A Sub-Section	...	Assault Group. Sub-section HQ Bren Group.
		Section HQ
B Sub-Section	...	Assault Group. Sub-section HQ Bren Group.

8

Drill No.	Ordered by	Order	Action
1	Instructor	Battle Drill—Fall in. Prove. Observe. Prepare to advance.	As for Sub-section.
2	Sec Comd	Section Advance.	Spring to attention, move off trailing arms.
3	A Sub Sec Comd	On the order " run," form line, Bren Group right or left.	Cautionary.
	B Sub Sec Comd	On the order " run," form file, Bren Group right or left.	
4	Instructor	Under effective small arms fire.	
5	A & B Sub Sec Comd	Sub-section run.	Sub-section Commanders halt. Sub-sections form as ordered " Run—cover —observe." Stand at ease. B Sub Sec Comd and section Commander move up behind A Sub Sec Comd.
6	A Sub Sec Comd	Sights—Target—Fire.	A Sub-section attention.
7	A Sub Sec Comd	A Sub-section STOP.	Stand at ease.
8	Instructor	Ground suitable for RIGHT flanking.	
9	Sec Comd	Enemy 300. Indication. We will kill all enemy. Right flanking. Smoke there— Bren Groups there—Assault Groups that way—Signals normal. Assault Groups prepare to advance (under cover theoretically)—UP— to the right Advance.	Assault Groups spring to attention, turn right and move off at double, canting rifle into left hand.
10	Sec Sgt	Gives fire order to No. 1 Bren Groups.	Usual Bren drill.
11	Sec Comd (as Assault Gp r e a c h e s flank)	Prepare to assault.	Assault Groups form into two waves and fix bayonets, on guard.
12	Sec Comd	Assault signal has been fired.	
13	Sec Sgt	Bren Groups switch.	Bren drill for switch.
14	Sec Comd	Charge.	Assault Group runs flat out, shouting, firing from hip.

The Assault Group advance through objective, wheel into the axis of advance. Halt on orders from Sub-section Commanders " cover—observe."

15	Instructor	Success signal has been fired.	
16	Sec Sgt	Bren Groups prepare to advance—UP—Double.	Bren Groups advance round objective and reorganise in sub-sections.

Sub-sections reorganise, prove and report Ammunition and casualties.

17	Sec Comd	Advance will continue there. Prepare to move. Advance.	Sub-section move off.

9

BATTLE DRILL FOR CLEARING A BUILDING.

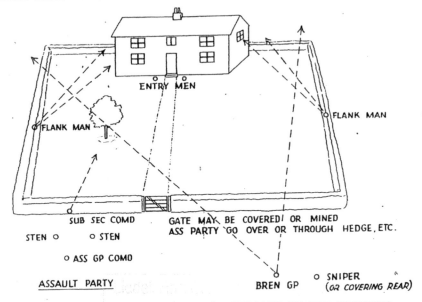

ENTRY MEN

FLANK MAN

FLANK MAN

SUB SEC COMD   GATE MAY BE COVERED! OR MINED
STEN o   o STEN   ASS PARTY GO OVER OR THROUGH HEDGE, ETC.

o ASS GP COMD

ASSAULT PARTY   o SNIPER
                            BREN GP   *(OR COVERING REAR)*

Drill for a Sub-section. Method :—1. THE APPROACH TO THE BUILDING.
                                  2. THE KILLING GROUND.
                                  3. FLANKMEN.
                                  4. ENTRYMEN.
                                  5. ASSAULT PARTY.

1. The Approach.

(a) The building must be carefully observed from an OP and positions chosen for LMG and FLANKMEN.

(b) DOORMEN and ASSAULT PARTY must then be detailed.

(c) Substantial outbuildings must be dealt with separately.

2. The Killing Ground.

The outside and rear exits of the buildings should be covered as far as possible by the Bren Group from some advantage point.

ANYONE leaving the building as the ASSAULT PARTY enter must be killed. The Bren Group must get into position UNSEEN. It is suggested that if the Sub-section has a Sniper he should be with the Bren Group, or he could work his way round to cover the rear, clear of the Bren arc of fire.

3. Flankmen.

A right and a left flankman should cover the windows to their flanks to prevent sniping by the enemy. The flankmen should be *concealed* in hedges, etc., and move to their positions UNSEEN.

4. Entrymen.

The two Entrymen, covered by the LMG and Flankmen, should move quickly to the wall, and move under cover of the wall to the doorway or entrance. Bayonets fixed—Open door—Right-hand Doorman holds rifle left-handed.

5. The Assault Party.

A Sten Gunner approaches first. The Sub-section Commander comes behind with a grenade to throw should the enemy be seen in entrance. The grenade is thrown if door opens into large hallway or room, or if enemy is known to be there.

The building to be searched systematically, starting from where the enemy is known to be. Entrances to other rooms being covered.

One Entryman can join in the assault, following in the Assault Group. The other acts as Look-out man at the entry and watches for any signals, etc.

BATTLE DRILL FOR CLEARING A SMALL VILLAGE.

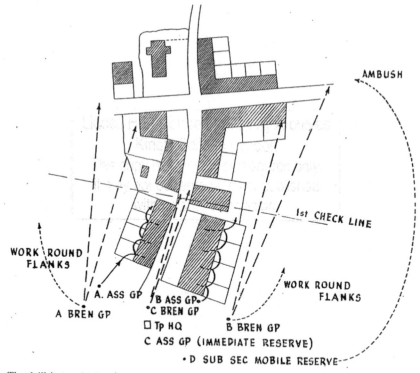

The drill is taught for dealing with the usual type of small village by a Troop. Not to be confused with Town Fighting or Fighting in City Centres.

Method :—1. FIRE GROUPS.

2. CHECK LINE.

3. MOBILE RESERVE.

4. ASSAULT PARTIES.

1. Fire Groups.

(a) The Leading Sub-section should place automatics to fire down the main road, killing anyone appearing in the streets.

(b) Flanking Sections should place LMGs to cover flanks of Village and any exits to the rear.

2. Check Line.

As houses are cleared, a signal such as handkerchief on bayonet is shown through windows leading on to the street.

A limit of advance should be chosen and the houses automatically cleared up to that line. The Fire Groups may then advance up the Village and a new advance can continue from the Check Line, which should not be too far ahead. It is essential that control is maintained and that there is always contact between the Fire Groups and the ASSAULT PARTIES.

3. Mobile Reserve.

A reserve should be ready to deal with bodies of enemy attempting to leave the Village.

4. Assault Parties.

(a) The dominant house in a row of buildings should be attacked first.

(b) Houses must be entered from the rear and the advance should be through the back gardens.

(c) The entry of individual houses should be performed as for " clearing a building."

(d) Care must be taken to clear all houses. If a dominant house has been cleared first, all smaller houses between this dominant one and the Fire Groups must be carefully cleared. If working back again, a picket should make sure that the dominant house is not re-occupied.

BATTLE DRILL FOR CLEARING STREETS OF A CONGESTED TOWN.

The congested area of a Town does not allow much freedom of movement or widespread fields of fire.

The most dominant positions for covering fire will be the roof tops.

Method :—

The leading Sub-section should immediately take up a position to cover and fire into the buildings on the left of the road.

The second Sub-section should immediately take up a position to cover and fire into the buildings on the right of the road.

The rear two Sub-sections should then enter the first house on each side of the road and establish themselves on the rooftops. These two Sub-sections will then take over Fire Groups, and the systematic clearing of the houses will be undertaken by the first two Sub-sections.

The covering fire of the Fire Groups should be one or two houses ahead of the assaulting Sub-sections.

The Signal that a house has been cleared can be given by showing handkerchief on bayonet out of window on to street and the cover then lifts and moves forward to the next house.

Assaulting Sections as well as Fire Groups can help to clear houses forward of the assaulting parties, by throwing grenades across the street into windows farther up the street on the opposite side.

Fire Groups should move along the roofs keeping just behind the assaulting parties. The Bren Groups should concentrate on the windows on the opposite side of the street. Rifle Groups should be responsible for flank protection.

PHASE 1.

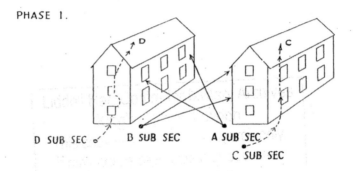

D SUB SEC   B SUB SEC   A SUB SEC
C SUB SEC

PHASE 2.

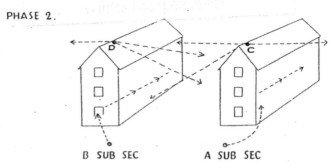

B SUB SEC   A SUB SEC

N.B.—It must be remembered that only a limited number of grenades can be carried, and as many as possible conserved for later stages of the battle.

13

BATTLE DRILL FOR WOOD CLEARING.

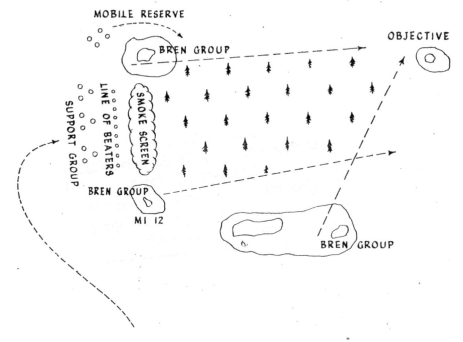

Method :—1. THE APPROACH TO THE WOOD.
        2. STOPS (TO ENCIRCLE WOOD WITH FIRE).
        3. BEATERS.
        4. SUPPORT GROUPS.
        5. MOBILE RESERVE.
        6. 2-IN. MORTARS.
        7. ORDERS.

1. The Approach to the Wood.

Points to be considered by the Commander (Troop or Section, depending on size of the ground).

(*a*) Decide on OP and make for it.   (Read Map.)

(*b*) Decide on method of beating—where to where—consider shape of wood—enter on a short front—not on a point—choose possible objective to make for, or if necessary, a possible CHECK LINE.

14

(c) Decide on positions for the STOPS.

(d) Decide how many BEATERS and detail them.

(e) Detail SUPPORT GROUPS.

(f) Detail MOBILE RESERVE.

(g) Decide on SUCCESS SIGNAL and on final rendezvous.

2. Stops.

(a) Task performed by LMGs who must get into position to perform whole task—must cover 360°, but use as few Brens as possible to preserve fire power—KILLING GROUND is the area outside the wood—ANYONE LEAVING the wood before the Success Signal will be KILLED.

(b) STOPS usually a Bren Group, but if necessary, just a No. 1.

(c) STOPS must get into position UNSEEN.

(d) They must cover the advance of the BEATERS and SUPPORT GROUPS into the wood.

(e) If the wood is long a check line may be given, and STOPS must move up to positions further forward on a pre-arranged Signal.

3. Beaters.

(a) Do not stint. Have as many as possible—should NOT be more than 5-6 yards apart.

(b) The Commander should be in centre of the line of BEATERS.

(c) All TSMGs should be with the line of BEATERS.

(d) Enter Wood in organized line, pace that of the slowest man.

(e) If line halts—BEATERS DOWN using cover and OBSERVE.

(f) Observe direct to front and look for FLASH, SMOKE or MOVEMENT.

(g) BEATERS to know their own SUPPORT GROUPS and to be able to call upon them easily.

(h) When enemy is encountered KILL HIM with bullets, bayonets or butts, if he is close enough. If he is beyond quick rushing distance, get down and fire, and call up Support Groups.

4. Support Group.

(a) Should never be less than 3 per group. There should NOT be less than 2 groups.

(b) Must keep contact with Beaters. Keep them in view.

(c) When enemy are encountered, beaters get down and give covering fire for Support Groups to come in with bullet from hip and bayonet. Line then reforms, Troop or Section Commander checking up, then FORWARD.

(d) Support Group best led by an NCO

(e) Watch Tree Tops. One man (the NCO) keeps contact with Beaters, others watch the trees.

5. Mobile Reserve.

(a) Strength depends on numbers available. If there is transport, use it. Stay on transport and OBSERVE.

(b) Chase the enemy should they succeed in crossing the Killing Ground alive.

15

6. 2-in. Mortars.

(a) Left under cover near OP.

(b) If necessary, give Smoke Cover to enable wood to be entered. If necessary, put down H.E. on edge of wood.

(c) Can be used by Mobile Reserve if necessary.

7. Orders.

(a) First given to STOPS, i.e., to No. 1 Bren Gunners.

(b) Then to " O " Group, i.e., Section Sergeant, Sub-Section Commanders, and No. 1 Mortars.

(c) Usual sequence of orders is STOPS—BEATERS—SUPPORT GROUPS—MOBILE RESERVE—MORTARS TASK—RENDEZVOUS—SUCCESS SIGNAL.

DISCIPLINE : NO ONE to leave the wood until Success.

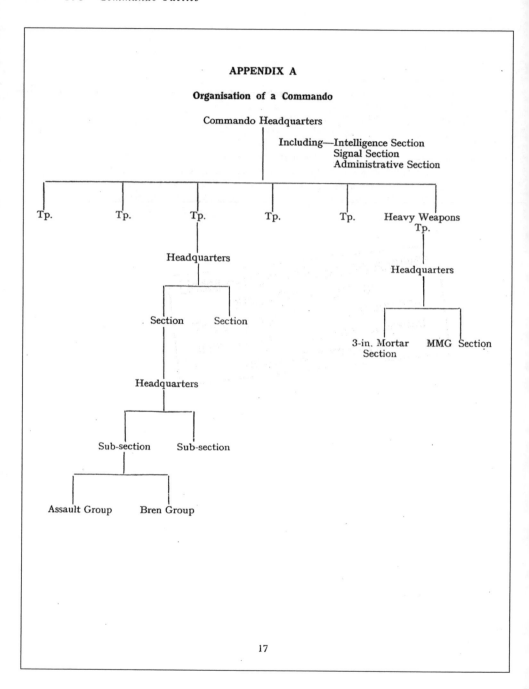

APPENDIX A

Organisation of a Commando

Commando Headquarters

Including—Intelligence Section
Signal Section
Administrative Section

Tp.   Tp.   Tp.   Tp.   Tp.   Heavy Weapons Tp.

Headquarters

Section   Section

Headquarters

3-in. Mortar Section   MMG Section

Headquarters

Sub-section   Sub-section

Assault Group   Bren Group

17

COMMANDO TROOP—ORG.

(Showing a normal method of allotting weapons)

Capt.
Two Subalterns.
TSM
Six Sgts.
Four Cpls.
Eight L/Cpls.
Forty-three Mnes. = Total 65 all ranks.

Tp. H.Q.—

Capt. ...	...	Pistol.
TSM ...	...	Rifle.
Runner	...	Sten. Pistol Sig.
Two Mnes.	...	PIAT.
		Rifle.
		Pistol.

(Att.—One RAMC Nursing Orderly)

Note.—One Cpl may be withdrawn from a Section for adm. duties at Tp HQ
One extra Bren may be carried in Tp HQ

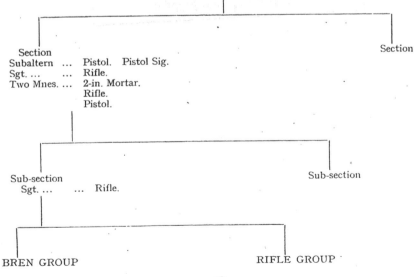

Section
Subaltern ... Pistol. Pistol Sig.
Sgt. ... ... Rifle.
Two Mnes. ... 2-in. Mortar.
Rifle.
Pistol.

Section

Sub-section
Sgt. ... ... Rifle.

Sub-section

BREN GROUP

RIFLE GROUP

18

L/Cpl.	Rifle	Cpl.	Rifle
Three Mnes. ...	Bren	Seven Mnes. ...	Five rifles (may include one
	Two Rifles		Sniper's rifle and one
	Pistol		EY rifle)
			Two Stens

Note : (a) *Org.*—It must be remembered that the allotment of personnel, weapons and equipment within the Troop will be varied at the discretion of the Troop and Section Commanders according to the Op.

(b) *Grenades.*—36 (4 section for hand throwing and 7 section for EY rifle), 68, 69, 75, 77 and 79 grenades are carried in a Cdo. The number and type carried in the Troop will vary according to the Op.

(c) *Weapons :*

	Carried in the Troop	In Cdo. HQ Pool for issue to Troops for a specified Op., at discretion of C O
Pistol .45 Colt Auto	15	25
Pistol Signal	3	14
Rifle, No. 4, Mk. I	38	45
Rifles, Snipers, Mk. I (T) No. 3	2	10
Rifles, No. 1, Mk. III or No. 3 (E.Y. rifle) ...	—	20
Brens	5	10
PIAT	—	10
TMG	9	40
2-in. Mortar (Ordinary)	2	5
(Airborne)	—	20
Vickers M.M.G.	—	2
3-in. Mortar	—	2

(d) *Equipment.*—The following equipment may also be carried according to the nature of the Op. :—

Toggle ropes.
Entrenching tools.
Mae Wests.
Bangalore Torpedoes and demolition equipment.
Climbing equipment.
Folding bicycles.
Rubber dinghies.
Handcarts.

(e) *Signals.*—One Signaller with a " 38 " set from Cdo. Sig. Sec. will normally be attached to Troop HQ for an Op.

(f) *Heavy Weapons Troop.*—A detachment of the Heavy Weapons Troop may be attached to a Fighting Troop at the discretion of the CO. Extra ammunition for the Heavy Weapons Troop (3-in. Mortar bombs and MMG ammunition) will normally be carried by the personnel of a Fighting Troop.

19

Effective Date—28th August, 1943

A COMMANDO—ROYAL MARINES

(To Command and Administer 5 Fighting Troops and One Heavy Weapons Troop).

War Establishment

(1) PERSONNEL

Detail	Commando H.Q.					Five Fighting Troops (each)					Heavy Weapons Troop				Total RM Commando
	Headquarters	Intelligence Section	Signal Section	Adm. Section	Total H.Q.	Troop H.Q.	Section H.Q.	2 Sub-sec. (each)	Total Section	Total Troop	Troop H.Q.	3-in. Mortar Section	MMG Section	Total Troop	
Commanding Officer (Lt.-Col.)	1	—	—	—	1	—	—	—	—	—	—	—	—	—	1
2nd in Command (Major)	1	—	—	—	1	—	—	—	—	—	—	—	—	—	1
Adjutant (Capt.)	1	—	—	—	1	—	—	—	—	—	—	—	—	—	1
Intelligence Officer (Lt.)	—	1	—	—	1	—	—	—	—	—	—	—	—	—	1
Captains	—	—	—	—	—	1	—	—	—	1	1	—	—	—	1	6
Subalterns	—	—	1	—	1	—	1	—	1	2	1	—	—	—	1	12
Administration Officer (c)	—	—	—	1	1	—	—	—	—	—	—	—	—	—	1
Total Officers	3	1	1	1	6	1	1	—	1	3	2	—	—	—	2	23
RSM	1	—	—	—	1	—	—	—	—	—	—	—	—	—	1
RQMS	—	—	—	1	1	—	—	—	—	—	—	—	—	—	1
CSM	—	—	—	—	—	1	—	—	—	1	—	—	—	—	5
Armourer Sgt.	—	—	—	1	1	—	—	—	—	—	—	—	—	—	1
Orderly Room Sgt.	1	—	—	—	1	—	—	—	—	—	—	—	—	—	1
Pay Sgt.	—	—	—	1	1	—	—	—	—	—	—	—	—	—	1
Sgt. RMSI	—	—	1	—	1	—	—	—	—	—	—	—	—	—	1
Transport Sgt.	—	—	—	1	1	—	—	—	—	—	—	—	—	—	1
Stores Sgt.	—	—	—	1	1	—	—	—	—	—	—	—	—	—	1
Intelligence Sgt.	—	1	—	—	1	—	—	—	—	—	—	—	—	—	1
Colour Sgts.	—	—	—	—	—	—	—	—	—	—	1	—	—	1	1
Sergeants	—	—	—	—	—	1	1	—	3	6	—	1	1	2	32
Total S.N.C.O.	2	1	1	5	9	1	1	1	3	7	1	1	1	3	47 (a)
Corporal RMS(1)	—	—	4	—	4	—	—	—	—	—	—	—	—	—	4
Corporal Intelligence	—	1	—	—	1	—	—	—	—	—	—	—	—	—	1
Corporal Clerks	1	—	—	1	2	—	—	—	—	—	—	—	—	—	2
Corporal Drivers IC	—	—	—	2	2	—	—	—	—	—	—	—	—	—	2
Corporal IC Despatch Riders	—	—	—	1	1	—	—	—	—	—	—	—	—	—	1
Stores Corporal	—	—	—	1	1	—	—	—	—	—	—	—	—	—	1
Corporals	—	—	—	—	—	—	—	2	4	8	—	2	2	4	44
Total Corporals	1	1	4	5	11	—	—	2	4	8	—	2	2	4	55
Tradesmen and Marines	6	5	18	33	62	1	1	11	23	47	3	11	13	27	324
Total Other Ranks	9	7	23	43	82	2	2	14	30	62	4	14	16	34	426
Total All Ranks	12	8	24	44	88	3	3	14	31	65	6	14	16	36	449
ATTACHED RAMC — Captain or Subaltern	1	—	—	—	1	—	—	—	—	—	—	—	—	—	1
Staff Sgt. or Sgt.	1	—	—	—	1	—	—	—	—	—	—	—	—	—	1
Lance Corporals	6	—	—	—	6	—	—	—	—	—	—	—	—	—	6
Privates	2	—	—	—	2	—	—	—	—	—	—	—	—	—	2
Total Attached	10	—	—	—	10	—	—	—	—	—	—	—	—	—	10
TOTAL INCL. ATTACHED	22	8	24	44	98	3	3	14	31	65	6	14	16	36	459

20

A COMMANDO—ROYAL MARINES

War Establishment

(2) DISTRIBUTION OF MARINES BY TRADES AND DUTIES

Page 2

DETAIL	Commando H.Q.					Five Fighting Troops (each)					Heavy Weapons Troop				Total RM Commando
	Headquarters	Intelligence Section	Signal Section	Adm. Section	Total H.Q.	Troop H.Q.	Section H.Q.	2 Sub-sec. (each)	Total Section	Total Troop	Troop H.Q.	3-in. Mortar Section	MMG Section	Total Troop	
							2 Sections (each)								
Tradesmen—															
Armourer	—	—	—	1	1	—	—	—	—	—	—	—	—	—	1
Clerk (MT Technical) ...	—	—	—	1	1	—	—	—	—	—	—	—	—	—	1
Equipment Repairer ...	—	—	—	1	1	—	—	—	—	—	—	—	—	—	1
Driver Mechanic	—	—	—	—	—	—	—	—	—	—	—	5	5	10	10
Fitter MV	—	—	—	2	2	—	—	—	—	—	—	—	—	—	2
Technical Storeman... ...	—	—	—	1	1	—	—	—	—	—	—	—	—	—	1
Shoemaker	—	—	—	1	1	—	—	—	—	—	—	—	—	—	1
Total Tradesmen	—	—	—	7	7	—	—	—	—	—	—	5	5	10	17
Non-Tradesmen—															
Batmen/Orderlies	4	—	—	1	5	1	1	—	1	3	—	—	—	—	20
Batmen/Drivers	—	1	1	—	—	—	—	—	—	—	2	—	—	2	4
Clerks	2	—	—	1	3	—	—	—	—	—	—	—	—	—	3
Despatch Riders	—	—	—	8	8	—	—	—	—	—	—	—	—	—	8
Drivers IC	—	—	—	14	14	—	—	—	—	—	—	—	—	—	14
Intelligence Section ...	—	4	—	—	4	—	—	—	—	—	—	—	—	—	4
Machine Gun Dets. ...	—	—	—	—	—	—	—	—	—	—	—	—	6	6	6
Mortar Dets.	—	—	—	—	—	—	—	—	—	—	—	6	—	6	6
Orderlies	—	—	—	—	—	—	—	—	—	—	—	—	1	1	1
Range Takers	—	—	—	—	—	—	—	—	—	—	1	—	1	2	2
Signallers (b)	—	—	17	—	17	—	—	—	—	—	—	—	—	—	17
Storemen	—	—	—	2	2	—	—	—	—	—	—	—	—	—	2
Marines	—	—	—	—	—	—	—	11	22	44	—	—	—	—	220
Total Non-Tradesmen ...	6	5	18	26	55	1	1	11	23	47	3	6	8	17	307

Notes :—(*a*) Includes 2 Clr./Sgts. in addition to the one shown in detail.

(*b*) Includes 2 RMS (1) and 15 RMS (2).

(*c*) This appointment to be held by a Quartermaster (R.M.), except when special authority is given by G.O.C., R.M., in which case this officer will be a Captain.

(*d*) Cooks and messing staff as set out below to be included in numbers of G.D. Personnel shown above in the case of a Commando overseas :—

O.M. Cook ...	...	...	...	1	
Cooks O.Rs. Mess ...	...	...	9	
Butchers ...	...	...	...	1	

(3) TRANSPORT

Detail	Headquarters	Heavy Weapon Troop	Total Commando
Bicycles	35	—	35
Motor-cycles, solo	9	—	9
Car, 4-seater, 4 × 2, G.S.	1	—	1
Cars, 5-cwt, 4 × 4	6	12	18
Trucks, 15-cwt, 4 × 2, G.S.	8	—	8
Lorr es, 3-ton, 4 × 2, G.S	3	—	3

21

APPENDIX B

SET PIECE ATTACK ON SMALL DEFENDED LOCALITY. THE COMMANDO SECTION IN THE ATTACK.

The Commando section is the smallest unit commanded by an officer, and is the smallest force which can be expected to launch an *organised* attack.

The method of attack laid down here is extremely simple. It is as simple as possible, but it combines the TRUE PRINCIPLES OF FIRE AND MOVEMENT. If every section within the Commando knows the basic attack, it is possible for a Commanding Officer to launch an attack on these lines from the size of one section to that of the whole Commando.

The method can be employed against enemy positions in depth and attacks against further enemy posts can follow the initial attack in rapid succession. A close study of following sections will explain this.

IT IS ESSENTIAL TO REMEMBER THAT THE TACTICS ARE SIMPLE, BUT THE EXECUTION OF THE PLAN MUST BE FIRST-CLASS.

In this attack both assault groups of one section carry out attack, whilst the second section are in Mobile Reserve. Even if the enemy position is held in very weak strength, it is still desirable to employ both assault groups for the following reasons :—

(a) It automatically ensures the German section which is 10 in strength is outnumbered.

(b) It facilitates control.

(c) It enables final assault to go in in two waves. Thus, the Section Commander has a reserve under his hand, even during the assault itself.

(d) It ensures the Section will not be " thin on the ground " when the inevitable counter attack takes place.

(e) Any augmenting of the Fire Group can be done by the Mobile Reserve.

On the Verey Light signal to lift supporting fire before the actual assault, the fire group continue firing but switch, this misleads the enemy and ensures he keeps his head down during the critical stage.

DRILL FOR ATTACK.

The Section or Troop should advance over the ground using as much caution as is compatible with the necessity for speed, and continue until the leading sub-section encounters fire from an enemy position. Care must be taken to ensure that a sniper alone does not hold up the advance, and the forward advance should continue until an actual stand by the enemy is encountered. As a guide, the advance should continue until aimed small arms fire at a range of less than 600 yards is encountered with an intensity sufficient to cause casualties unless action is taken.

When such an enemy is encountered, the Commander of the leading section must decide whether he can neutralize the enemy by his own immediate action, or whether the Troop Commander must be brought in. In the first case he will at once attack.

A. Drill for Section Acting on its own Initiative.

1. *Leading Sub-section is fired on :—*

Action of remainder of section	...	Run to cover.
Action of leading Sub-section	...	(a) Run to cover indicated by Sub-section Commander (or Section Commander if up with them).
		(b) Adopt fire position.

In adopting fire positions, remember cover from view is NOT cover from fire if you are seen getting there.

DON'T BE PIN-POINTED. THE LEADING SUB-SECTION MUST BE AGGRESSIVE.

2. *Action of Section Commander.*

   (a) Comes up as close as possible and identifies the enemy position (from Sub-section Commander, if necessary).

   (b) Makes quick appreciation of the situation and plan and issues QUICK orders.

3. *Orders of Section Commander.*

   These might be :—" Enemy in copse 300 yards direction my arm—We will kill all enemy—Right (or Left) Flanking—Smoke there—Bren Groups there—Assault Groups that way—Signals normal."

   Note 1.—The descriptions of positions must be as brief as possible consistent with being thoroughly understood.

   Note 2.—When the Bren Groups are left as Fire Group, the Section Sgt. would remain and control their fire.

   Note 3.—The Section Commander will lead the Assault Group.

4. (a) *2-in. Mortar.*

   (i) If ordered, smokes target at once. This serves to cover the move of the Assault Group and also to act as a landmark to pinpoint the enemy when the Assault Group reach their forming-up position.

   (ii) Then joins Fire Group and thickens their fire with HE if necessary.

   (b) *Action of the Fire Group.*

   (i) Steady—accurate—controlled—AGRESSIVE Fire.

   (ii) Foot on the ground whilst Flankers move.

   (iii) Engage full attention of the enemy.

   (iv) Work forward frontally when possible to get more accurate field of fire.

   (v) On success signal, come up and reorganise.

   Note.—The Bren Group of the leading Sub-section must fire if necessary to allow the rifle group to withdraw for flanking.

   The Fire Group should try to help the Flankers forward by firing at PSYCHOLOGICAL moments, and observe exactly when the assault is going in. On the Assault Group approaching the objective, fire of Bren Groups must switch to any convenient target—it must not STOP—thus making the enemy think he is still being fired on and so keeping his head down.

5. *Action of Flanking Assault Groups.*

   (a) Lead by Section Commander round flank through covered approaches, covered by fire of Fire Group.

   (b) On reaching position from which assault is to be made, form up for assault (usually in two waves, one passing through the enemy and the other clearing up behind them).

   (c) Verey light or normal signal for assault fired by Section Commander, and Fire Group switch IMMEDIATELY.

6. *The Assault.*

   (a) The crucial moment—On Guard—Run FLAT OUT.

   (b) Stens fire to take place of Brens which have switched.

23

(c) SHOUT.

(d) Fire from hip and add 20 yards on the bayonet.

(e) Wheel into the original axis of advance when through the objective.

(f) Section Commander must fire success signal as soon as objective is taken to ensure speedy reorganisation.

7. *Re-organisation.*

(a) Must take place immediately the assault is successfully completed, in order to repel any counter-attack.

(b) Must be in original axis of advance. This is the direction a counter-attack is most likely to come from.

(c) Get well off the objective. The enemy will mortar it as soon as they realise it has been taken.

(d) All-round protection.

(e) Bren Groups must come up quickly. Their fire power will be needed to repel any counter-attack.

(f) Leave room for the following Section and Troop HQ, when they come up, well clear of objective.

B. Drill for a Troop.

Note that even in the case of a leading Section taking immediate action on its own, the Troop Commander will play his part and can help the action forward with supporting fire from the remaining Section, when he sees an opportunity by observation.

1. *Troop Commander's Orders.*

(a) When the leading Sub-section is committed, the Troop Commander should come up as close as possible. Make a quick plan and issue quick orders.

(b) The Troop " O " Group should move up behind Troop HQ, so that orders may be shouted to them.

(c) The orders follow a similar pattern to those given by the Section Commander.

2. *The Re-organisation.*

(a) The first section in at the Assault should reorganise forward and become the leading section in the continued advance.

(b) The second section should reorganise in rear with a sub-section on right and left. This makes for better all-round protection.

(c) On reorganisation, the " O " Group should immediately take up their position behind Troop HQ

(d) After the reorganisation, Section Commanders should report all casualties to Troop HQ and inform Troop HQ of their ammunition supply.

24

(5141/682) Wt. 48030/P7578 750 2/45. T. & B. Gp. 8.

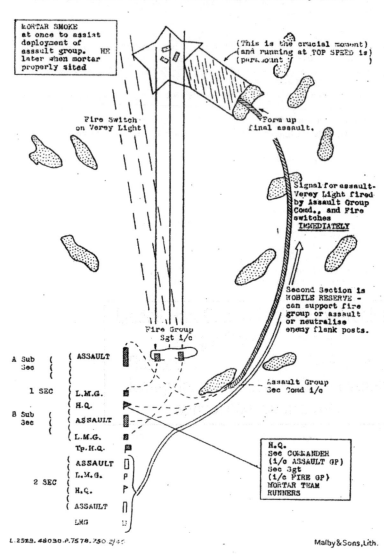

SET PIECE SECTION ATTACK ON
SMALL DEFENDED LOCALITY
(Increased to Troop attack where necessary)

NOTE: The Commando Section is the same size as an Infantry Platoon.

MORTAR SMOKE
at once to assist
deployment of
assault group.   HE
later when mortar
properly sited

(This is the crucial moment)
(and running at TOP SPEED is)
(paramount   )

Fire Switch
on Verey Light

Form up
final assault.

Signal for assault.
Verey Light fired
by Assault Group
Comd., and Fire
switches
IMMEDIATELY

Second Section is
MOBILE RESERVE -
can support fire
group or assault
or neutralise
enemy flank posts.

Fire Group
Sgt i/c

Assault Group
Sec Comd i/c

A Sub Sec	ASSAULT
1 SEC	L.M.G.
	H.Q.
B Sub Sec	ASSAULT
	L.M.G.
	Tp.H.Q.
2 SEC	ASSAULT
	L.M.G.
	H.Q.
	ASSAULT
	LMG

H.Q.
Sec COMMANDER
(i/c ASSAULT GP)
Sec Sgt
(i/c FIRE GP)
MORTAR TEAM
RUNNERS

L.2529. 48030.P.7578.750 2/45

Malby & Sons, Lith.

Bibliography

Memoirs, manuals, and other primary sources

Anon. 'List of Officers and Men of No. 4 Commando who attacked and Destroyed the Hess Battery at Varengeville', Queen's Lancashire Regiment Museum, 846/2.2.

Anon. *Manual of Commando and Guerrilla Warfare: Unarmed Combat*, London, undated (*c.* 1941).

Anon. *The Sten Machine Carbine*, Aldershot, undated.

Anon. *The Thompson Submachine Gun*, Aldershot, undated.

Austin, A. B. *We Landed at Dawn*, London, 1943.

Bertram B. B. & G. C. L. *Handbook on Clothing and Equipment Required in Cold Climates*, War Office/Ordnance Survey, 1941.

Brereton, J. M. 'Memories of his Service in the Royal Marines During the Second World War [...] 30th Assault Unit', Sound recording, Dorset History Centre, DSA/143/1.

Chant–Sempil, S. *St Nazaire Commando*, London, 1985.

Churchill, T. *Commando Crusade*, London, 1987.

Durnford-Slater, J. *Commando*, London, 1953.

Embleton collection. *Commando: Where Next?*, *c.* 1943. Liddell Hart Archive 2/3/1–22.

Fairbairn W. E. *All-in Fighting*, 1942.

Fairbairn W. E. & Sykes E. A. *Shooting to Live*, 1942, reprinted Boulder, 1987.

Forfar, J. *From Omaha to the Scheldt: The Story of 47 Royal Marine Commando*, East Linton, 2001.

General Staff (India). *Close Quarter Battle*, Small Arms Training, Volume 1, Pamphlet 2, Delhi, 1945.

Gooch, F. 'Papers of Lance Corporal Frederick Gooch, No. 4 Commando', Surrey History Centre, ESR/25.

Gubbins, C. M. *Partisan Leader's Handbook*, London, 1939 (reprinted San Francisco, 1981).

Haydon, J. C. 'Papers of Major General JC Haydon', Imperial War Museum Archive, 2397, JCH 1/1–7.

Haydon, J. C. (et al) *Raid on Military and Economic Objectives in the Lofoten Islands*, Official Despatch, March 1941.

Hickman, R. J. 'Papers of Frederick Raynard James Hickman, No. 1 Commando Brigade', Berkshire Records Office, D/EX 1201–1300.

Holman, G. *Commando Attack*, London, 1942.

Lawson, V. E. *Ranger–Commando Junior*, New York, 1944.

Mackenzie, A. *44 (RM) Commando*, Brighton, 1996.

Military Intelligence (US) *British Commandos*, War Department, Washington, 1942.

Mills-Roberts, D. *Clash By Night: A Commando Chronicle*, London, 1956.

Mills-Roberts, D. *Lessons Learned on Combined Operations*, undated, Liddell Hart Archive, Mills-Roberts, 1/5.

Mitchell, R. *Marine Commando*, London, 1988.

Mitchell, R. *Commando Despatch Rider*, London, 2001.

Montanaro, C. S. *Personal and Military Papers 1916–1976*. Liddell Hart Centre for Military Archives, King's College London, unpublished.

Morris, C. *The Diary of a Commando Soldier*, Mills-Roberts Collection, Liddell Hart Archive, 3/18.

Mountbatten, Lord L. *Combined Operations: The Official Story of the Commandos*, New York, 1943.

National Archives (UK) 'British North West Expeditionary Force, Norway, War Diaries 1939–1940', WO 168.

National Archives (UK) 'North West Expeditionary Force, Norway. Military Headquarters Papers, 1940', WO 192.

National Archives (UK) 'Combined Operations Headquarters, Records 1937–1963', DEFE 2.

National Archives (UK) 'Special Services War Diaries', WO 218.

National Archives (UK) 'War Crimes Case File' (Commando Order 1942), WO 235/560.

National Archives (UK) 'History of 30 Commando 1942–1946'. HW8/104.

National Archives (UK) 'Operation FROG; 46 (RM) Commando, 1944', ADM 202.

National Archives (UK) 'Second Echelon Commando Wing, Central Mediterranean Forces, 1945', ADM 202/86.

National Archives (UK) '44 (RM) Commando, 1945', ADM 202/96.

National Archives (UK) '47 (RM) Commando, 1943', ADM/107.

National Archives (UK) *Source Sheet 24: Dieppe Raid (Operation Jubilee)* list of 75 documentary sources from the archive, also web published.

Nutting, D. C. & Glanville T. J., *History of 30 Assault Unit 1942–1946*, Liddell Hart Archive, GB99 KCLMA.

Royal Marines, *Royal Marine Training Pamphlet No. 2: Commando Battle Drill*, 1945.

Ryder, R. E. D. *The Attack on St Nazaire*, London, 1947.

Stokoe, E. G. *Lower the Ramps: Experiences with 43 Royal Marine Commando in Yugoslavia*, Maidstone, 1974.

US War Department, 'Organisation and Training of British Commandos', in *Tactical and Technical Trends*, No. 1, 18 June, 1942.

US War Department, 'Devices for Crossing Streams, in *Tactical and Technical Trends*, No. 14, 17 December, 1942.

US War Department, 'Notes on Street Fighting – taken from a lecture given by a British Major to soldiers attending the Commando School' in *Tactical and Technical Trends*, No. 17, 28 January, 1943.

US War Department, 'Scouts and Observers – based on a lecture given by a British Officer at a Commando School' in *Tactical and Technical Trends 18*, No. 11, February, 1943.

US War Department, 'Commando Raid on Varengeville, France', in *Tactical and Technical Trends*, No. 28, 1 July, 1943.

War Office (UK), *Commando Training Instruction No. 1*, 15 August, 1940.

War Office (UK), *Surprise – The First Principle of Attack: A Handbook for NCOs*, General Staff Publication 592, 1941.

War Office (UK), *Individual Battle Practices*, Small Arms Training Volume I, Pamphlet No. 18, Supplement 1, General Staff Publication 925, 1943.

War Office (UK), *Grenade*, Small Arms Training Volume I, Pamphlet No. 13, 1942, reprinted General Staff Publication 1570, 1946.

War Office (UK), *Combined Operations: RA*, Pamphlet 34, General Staff Publication 911, 1943.

War Office (UK), *Notes From Theatres of War, No. 11, The Destruction of a German Battery by No. 4 Commando During the Dieppe Raid*, General Staff Publication 905, 1943.

War Office (UK), *The Machine Carbine*, Small Arms Training Volume I, Pamphlet No. 21, General Staff Publication 1115, 1944.

War Office (UK), *Infantry Training*, General Staff Publication 1076, 1944.

War Office (UK), *Rafting and Bridging: Military Training pamphlet 74, Part III, Assault Crossing Equipment*, General Staff Publication 1067, 1944.

Ward, D. C. R., 'My Time with 45 (RM) Commando', King's Own Scottish Borderers Museum, T1/1–37.

Weatherall, S., 'Papers of Lt. S. Weatherall', Imperial War Museum Archive, 2088, 76/143/1.

Young, P., *Storm from the Sea*, London, 1958.

Histories and Secondary Works

Anon, *The Story of 45 Royal Marine Commando*, London, 1949.

Allan, S., *Commando Country*, Edinburgh, 2007.

Atkin, R., *Dieppe 1942 – The Jubilee Disaster*, London, 1980.

Brown, G. A., *Commando Gallantry Awards of World War II*, (place of publication unspecified), 1991.

Butler, J. (ed.), *History of the Second World War*, United Kingdom Military Series, multi-volume, 1952–1972.

Butler, R., *Hand of Steel: the Story of the Commandos*, Feltham, 1980.

Carman, W. Y., 'The Distinctions of the Army Commandos, 1940–1945', in *Military Illustrated*, numbers 10 and 11, 1988.

Chappell, M., *Army Commandos 1940–1945*, London, 1996.

Cooksey, J. *Commandos: Operation Chariot, the Raid on St Nazaire*, Barnsley, 2005.

Cruickshank, C., *The German Occupation of the Channel Islands*, (New Edition), Stroud, 1990.

Davis, B. L., *British Army Uniforms and Insignia*, London, 1983.

Defelice, J., *Rangers at Dieppe*, New York, 2008.

Derry, T. K., *The Campaign in Norway* (Official History of the Second World War), London, 1952.

Dorrian, J. G., *Storming St Nazaire*, London, 1998.

Duffield, A., 'The Royal Marines', Imperial War Museum, Recommended Reading List 134, 2001.

Dunning, J., *The Fighting Fourth: No 4 Commando at War*, Stroud, 2003.

Ford, K., *D-Day Commando: From Normandy to the Maas with 48 Royal Marine Commando*, Stroud, 2003.

Fowler, W., *The Commandos at Dieppe*, London, 2002.

Gilchrist, D., *Don't Cry for Me: The Commandos, D-Day and After*, London, 1982.

Gilchrist, D., *Castle Commando*, 1960.

Henry, H. G., *The Planning, Intelligence, Execution and Aftermath of the Dieppe Raid*, unpublished PhD thesis, Cambridge University, 1996.

Hobbs, B., 'British Commandos in the Field, 1942–1945', in *Military Illustrated*, numbers 26 and 30, 1990.

Hunter, R., *True Stories of the Commandos*, London, 2000.

Keyes, E., *Geoffrey Keyes*, London, 1956.

Ladd, J. D., *Commandos and Rangers of World War II*, London, 1978.

Ladd, J. D., *Royal Marine Commando*, London, 1982.

Landsborough, G., *Tobruk Commando*, London, 1956.

Langdon, J., 'Too old or too bold? The Removal of Sir Roger Keyes as Churchill's First Director of Combined Operations', in Imperial War Museum *Review*, number 8, undated.

Lee, D., *Beachhead Assault: The Story of the Royal Naval Commandos in World War II*, London, 2004.

McDougall, M. C., *Swiftly they Struck*, London, 1988.

Michelli, A., *Commando to Captain General: The Life of Brigadier Peter Young*, Barnsley, 2007.

Moreman, T., *British Commandos 1940–1946*, Oxford, 2006.

Moulton, J. L., *The Royal Marines*, London, 1972.

Neillands, R., *By Sea and Land: The Story of the Royal Marines Commandos*, London, 1987.

Neillands, R., *The Raiders: The Army Commandos 1940–1946*, London, 1989.

Neillands, R., *The Dieppe Raid*, London, 2005.

Nutting D. and Glanville J., *Attain by Surprise: the Story of 30 Assault Unit*, Chichester, 1997.

Oakley, D., *The Commandos*, Poole, 1987.

Preston, E., *The Commando Raids on Sark*, Dartmouth, 2007.

Ramsay, W. G., 'Dieppe', in *After The Battle*, number 5, London, 1974.

Ramsay, W. G., 'Operation Ambassador', in *After The Battle*, number 32, London, 1981.

Reeves, D., *Special Service of a Hazardous Nature: The Story of Liverpool Scottish Involvement in Special Forces Operations*, Liverpool, 2007.

Schofield, S., *Musketoon Commando Raid, Glomfjord 1942*, London, 1964.

Scott, S., *Fighting with the Commandos*, Barnsley, 2008.

Shortt, J. G., *Special Forces Insignia: British and Commonwealth Units*, London, 1988.

Thompson, J., *War Behind Enemy Lines*, Imperial War Museum, 1998.

Thompson, L., *Commando Dagger*, Boulder, 1985.

Wallis, J., *With God's Blessing and a Green Beret*, Poole, 1994.

Young, P., *Commando*, London, 1974.

Young, P., *The Commando Memorial Spean Bridge*, 1978.

Index

'A' Commando (see also 40 RM Commando) 59, 66–7
Abbott, J. 65–6, 153
Abwehr Englisher Gangster-Methoden 122
Achnacarry 60, 97–106, 165, 173–5, 177
Achnacarry Castle 97
All-in Fighting 111–20
Ambassador, Operation 20–2
Amfreville 153
Andrews, Corporal (RM) 139
'Anklet', Operation 34, 173
Anti-tank rifles 7, 46
Applegate, Colonel Rex (US) 120
Appleyard, Lance Corporal Frank (RM) 145
Appleyard, Major 79, 83–4
'Archery', Operation 34–43
Artillery, and Combined Operations 131–2, 145
Assault craft 19, 28, 29, 46, 63, 66, 99–100, 179
Austin A. B. 60–1, 72, 169
Awrology 120–21

Badges 16–7, 98, 101, 167
Balloche, Sergeant François 60
Bangalore torpedoes 92, 131, 200
Barber, Samuel 98
'Basalt', Operation 79
'Battle drills' 95–6, 124–8, 182–206
'Battle inoculation' 85
Beach Commando, Beach Master 133–4
Beret, green/blue (see also 'Headgear') 98, 101, 138, 175
Bergen rucksacks, use on D-Day 137–8
Berneval 58, 62, 64
Bevin, Marine Reginald 67
Bidmead, Private W. 160
Birney, Captain 52

Bissell, Stanley 119
Blunden, Corporal C. 75
Bourne, Lieutenant General A. 12–3, 22
Bradley, Captain 40–2
Breen, Marine T. 67
Bren guns, additional provision of 137
British Commandos (1942) 129, 171, 176
Brooke, General Sir Alan 43
Bryen, C. L. G. 172–3
Buckee, Lieutenant (RNVR) 63–4
Burn, Captain M. 47

Campbell Hardy, Lieutenant Colonel 149
Campbeltown, HMS 47–56
Campbeltown, HMS, explosion of 54
Carr, Captain 'Muscles' 159
'Cauldron', Operation 68–78
Channel Islands 20–2, 79–80
Chant, Lieutenant S. W. 48, 51
'Chariot', Operation 45–56
Chasseur boats 66
'Chopper', Operation 34
Churchill, Colonel John M. T. F. ('Mad Jack') 12, 36–8, 83, 170
Churchill, Randolph 168
Churchill, Tom 101–02
Churchill, Winston viii, 1–3, 20, 22–4, 26, 29, 33, 43, 58, 78, 107, 164, 168, 171, 175, 178
Clarke, Colonel Dudley W. 3, 8–11, 15–6, 18–20
'Claymore', Operation 29–34, 167, 173
Clement, Lieutenant 36
Cliffe Cooling Marsh ranges 127
Climbing 84, 105–06
Clothing, uniform, and clothing civilian 7, 82, 98, 179–180

'Collar', Operation 19–20
Combined Operations Development Centre 103
Commando:
  Army disbandment of 178
  as 'brand' viii, 171–2
  Association 12
  Commando Attack 169–71
  Basic Training Centre (CBTC) 97, 174
  Commando Battle Drill (1945) 127, 166, 182–206
  birth of 1–28
  Boer 9–10, 172
  derivation of term 9–10
  March 98
  memorandum 8–9
  memorial (Westminster Abbey) 164
  mythology of viii–ix, 1
  as 'national force' 167
  'Order' 80–2, 174
  organisation – *see* 'Organisation'
  units – *see* 'Units'
Communications 43
Copland, Major W. C. 50, 52, 55
Cousins, Captain (RM) 142
'Covering fire', instruction regarding 125
Crete 69
'Crusader', Operation 44

D-Day 133–162
Darby, Major William (US Rangers) 59
Dawson, Lieutenant Colonel Robert 123, 134, 157–9
'Deepcut', Operation 34
Demonstration troop (see also 'Achnacarry') 98
Dewing, Major General R. H. 10
Dieppe, raid on 57–82, 165, 169
Diet – *see* 'Food'

'Doubling week' 104
'Dryad', Operation 79
Dunkirk 1, 8
Dunning, Captain James 31, 87, 99
Durnford-Slater, Colonel John 13–4, 22, 26, 30, 32, 34, 39–42, 62, 83, 176
Durrant, Sergeant T. F. 54

Eisenhower, General D. 59
Equipment, general 7, 17–8, 28, 37, 46, 61, 64, 130–1, 136, 138, 150, 179–80, 200
Eureka boats 62
'Euston Bridges', '1' and '2' 135

Fairbairn, Colonel William Ewart 109–11, 113–9, 171
Fairbairn-Sykes, see also 'knives' 60, 109–10, 115–9
Fawcett, Troop Sergeant Major (RM) 148
'Field Firing' 85
Film, and propaganda value of 170–1, 173
Finney, William 74
'Fire and movement', development of 125
Floss 34
Flunder, Major (RM) 139
Food, messing and diet 15–6, 37, 87–91, 97, 174
Forfar, John 142
Forrester, Algy 39
Frankton Raid 100
Fraser, Simon J. – see 'Lovat'

Garnon-Williams, Captain C. (RN) 11
Get Tough – see All-in Fighting
Goatley boat, and Fred Goatley 100
'Gold' beach 135
Gray, Marine Douglas 143
Grey, Major (RM) 150–2
Gubbins, Colonel C. M. (1896–1976) 3–9, 163, 166
Guerrilla fighting, and principles of 4–5, 82, 95, 111, 114–15, 163, 167–8

Hargreaves-Heap, Captain 133
Haydon, Major General Joseph C. 14, 27, 29–30, 34, 49, 55, 85, 102, 126
Headgear 16–7, 61, 98, 101, 138
Hipkiss, James 119
Hitler, Adolf 80, 82, 168, 174
Hodgson, Captain 47, 50
Holland, Colonel J. F. C. 3
Hooper, Captain 36, 40
Hopkins, Private 64–6
Houghton, Major R. D. (RM) 67–8
Howes-Dufton, Captain Peter T. (RM) 148
Hunt, Major John 106
'Huskey', Operation 32
Hutton, Lieutenant 31

Independent Companies (see also 'Units') 3–8, 18–21, 26
Individual Battle Practices 125–7
Infantry Section Leading (1938) 125
Infantry Training (1944) 125, 156
'Instinctive aim' 112–3
Instructor's Handbook on Fieldcraft and Battle Drill 125
Inveraray 43, 84, 106
'Ironclad', Operation 134
Irregular Warfare School 85
Ismay, Major General Sir Hastings (1887–1965) 2, 20, 22–3

Jeeps 136
Jenkins, Lieutenant W. G. 104–06
Jiu-Jitsu 109, 119–20, 169
Jodl, General Alfred (1890–1946) 82
'Jubilee', Operation 57–82
'Juno' beach 133, 135, 143–6, 149

Keyes, Lieutenant Colonel Geoffrey 44
Keyes, Admiral Sir Roger (1872–1945) 22–3, 26, 33, 43–4, 97, 168
Kieffer, Commandant E. Muselier 101, 134, 139, 157–8
King, Captain Lorrington, and fiction 172
'Kitbag', Operation 172
Kite, Sergeant J. 137

Knives 46, 60, 109–10, 115–9, 121
Komrower, Arthur 39
Koons, Corporal F. M. (US Rangers) 75, 78

La Beche 149
Landing craft 34, 37, 67, 103, 138–9
Lassen, Anders 79
Laycock, Major General Robert 44, 69, 132, 165
Layforce 69, 132
Le Hamel 149
Le Plein 151–3, 157
Le Touquet 19
Leicester, Major General Bernard (RM) 89, 133
'Lessons learned' 128–32, 165
Levick, Surgeon Commander G. M. (RN) 88, 90–1
Linge, Captain Martin 30–1, 33, 39
Lion-sur-Mer 148
Lister, Colonel 16
Lochailort 85
Lofoten Islands 30–3, 36, 107, 169, 173
Loustalot, Lieutenant (US Rangers) 63, 78
Lovat, Lord (Fraser Simon J.) 31, 61, 68–78, 85, 107, 133, 153, 155, 157
Lovat Scouts 6, 107
Lund, Brigadier Otto 11
Lyons, R. M. 86

Maaloy Island 36–7, 40, 42
Mad Jack – see 'Churchill, John'
Madden Committee 103
Mair, Sergeant Ian (RM) 144
Mann, Lance Corporal 71
March-Phillips, Major Gustavus H. 'Gus' 18, 79
Martel, Lieutenant 20–2
Masters, Lance Corporal 156
McDonough, Gunner 72–3
Medals, for raids 170
Media – see 'Publicity' and 'Film'
'Menace', Operation 27
Merville Battery 135, 150–1, 154
Middle East Commando 28, 69
Milch, Field Marshal Erhard 123

Millin, Piper Bill 107, 141, 157
'Milling' 100–01
Mills-Roberts, Brigadier Derek 61,
  68, 70–2, 76, 96, 123, 137, 155, 175
Montanaro, Captain G. Charles 17,
  84
Morris, Private Alex 136
Morris, Lance Corporal C. 155–6
Motor Launches, (MLs) 46–55
Moulton, Lieutenant Colonel (RM)
  134, 143–4, 146–7
Mountbatten, Lord Louis
  (1900–1979) 8, 57, 165, 169
Murray, Captain Roy A. (US) 60

Newman, Lieutenant Colonel 47,
  53, 55, 86
Niven, Captain David 11, 20, 69
Non-Commissioned Officers,
  numbers and training of 14–5,
  28, 83
Norway, 1940 campaign in 5, 7–8
Norway, raids 29–44, 172–3

O'Flaherty, Lieutenant Denis
  W. V. P. 40, 165–6
Organisation 4, 6, 10–6, 26–8, 29,
  46, 132, 176, 178, 181, 186,
  198–9, 201–02
Osmond, Captain 63
Ouistreham 135–6, 158–9
'Overlord', Operation 133–162

Paget, Sir Bernard C. T.
  (1887–1961) 3
Partisan Leader's Handbook 4–5
Paton, David 51
Pedder, Major 6
Pegasus Bridge 135
Perrigard, Gordon E. 120
Perry, Captain James L. (RM) 146
Phillips, Lieutenant Colonel J. P,
  (RM) 67
PIAT (Projector Infantry Anti
  Tank) 136, 150–1, 155, 158, 180,
  200
Pinckney, Captain P. 173
Pistol-shooting technique 111–4
PLUTO (Pipe Line Under The
  Ocean) 143
Pollock, Lieutenant Alan 154

Pooley, Major John B. V. 154
Port en Bessin 135, 142–3
Porteous, Captain Pat A. 75–6
Prisoners, treatment of 80–2, 94
Promotion of officers 176
Publicity and propaganda
  (Commando) 42, 114, 119–22,
  129, 163, 167–76, 178
Purdon, Lieutenant 52–3

Rangers, US 58–60, 75, 78,
  101–02, 167, 171
Rations – *see* 'Food'
Rebel Force 30
'Returned to Unit' (RTU) 18, 177
Reynolds, Michael 145
Ries, Lieutenant Colonel (RM)
  150
Rommel, Field Marshal Erwin, raid
  on 44, 69
'Rommel', Exercise (1942) 82
Rowley, Company Sergeant Major
  Jack 99–100, 105
Royal Marines (see also 'Units') 3,
  66–7, 102–04, 134, 141
Rubenstein, Lieutenant (RM) 146
'Rutter', Operation – first plan for
  Dieppe 57
Ruxton, Captain 64, 66

Salerno 103
Sallenelles 150
Salt, experiments with 90
Samian, Bryan (RM) 139–41
Scouts 92–3
Selwyn, Captain 64, 66
Shanghai Municipal Police, 'SMP'
  109–10
Small Scale Raiding Force, 'SSRF'
  79, 132
Smatchet 116–17
Special Companies – *see*
  'Independent Companies'
Special force, special service viii,
  10, 26, 29, 167, 178
Spitzbergen 34, 169
Spring Training Instructions (1941)
  85
Stalin, Joseph 57, 175
Stempson, Staff Sergeant K. D.
  (US Rangers) 60

Stevens, Captain T. M. P. (RM)
  149
St Aubin 145
St Nazaire, and bombing 45–6, 49
St Nazaire, raid on 45–56, 58, 170
St Nazaire, strategic position of 45
Stirling, David 107, 111
Stockdale, Troop Sergeant Major
  75
Storm Troops (British) 2–3
Street-fighting 39–42, 85–6, 93–5,
  101, 104–05, 127–8, 191–4
Sturges, Major General R. G. 133,
  144
Style, Lieutenant 71–2
Submachine guns 17 –8, 28, 46, 77,
  137
Subsistence payments 15
Svolvaer 31
Swayne, Lieutenant Ronald 19, 47
'Sword' beach 135, 149
Sykes, Eric A. 109, 111–12

Tactics ix, 5, 24, 48, 77, 108,
  110–22, 125–32, 138, 147, 155–6,
  161, 165–6
Thompson, 'Tommy Gun' – *see*
  Submachine guns
Tilney, Company Sergeant Major
  (RM) 148
Timmins, Harry 140
Tirpitz 45, 56
Tod, Major R. J. F. 18–20
Toggle rope, description of 85
'Tomato', abortive operation 23
Training 7, 18, 24–5, 61, 82–108,
  110–28, 130, 134, 169, 174
  accidents 85, 104–05
  close combat 109–20
  jungle 107–08
  mountain and snow 106
  Physical 'PT' 84–5, 99
  schedules and syllabus 83–5, 87,
  92, 98–9, 104, 108, 110–11,
  115
Transport 15–6, 25, 179, 202
Travers, Troop Sergeant Major 143
Truscott, Colonel Lucien (US) 59

*Unarmed Defence for the American
  Soldier* 120

Units, Commando:
  1 Commando 47
  2 Commando 11, 13, 27, 34,
    47–56, 86–7, 102, 177
  3 Commando 14, 18, 30, 32, 34,
    47, 58–66, 84, 133, 137, 151,
    153–4, 164, 177
  4 Commando 18, 30, 34, 47, 58,
    68–78, 123, 133, 135–6, 157,
    159–60, 177
  5 Commando 34, 47, 51, 123
  6 Commando 14, 16, 34, 84, 133,
    135, 153–7, 166
  7 Commando 102
  8 Commando 14–5, 69, 102, 166,
    168, 177
  9 Commando 34, 47
  10 Commando 59, 101, 134, 152,
    156–7, 166, 167
  11 Commando 86
  12 Commando 27, 34, 47, 173,
    177
  14 Commando 167
  30 Commando 133, 166
  40 RM Commando 59, 66, 102
  41 RM Commando 103, 133,
    148–9
  42 RM Commando 103
  43 RM Commando 104
  44 RM Commando 103–04,
    107–08, 176–7
  45 RM Commando 133, 135,
    140, 149–54
  46 RM Commando 133, 149
  47 RM Commando 102, 133,
    139, 141–2
  48 RM Commando 102–03, 106,
    127, 133, 134, 140, 143–7
  50 Commando 28
  51 Commando 28
  52 Commando 28
  62 Commando 79, 166
  Royal Navy Commandos 133,
    166
Commando Brigades/SS
  Brigades:
  1st Commando Brigade 123,
    166
  Special Service Brigade 132
  1st Special Service Brigade
    133, 149, 160, 164
  3rd Commando Brigade 164
  4th Special Service Brigade
    133, 138
Independent Companies:
  Independent Companies 6–7,
    11, 13
  4th Independent Company
    6–7
  5th Independent Company 6
Units, General:
  21st Army Group 133
  30 Assault Unit 133
  52nd (Lowland) Division 6
  55th (W. Lancashire) Division
    6, 18
  125th Infantry Brigade 123
Commando units, 1940 11
Layforce 69
Lovat Scouts 6
Royal Navy Commandos (Beach
  Commandos), 33

Special Service Group (1944) 133
Territorials 6

Vaagso, South Vaagso 34–6, 38–43,
  96, 128–9, 170
Varengeville, Varengeville battery
  58, 68
Vaughan, Lieutenant Colonel
  Charles 97, 173–4
Veasey, Lieutenant A. S. S. 74
Venereal disease 96
Vickers 'K' guns 136, 158–9

Walbridge, Captain P. N. 115,
  117–8
Walcheren 89, 144
Warlimont, General Walter 82
Waugh, Evelyn 168
Weapons 2, 12, 17, 21, 37, 46, 60, 64,
  71, 76–7, 99, 108, 110–21, 125–7,
  136–7, 158, 179–80, 181, 200
Weatherall, Lieutenant S.
  (Commandos and SBS) 14
Web, Lance Corporal 50
White, Corporal E. G. 'Knocker' 39
Wigram, Major Lionel 95, 125
Wilkinson, Wilkinson Sword 110
Wills, Captain R. L. 63
Woodcock, Lieutenant 48

X-Troop 101, 134

Young, Brigadier Peter 14, 16,
  21–2, 33, 37–8, 40–1, 62–6, 83,
  123, 137, 153, 164, 175
Yugoslavia 12